How to Raise More Money for Any Non-Profit:

The Definitive Fundraising Guide

By Joe Garecht

Fundraising Authority Press

How to Raise More Money for Any Non-Profit: The Definitive Fundraising Guide

Published by Fundraising Authority Press. No part of this publication may be reproduced or transmitted in any form or by any means – electronic, mechanical, photocopy, recording or otherwise, without prior permission of the author.

www.TheFundraisingAuthority.com

ISBN:
0615923178

ISBN-13:
978-0615923178

This book is dedicated to
Ashley, Haley, Emily, Caleb and Liam

Table of Contents

Introduction:
Thinking Big in Fundraising

If there's one thing I don't like, it's thinking small. Far too many people spend their time and energy thinking small. That's true in the wider world, and it's true in fundraising.

There are a lot of fundraisers in the world – some professional, some volunteer. Some work on staff, some consult, some are on boards, some do it as a favor to a friend. People come at fundraising from all different angles... but there's one thing that 99% of fundraisers have in common — most of us think small-scale.

If there's one area where there's really no excuse for thinking small, it's fundraising. As fundraisers, we fight for and fund important, often earth-shattering causes. (If you're not working on causes that matter..... well, why not?)

No matter how small your cause or organization seems, chances are it's important... much more important than you give it credit for.
Your organization may be providing meals to the homeless in one small corner of one small city — but to those you feed, you're doing the most important work in the world.

You may be raising money to battle one disease out of thousands – but to those who are afflicted by that disease, your fundraising is the only hope they have of finding a cure and staying alive.
So why do we think small about the work that we do?

If the work that you are funding is important... if it matters, if it makes a difference... then the time has come to stop thinking small. Your board may be thinking small. The executive director (or development director, or program staff) may be thinking small. Your volunteers and event hosts may be thinking small. But it's time for *you* to start thinking big.

What does thinking big look like? It might be launching a new program, a new fundraising campaign, a new event. It might be reaching out to new funding streams, dipping into a new donor universe, or hiring a new development officer even though you've never had one on staff before.

Thinking big looks different in every organization, but no matter what cause you are fundraising for, big thinkers always share one trait in common: they're willing to step outside the confinement of past strategies to cast a new and bold vision for their causes and organizations... one that will literally change the way the game is played.

Isn't it time *your non-profit* started thinking big?

Chapter 1:
The Basics of Non-Profit Fundraising

Before delving into advanced fundraising strategies and tactics, let's go over some of the most important basic fundraising principles that are applicable to every organization, and to every fundraising strategy. These ideas are the bedrock of strong fundraising programs, and essential to everything you do in non-profit development.

Principle #1: Fundraising Isn't Evil

You'd be surprised how many people, including those who fundraise for a living, need to hear this... fundraising isn't evil! It's not bad, it's not dirty, it's not slimy or beneath you. Sure, most folks don't think non-profit fundraising is literally evil, but I can't tell you how many executive directors, board members, and even development staff members feel icky about making an ask.

Here's the thing: What your non-profit does matters. It's as simple as that. Take a moment to think about your organization's mission... what it is it that you do? Do you give the homeless a place to sleep? Do you fund cutting edge cancer research? Do you educate young minds? Whatever the mission of your non-profit, it matters (otherwise you wouldn't or shouldn't be working there).

If your mission matters, then your fundraising matters. You wouldn't be able to serve the people you serve, or do the work that you do, without fundraising. Without fundraising, a homeless shelter can't put in more beds. Without fundraising, a research hospital can't find a cure for ALS. Without fundraising, you *can't do* what you do!

Think about it. In general, with *more* fundraising revenue, you could do even *more*! You could serve more people, do more good in the world. When it is put that way, doesn't it sound like fundraising is extremely important? Fundraising leads to lives saved, lives changed, children educated, research completed, church doors opened, good things getting done.

If you make an ask, and the person says no, you shouldn't feel icky or smarmy. You should feel good about yourself and your organization, because you tried to raise money to change lives. Sure, you can go back and look at your cultivation process to see if it was lacking somewhere, but you should never, ever feel bad about fundraising.

How does your team feel about raising money? Maybe it's time to have a talk with your board and staff about the importance and *goodness* of fundraising.

Principle #2: Plans Matter

Most non-profits get started on a wing and a prayer... the founding board members pull together and will the organization into existence, raising whatever is needed to start the charity through personal connections and maybe a small fundraising event. The organization gets off the ground and low and behold, the fundraising activities continue, without much of a plan.

As the non-profit grows, some plans get sketched out (usually revolving around when to hold events or send out letters) but they are done piecemeal and often without much thought about a comprehensive strategy. When the non-profit matures, it will often take the time to write out a full, comprehensive plan (sometimes using paid consultants), and then will bind up the plan, put it on the shelf, and not look at it for another 5-10 years, until someone on the board says, "what's our fundraising plan again?"

The process outlined above is a mistake. Having a good plan matters to your fundraising efforts. A plan provides a guide your efforts, makes sure everyone is on the same page, defines which activities you will carry out and which you will avoid, and provides a reference point in the heat of battle, allowing you to look at the overall strategy in the midst of daily activities and issues.

A good fundraising plan:

...is written down. Fundraising plans that exist only in the mind of the Development Director or Board Chair are apt to fail.

...is constantly evolving. Don't write a plan and expect it to last for the next two decades. You will need to take your fundraising plan out and look at it and tinker with it on a regular basis. Things change... so should your plan.

...clearly defines goals and deadlines. A plan that simply says "we will send out direct mail pieces twice per year" is a recipe for failure. Far better to say, "we will send out a direct mail piece the third week of February and the third week of September this year. The Development Director will be responsible for writing the copy and developing the lists, and our print shop will handle design, printing, and mailing."

Does your non-profit have a written fundraising plan? When was the last time you looked at or updated it?

Principle #3: Fundraising Is Everyone's Responsibility

Because fundraising is so important to the success of your non-profit, it needs to be made clear to your entire board and staff that fundraising is everyone's responsibility. Yes, you should have a Development Director or development team that spends 100% of their time fundraising (or, in smaller organizations without a development staff, an Executive Director who spends a significant portion of his/her time raising money), but everyone should have "assisting with fundraising" as part of their job description.

For your program staff, this means that they should be willing and able to help at fundraising events and with fundraising presentations like tours and roundtables (donors love to hear from the folks who are actually providing the services they are funding, instead of just the development staff). It also means that your program staff should constantly be on the lookout for fundraising opportunities in the course of their daily responsibilities.

Likewise, everyone on your board should be expected to help fundraise. This means making personal asks, selling tickets to events, and providing contacts for your fundraising mailing list.

Yes, some board members will be primarily responsible for fundraising (such as your development or event committees) and some will not take a leading role with fundraising (focusing more on programs, governance, government relations, etc.) but everyone on your board should understand that they are expected to fundraise.

Because you are expecting your board and non-development staff to help with fundraising, and because these folks may not have a fundraising or sales background, it is imperative that you offer fundraising training to your board and entire staff on a regular basis. My suggestion is that you hold an annual board retreat that is 50% focused on vision, strategy, and programs and 50% focused on fundraising training and strategy.

Likewise, I suggest that you hold at least one, if not more 1-2 hour fundraising training sessions for your program and administrative staff each year.

Does everyone at your non-profit understand that fundraising is part of their job description? Does everyone on your board help with fundraising?

Principle #4: The Best Fundraising Efforts are Scalable

Cultivating a prospect and making an ask takes time. If you only have one development person on your staff, there's a limit to the number of new prospects he or she can contact or the number of asks he or she can make on a yearly basis. Similarly, writing grants, holding events, and sending out mail takes time. No matter how many development professionals you have on your staff, there will never be enough time or resources for them to reach out to every person, business or foundation in your community for financial support. This is doubly true if you don't have any full-time development staff and are relying on the Executive Director or volunteers to head up your fundraising efforts.

Getting your board, volunteers, and entire staff involved in your fundraising (as mentioned above in Principle #3) certainly helps, but it is still not enough. You'll still need more help to raise the money you need to carry out your mission. That's why the best fundraising efforts are scalable... meaning they are designed in such a way that you are able to recreate them over and over again while getting others to do your fundraising for you.

For example, one non-profit I know puts a special focus on getting board members and other friends of the organization to host fundraising events on their behalf. This non-profit has only one full time development staff member, who could never coordinate more than a couple of small fundraising events per year, given her additional work load. So, the development director put together a "how to hold a fundraising event for us" guide, along with a set of pre-packaged materials like plug-n-play event invitations, an Evite template, and guidelines for putting together an event host committee. The organization uses this kit to help it scale its fundraising efforts, and last year held over two dozen small fundraising events around its region that raised 25% of the non-profit's overall budget for the year.

Another example of a scalable fundraising effort is an affinity group. Many non-profits have found great success putting together "Young Friends of..." or "Doctors for..." or other types of affinity groups for their organization that go out and hold events and raise money on a volunteer basis. This allows the non-profit to spend time on other fundraising efforts while the affinity group multiplies its efforts by working in parallel on different fundraising projects.

How scalable are *your* fundraising efforts? Have you built affinity groups? Are you making it easy for other people to fundraise on your behalf?

Principle #5: Relationships = Success

The fifth and final basic fundraising principle that every non-profit needs to understand is that building strong relationships is fundamental to fundraising success.

Fundraising is all about relationships.

Sure, you can buy a direct mail list and send out a fundraising appeal and make money, but the real money comes on the back end, as you develop relationships with those donors who responded to your initial prospecting letter. Ditto for personal asks, foundation support, online fundraising… the real money is in the relationship.

Your development staff (and your board) should be in the relationship-building business. That's why the fundraising funnel that we'll talk about later is so important. The goal of your fundraising efforts should be to identify people who might want to donate to your organization if they knew more about it, and then to develop a relationship with them through cultivation activities. It is only after the relationship is built that an ask should be made… making an ask before there is a relationship might lead to a gift, but it will be far smaller than one that is made after the relationship is established.

One a relationship is established and a gift is made, the non-profit will need to work hard at stewarding the donor to maintain the relationship in order to receive follow up donations, like annual gifts, bequests, etc.

Donors want to feel like a part of your team. When they do, they will be inclined to give again and again. Build relationships with your donors, and turn them into friends for life.

Vision: The Most Important Ingredient

All of the principles that we talked about are important, but even when you design your fundraising program in accordance with all five principles, you will never truly reach your fundraising potential unless you cast a big vision for your prospects and donors. Vision is the most important ingredient in supersizing your fundraising.

Having a vision means that your non-profit has a distinct view of the world. You know what the problem is that you are trying to correct – you know how you are trying to make the world a better place. You know what you need to do to reach the outcomes that you want to reach. You have a plan to do those things. You are pushing ahead with that plan. That's what it means to "have a vision" at your organization.

Of course, there are visions, and then there are VISIONS. Your non-profit's vision could be to serve 1,000 meals per month to the homeless people of Cincinnati... or your vision could be to *end* hunger among the homeless of Cincinnati. Which vision sounds more exciting?

People (donors, staff, prospects, volunteers, reporters... everyone!) are looking to get caught up in a vision. People are looking for a narrative of their life, a story... a way to give their lives meaning, and a way to make a difference. Your donors want to get caught up in a larger story, a larger vision, and work towards a common (and amazing!) goal. That's why you need to have a BIG vision for your non-profit.

Sure, your *plan* may call for serving 1,000 meals per month to the homeless, but your VISION is to end hunger in your city. You *plan* may call for providing $250,000 in scholarships to high school students in your town next year, but your VISION is making sure every single child in your town gets a great education (not a good education... a GREAT education). Those are big visions.

Having a big vision makes it easier to raise money because people are drawn to large visions. People want to make a huge difference in the world, and if your non-profit will allow them to do that, they will want to be a part of it.

Once you have a big vision in place, you can create a plan to accomplish it that allows your staff and donors to bite off manageable chunks. For example, if your vision is to provide a great education to every child in your town, you may ask donors to sponsor one scholarship this year... as part of your plan to offer 500 scholarships this year and 1,000 the next year... If your vision is to end hunger in Cincinnati, you may ask a donor to · make a commitment to donating $4,000 per year for three years to pay for the fuel for your food delivery van, as part of your goal of having 20 vans on the street by 2018, as part of your plan to end hunger in the city.

It all starts with a big vision.

Of course, you should only cast a big vision if you and your team are committed to seeing it through. If you say you are committed to ending hunger for the 1,000 homeless people in your city, and you provide meals for 400 homeless people per year this year, next year, and the year after, donors will know that your *real* vision is to feed 400 homeless people per year. A good, laudable vision, but not the same as the BIG vision of *ending hunger* If, on the other hand, you feed 400 this year, 600 the next year and 800 the year after, donors will see that you *are* committed to your vision, and are working hard to accomplish it.

What is *your* non-profit's vision? Is it BIG enough?

Casting a Vision vs. Writing a Plan

As you can see, there's a big difference between casting a vision and writing a program or fundraising plan. Your vision should be a mission statement that encapsulates everything you want your non-profit to do:

"The mission of the End Lung Cancer Foundation is to find a cure for lung cancer by 2035."

"The Lawncrest School exists to offer the students of our town the best education available anywhere in the state of Pennsylvania, without regard to a family's ability to pay."

"DePaul Mission Houses seek to end homelessness in Kalamazoo by providing shelter to everyone in our city who needs it."

Cast a vision – a big one – and mean it. Every non-profit, no matter how small, can cast a big vision.

What Do You Do With Your Vision, Once You Have It?

Once your non-profit creates (or re-creates) its "big vision," it should be part of everything you do. Everything your non-profit says or does, including events, fundraising appeals, letters, PR, newsletters, websites, e-mails... everything... should refer back to your vision. Do you have a letter going out asking for money for a specific project? Tell how it relates to your BIG VISION. Getting ready for your annual fundraising event for general operating expenses? Tell how those expenses help you serve your BIG VISION.

You see, it will take prospects, donors, and the general public a while to understand what your vision is, no matter how clear you make it. Political consultants estimate that it takes a voter between five and seven times actually seeing/hearing/reading a candidate's name and campaign message before that message sinks in. The same is true of your non-profit. You'll need to reinforce your vision over and over again. Eventually, after enough repetition, your prospects and donors will come to associate your organization with that vision and understand your commitment to it.

A Leisurely Walk down the Fundraising Funnel

In the next four sections of this book, we're going to be talking about the Fundraising Funnel – this is the path that your non-profit should be taking with all new prospects, whether they are referrals from a board member, donors from a prospecting mailing, people who come to a non-ask event, or folks who walk in off the street to make a small donation.

Each and every prospect that comes into your orbit should be walked down a tried and true path to generate revenue for your organization. The specific tactics you will use for each prospect will differ (for example, you may never pick up the phone and call a $50 per year donor, but you may call a $100,000 capital campaign donor three times per year), yet the strategy remains the same no matter the donor/prospect.

The point of this funnel is to avoid "one and done" donors who are strong-armed into giving by their boss, friend, family member, or someone they owe a favor to. Instead, we're going to be creating *lifelong* donors who develop an honest-to-goodness relationship with your non-profit organization, slowly get more involved, and make gifts to you year after year.

The four steps of the Fundraising Funnel are:

1. Prospect

Find new individuals, foundations, businesses and organizations who might be interested in your non-profit if they knew more about you. Figure out what makes them tick, who you know that knows them, and what is the best way to begin a conversation with these new prospects that won't turn them off before you've even begun.

2. Cultivate

Once you've developed new prospects and had initial conversations to gauge interest, it's time to build relationships. What are the best ways to draw prospects closer to your organization, get them involved, and build a personalized yet scalable cultivation system? How can these prospects help you bring in new prospects as the cultivation process marches on?

3. Ask

Now that a relationship has been built and the prospect becomes a supporter (in terms of time, energy and advocacy), what is the best way to make an ask? How much should you ask for? What will appeal most to the donor? Who should make the ask and what should they say? Is this an in-person ask, a mail ask, a phone ask, an event ask?

4. Steward

Great, the person / foundation / business made a gift. Now what? How do we continue to cultivate (steward) our donors, communicate with them, deepen our relationship with them, and encourage them to become regular givers to our organization? How can we get these donors to reach into their own networks to fundraise on our behalf?

We're going to delve deeply into each of these topics in order to build a strong understanding of these four steps. Once you master each of these steps, you'll be able to apply them to any donor at any non-profit, as well as utilize them in all kinds of fundraising tactics including direct asks, mail, online fundraising and more.

Chapter 2:
How to Find New Prospects
for Your Non-Profit

The fundraising process starts with the prospect. Prospects are the fundamental starting point for the fundraising funnel. Without prospects, you have no one to cultivate, and without people to cultivate, you have no one to ask for a gift. Simply put, new prospects are the lifeblood of your fundraising effort.

If your non-profit is having trouble raising enough money year after year, chances are you have a problem with your prospecting system. Sure, it could be that your cultivation strategy is flawed, or that you are having problems with making good asks… but it is far more likely that you simply are not feeding enough prospects into your system to allow your cultivation and ask strategies to work.

The goal for this section is to explain the prospecting process, and talk about the key paths that prospects take to reach your non-profit organization, with a particular focus on building strong and sustainable fundraising networks. Once you have enough prospects entering the funnel, you will have far more opportunities to cultivate support and ask for gift to support your mission.

What Is a "Prospect?"

The best place to start is by asking, "What *is* a prospect?"

Many organizations answer this question by saying, "everyone is a prospect." I disagree. It takes real time and effort to figure out how to approach prospects, cultivate them, and move them into your fundraising funnel. If you aren't sure who your prospects are, or want to target "everyone," you will never, ever have the time and resources necessary to effectively move people through your system. It's just not practical. That's why I advocate "targeted prospecting."

Simply put, targeted prospecting means setting up your prospecting system with certain donor profiles in mind. Because your non-profit won't have the time and resources to focus on everyone in the world as a prospect, you will need to find the "low hanging fruit," those prospects who are most likely to give to your organization once they understand your mission. These people are true prospects, because they really are potential donors to your organization. You have a reasonable belief that you can move them to an ask with a minimum amount of introduction and cultivation.

So, who *really* is a prospect (potential donor) to your organization? Who is likely to give once they hear about your organization?

Good, solid prospects might already know about your non-profit (they may be graduates, if your organization is a school, or patients, if you are raising money for a hospital). Or, they might not know about your organization, but be inclined to give because someone they do know is involved with your board, received services from your organization, or otherwise support you. Your non-profit also has a sizeable pool of prospects that doesn't know about your organization or have a relationship with someone connected to your non-profit, but who may be inclined to support you for other reasons, such as an affinity for your cause, a personal belief system, etc.

Your goal as a fundraiser is to use the tools at your disposal to figure out and/or expand the prospect universe your non-profit is targeting.

The Fundamental Rules of Prospecting

In addition to understanding the donor funnel, there are several fundamental rules of prospecting that you will need to grasp in order to have the greatest amount of fundraising success:

Rule #1: People Give Based on Relationships

Humans are relationship driven. We seek out relationships and make decisions based on relationships. It's no different with philanthropy – people give based on relationships. Before someone gives to your non-profit, there has to be some sort of relationship which gives the prospect a reason to give. That relationship can be interpersonal, or organizational.

Some people give because of interpersonal relationships: they know and trust someone on your board, or one of your volunteers, or someone that you helped. Their relationship with that person (and that person's positive recommendation of your non-profit), encourages them to make a gift.

Some people, on the other hand, give because of an organizational relationship with your non-profit. They hear about your organization, you cultivate them and build a relationship with them, and then they give.

Either way, a relationship must exist or be built before a check will be written.

Rule #2: Strong-Arm Fundraising Doesn't Work

Having read Rule #1, many non-profits may think, "great! I'll just tell my board and volunteers that they have to get all of their friends to write checks. They can just go through their rolodex and tell people, 'I need you to write a $1,000 check.'" This is called "strong-arming your rolodex," and it doesn't really work.

Sure, you *can* raise money this way, at least for a time. Your board and supporters can call in favors from friends and colleagues and make it a point of personal friendship or professional association for donors to give to your group. And some of those people will in fact give. Once. But it's not sustainable, and doesn't generate the huge returns that can be had by relationship-based prospecting.

Instead of asking your board to strong-arm their contacts into making a donation, ask your board to invite three people they think may be interested in your non-profit to a non-ask event or a tour of your facility... or ask them out to lunch with the Executive Director... or get them involved in a volunteer activity. This slow-but-steady approach to prospecting builds long-term donors who give more money, year in and year out, than the one-time gifts that can be had through strong-arming your board's rolodexes.

Rule #3: Mission Matters to Prospects

No matter how you come across a prospect – whether that person is a former client of your agency, a patient at your hospital, a friend of your board chair, or simply a businessperson with a heart for your particular issue, know that mission matters to your prospects.

Some prospects will want to give to your organization because they support your mission. Other prospects will decide not to give because they don't support your mission or disagree with your approach to tackling your mission. Either way, your mission matters to them. For that reason, you should make your mission, and the work you do, central to your prospecting conversations and communication.

Rule #4: Prospecting is a Deliberate Process

Prospecting should be a deliberate process. Far too many non-profits prospect without any real strategy or plan. This leads to haphazard prospecting at best, and a disorganized and ineffective fundraising organization at worst.

Have a written prospecting plan. What are your prospect profiles (who is likely to give to your organization)? Where can you find those people? How can you reach them?

Similarly, track your prospects through the fundraising funnel. My favorite strategy for doing this (in addition to keeping accurate and detailed notes in an organization's fundraising database) is to visually track major prospects through the funnel on a whiteboard that allows your entire team to see, on a daily basis, where each prospect stands in your funnel.

Rule #5: The More You Ship, the More You Will Receive

How many newsletters does your non-profit send out? How many non-ask events do you have? How many tours do you offer of your facilities per month? How often do you provide volunteer opportunities? The more often you "ship" things out into the world, the more prospects will seek you out.

For example, over the course of one year, one non-profit I know went from shipping almost nothing to offering quarterly facility tours, monthly e-newsletters and press releases, and renewed focus on volunteer activities, which were heavily publicized. As they implemented this plan to ship more out into the world, they not only generated additional buzz among their own supporters and friends, but they started to have new prospects approach them, simply because the prospect had heard about all of the good work the non-profit was doing.

Ship more, receive more.

The Concentric Circles Theory of Prospecting

Because all fundraising is based on relationships, and because the goal of your prospecting should be to reach the lowest hanging fruit first, maximizing your fundraising by starting with those most likely to give and moving out from there, I often like to think of your prospecting universe as a series of concentric circles.

At the center of the ring stands your non-profit, which needs financial support in order to do its work and serve its mission.

In the ring directly around your non-profit live your closest supporters: your board of directors and key fundraisers. In the next ring out are the donors who give annually, and your key volunteers. Next come those who occasionally give, and those who occasionally volunteer... and so on, and so on, until you reach the final layer... those who have never heard of you and wouldn't like your organization, even if they did (your non-prospects).

How your organization groups its prospects will depend on the size of your organization, how long you have been around, the level of support you enjoy in the community, etc. For the purposes of this discussion, who you decide to put in each concentric circle isn't important – what *is* important is that you start to think of your prospect universe in terms of concentric circles emanating out from your organization, with the closest group containing those most likely to give, the next group containing those a little less likely to give than the first group, etc.

It's also important that you segment your prospects this way – who is most likely to give to my organization right now?

Finally, it is important to remember that each of your prospects has their own group of concentric circles... their own network. In the closest ring they may have their family and friends, then their co-workers and golf partners, then their vendors and clients, then their employees and high school buddies... etc. This is important to remember because later in this book, we're going to be talking about building a fundraising network for your organization to increase your prospect pool. The best way to do this will be to go to your donors and supporters and ask them to reach into their own networks on your behalf, so you will want to help them take a look at their own concentric circles to see who they can approach.

Remember – your prospect universe is like a series of concentric rings. Inside each ring is a group of people who are more or less likely to give to you. As you move out from the center, the people in each ring are less likely to give to you than the people in the ring preceding it. Each ring contains people – either real, identifiable people (like your board or that woman you met at the trade show who was interested in your mission), as well as groups of people (for example, you might say "anyone who graduated from our university," or "Catholic men aged 35-55").

Each person in your circles has their own circles, too. Once you get a person involved in your organization and start to cultivate them and move them down the fundraising funnel, you may also be able to get *their* circles involved by asking them to reach out to their network on your behalf.

Creating Prospect Diagrams

I am a firm believer in writing things down. Understanding the concepts is great, but it's hard (impossible, actually) to keep track of a prospecting program in your head. It's imperative that your non-profit sits down and actually maps out it's prospect universe. Figure out who is likely to give, and what priority to give them, based on the fundraising circles theory presented above.

At a minimum, ask yourself the following questions:

- Who are my current donors? Who are my largest donors? Who are my most consistent donors?
- Who are my lapsed donors?
- Who are my current volunteers? Who are my best volunteers? Who are my most consistent volunteers?
- What groups of people are most likely to give to our organization? What are the profiles (age, gender, occupation, interests, etc.) of people who are likely to give to our organization?
- What types of people give to other organizations that do work similar to our non-profit?

Write your answers down, and start creating a concentric circles prospect diagram. Remember, your diagram (and your prospect list) is a work in progress – don't wait until it is perfect before you right it down and start acting on it. Get started now, and keep adding people as time goes on and as new opportunities present themselves.

Reaching Prospects by Finding the Path of Least Resistance

Once you have a list of prospects that you want to approach, one of the key questions that will need to be asked is: how do I reach out to each person, company, or foundation on this list to start building a relationship with them? How do I get them into my prospect funnel?

I tell non-profits all the time: the best way to reach a new prospect is by finding the path of least resistance. Because people give (and get involved) based on relationships, the path of least resistance usually involves a relationship the prospect already has... so ask yourself, for each of your top donor prospects... who knows this person? Who on our board knows them? Which of our current donors know them? Do they sit on a corporate board with someone that we know? Are they involved in a service club, country club, or other organization where we know members?

<u>Do we as an organization have a relationship with anyone that already has a relationship of some kind with this prospect?</u>

If the answer is yes, than the path of least resistance is to utilize that relationship to build a new relationship directly between you and the prospect, with the help of the person who already has a relationship with the prospect.

Utilizing the concentric circles theory presented above, most of the prospects you will approach will be people or companies with whom someone you already know has a relationship, no matter how tenuous. You'll be contacting friends and colleagues of those people who already have a relationship with your non-profit.

For those prospects with whom you do not have any shared pre-existing relationships, you will need to develop a new relationship from scratch. For these prospects, the path of least resistance is generally a non-threatening, not-committal entry point: a way for the person to get to know the organization and its mission without getting scared off by being asked to make any sort of commitment. Non-ask events work well (these are informational events where no admission price is charged) as do tangential presentations and classes (for example, if you are raising funds for a soup kitchen, offering an informational seminar for the local bar association around the plight of the homeless in your city may attract a crowd of people who are great prospects for your organization).

Actually Getting Prospects into Your Funnel & Determining Interest

Once you have your prospect list, the best way to actually kick of the relationship is a meeting of some kind. If you know someone who knows the prospect (or knows a key person at the business you are considering a strong prospect), try to set up a lunch with someone from your organization, the prospect, and the mutual acquaintance. Alternately, have the mutual acquaintance invite (and accompany, if possible) the prospect to a non-ask event or on a tour of your facility. As mentioned above, if you and the prospect do not share any mutual acquaintances, the best way to start building the relationship is to invite the person to a non-threatening, non-ask event.

Once the relationship starts, the first task for your non-profit is to gauge the interest of the prospect – once the person learns about your organization and your mission, how interested are they in getting involved? Do they seem moved by your mission and work, or just polite and uninterested?

I always suggest gauging interest by being direct in your follow-up. Meet with a new prospect, then call the following week to thank the person for the meeting and ask if they have any questions. Ask for their thoughts about your work. If the person seems supportive, ask them something like, "would you ever see yourself getting more involved with us?" This is a fairly non-threatening way to deepen the relationship. If the person says "no," you know not to waste your time and energy on building that relationship. If the person says "yes," you can move on to the cultivation phase. Most people, of course, will say, "I'm not sure," or "maybe." These folks are still good prospects, and you should continue building the relationship through cultivation until they reach a decision point.

Building a Fundraising Network to Increase Your Prospect Pool

The single best way to build your prospect pool is by getting your non-profit's donors, volunteers, board members and friends to reach into their *own* networks to find new prospects on your behalf.

Remember what we said above: each of your donors and friends has their own network of concentric circles, people they know, people they do business with. The best way to build your prospect pool is to have your donors and friends reach into their own concentric circles to help you build relationships with the people inside. Then, as you cultivate and make asks of those people, you can reach into *their* networks to find even more prospects... so on and so on, continually growing and involving ever more people. This is called building a fundraising network, and it's the number one way to build a sustainable fundraising organization.

So... how do you convince your donors and friends to reach into their own rolodexes on your behalf? It's simple... you ask! The best way to get people to open up their network to you is to ask them to do so.

Many non-profits don't take this step, with the exception of asking the board to give them names for the annual appeal letter or fundraising event mailing list. This is a mistake. All non-profits should be sitting down and taking a look at their donor, volunteer, and supporter lists to determine who they want to approach with the request that they help build your fundraising network. Then, for each person targeted, there should be a direct appeal, such as a phone call from the Executive Director asking the person to help you raise money by setting up some meetings for you, or by inviting people to a non-ask event, or by hosting an informational meeting in their home or office on your behalf.

For non-board members, a great way to ask a person to open up their network to you is by asking them to serve on a development committee or an event committee that is focused on bringing in new prospects. Board members, on the other hand, should all be expected to reach into their rolodexes on your behalf.

Then – and this is crucial – you need to show them how to do it, and offer them support in their efforts. It's not enough to simply ask someone to open up their network to you – you need to help them think through who they can approach, and give them the tools they need to succeed, including ideas on how to ask for support.

Ask your supporters to serve on a development committee, and then help them walk through their own concentric circles. Who do they know that might be interested in supporting your non-profit? Who do they do business with? Help your supporter hold a non-ask event at their office, provide them with literature, have your staff come to the event to talk with the guests. Make it as easy as possible for your supporters to build a fundraising network on your behalf.

Affinity Group Prospecting

Another great way to prospect through fundraising networks is by building affinity groups. Simply put, an affinity group is a group of people or companies who share a common trait, and who come together to support your organization. Some examples include:

- Young Professionals Groups

- Attorneys Groups
- "Women for" Groups
- Industry-Based Groups (e.g. restaurants banding together to support a cause, etc.)
- Common Interest Groups (e.g. fans of a sports team supporting a non-profit, etc.)

Affinity groups are great because they are an easy way to get new prospects involved. For example, if you have a young professionals group (or young friends of... group) that holds great events at up and coming bars in your town, it's relatively easy for members of that group to get their friends to attend the next non-ask event.

Just be sure that all of your affinity groups are mission-focused, meaning that while your attorneys group may talk a lot about the big recent ruling at the courthouse and the young professionals group you set up may like to eat, drink and be merry, both need to place a lot of focus and energy into supporting your non-profit.

Building a Sustainable Prospecting System

It is essential to the long term health and stability of your organization (as well as your staff!) that you build a sustainable prospecting system. This means setting up a system where you are constantly looking for new prospects to feel into your fundraising funnel. For example, one organization I know sponsors monthly non-ask events, and has a set system for approaching donors and friends to help them get people to these events, which are the launching point of their cultivation process.

What processes can your organization put in place to make sure that your prospecting goes from one-off initiatives into a sustainable, scalable, repeatable system?

Chapter 3:
Cultivation - How to Turn
Prospects Into Donors

In the section above, we talked at length about finding new fundraising prospects... i.e. where to look for new people to get involved with your non-profit. In this section, we're going to answer the question, "Now that I have a list of new prospects... what should I *do* with them?" Or, to put it even more simply: "how do I turn prospects into donors?" The process for turning prospects into donors is called *cultivation*.

What is Cultivation?

Cultivation is everything your non-profit does from the time you identify a person, business, or foundation as a good prospect for your organization until the time you make an ask of that person or entity. Cultivation is what happens in between... it is all of the communication and interaction that occurs between your non-profit and your prospect.

It's important to remember that the cultivation process has one major goal, and lots of minor goals. The big goal that the entire process is focused on is the ask: your cultivation efforts should move the prospect closer and closer to the organization, for the purpose of making an ask (the ask is usually for money, but can also be for other things, like asking the person to open up their network to you, etc. But usually, it is an ask for money).

The cultivation process also has a number of minor goals: you'll hopefully be creating new evangelists for your organization (people who are willing to spread the word about your good work), making new connections (friends of the prospect will often come into your orbit) and generating new support in the form of volunteers and committee members. That being said, the reason your non-profit will need to spend so much time on the cultivation process is because the major goal of the entire endeavor is to make an ask... and asks produce the money that your non-profit needs to carry out its mission.

The Hidden Agenda of Cultivation: Weeding Prospects Out

Most of your cultivation efforts are spent building relationships to *convince* people to give to your organization. However, the cultivation process has another, somewhat hidden agenda: to weed out prospects that are not a good fit with your non-profit.

As fundraisers, we like to think that everyone will want to give to our organization, if we can just get them into the room to hear about our work. But the truth is that some people will not want to give to your organization, no matter how much you communicate with them. The fact that they do not want to get more involved with you does not make them a bad person... their interests may lie elsewhere, or they may not have the financial capacity to give at the level that you thought. Thus, while you originally thought the person or business was a great prospect for your non-profit, it turns out that they are really not.

The cultivation process helps by allowing you to identify those prospects who are not likely to give (or are unable to give) so that you don't have to spend time trying to get them to do something they are not going to do. Cultivation takes time: there are phone calls, events, letters, emails, and more. You've got limited staff resources. Don't spend time trying to cultivate people who just aren't interested in getting involved with your organization. Instead, use the cultivation process to weed out the people who aren't going to give. These folks will self-identify, if you ask the right questions and do the right things. They'll skip your events and avoid your phone calls. When you ask them if they'd like to get more involved with your organization, they talk about how busy they are. When you send out a survey, they don't respond. Be alert. When it is clear that someone does not want to walk down the cultivation highway with you, stop the process, and part as friends.

Generally, your cultivation process should look like a funnel. At the one end, you have a large group of potential prospects. As you walk down the process, you have fewer and fewer prospects, until you come to the other end, where you have the smaller group of people who have demonstrated their interest in your organization. This is the group you will ask for a monetary gift.

The 8 Keys to Understanding the Cultivation Process

Now that we've defined exactly what cultivation is, let's review the 8 keys to understanding the cultivation process:

Cultivation is a process.

It is important to note, from the outset, that cultivation is, in fact, a process. It is not a one-shot deal. If you meet a new prospect at an event and she tells you she wants to make a $10,000 donation to your organization, you didn't cultivate the prospect, you just got lucky. That doesn't mean you should turn down the donation, it just means you should realize that that particular circumstance is rare and is not a scalable proposition.

Cultivation takes time to do properly. It doesn't need to cost a lot to cultivate prospects, but it does take a lot of time and work by your staff, board, and/or volunteers. Have patience, and resist the urge to rush people towards the ask. Build the relationship first, then make an ask (but make sure you have an endgame: don't keep putting off the ask just because you want to lengthen the cultivation period. Take your time to cultivate, but when it is time to ask, go make an ask!)

It's all about building relationships.

People give to non-profits because they have developed a relationship of some sort with that organization. Relationship-building is the goal of the cultivation process. Everything you do to cultivate a prospect could also be called "building a relationship." The stronger the relationship is, the more likely the person is to make a gift to your organization and become a lifelong donor / supporter of your cause.

Relationships build and strengthen over time.

Just as with any relationship, donor relationships build and strengthen over time. Realize this, and give your donor relationships the time they need to mature. As you walk a prospect down the cultivation highway, the relationship between the prospect and your organization will slowly but surely strengthen.

Relationships are built with people.

All true relationships are built between people. If your prospect is a business, understand that it is impossible to build a lasting relationship between your non-profit and a business entity. Yes, the business may support your organization financially, offer staff volunteers to work your events, etc... but in almost every case that help will be driven by one or two people at the business who have a relationship with the staff of your non-profit – a relationship that was built through cultivation.

For that reason, when you are cultivating a business or other organization, it is important that your staff identifies one or two key decision makers at the business or organization to build a relationship with. Once you get the decision maker on board, you will get the business on board. As your relationship with the *person* strengthens, so too will your organization's relationship with the *business*.

Relationships are built person to person.

No two people are alike, but your process must still be scalable. Cultivation can be a tricky proposition. On the one hand, no two people on this Earth are exactly the same. This means that no two people will react exactly the same way to your cultivation process.

On the other hand, it is impossible to develop a new cultivation process for each prospect that is completely individually tailored for their likes and dislikes. You just don't have the time and resources. Your cultivation process needs to be scalable so that it can be used in multiple situations without constantly re-crafting it.

I have found that the best way to make sure that your cultivation process is both individualized and scalable is to make sure that you have a couple of standard cultivation processes in place and that you remain flexible.

For example, you may have a cultivation process in place for new major donor prospects, one for business prospects, one for planned giving prospects, and one for lower-level donors. I suggest that every non-profit have several different cultivation "paths" that they have laid out in advance (in writing). Additionally, organizations should remain flexible, should an individual donor need a different path.

If your cultivation paths are well designed, you will be able to use them for the vast majority of prospects, but will also feel comfortable deviating from them (particularly for major donor prospects with individualized needs).

People like to feel like part of a team.

The final three keys are a pseudo-psychology lesson on donors and prospects. The first lesson is this: people (all people!) like to feel like part of a team. Everyone on Earth wants to feel like they are joined in a relationship with other people who are all marching towards a common goal.

Thus, one of the key strategies for your cultivation efforts should be to make people feel like part of *your* team. Ask them for their suggestions. Keep them constantly in the loop. Invite them to exclusive events. Give them branded materials that show the world that they are part of your team (Buttons? Bumper stickers? Pens?) Make them feel like you're all one big team working towards a common vision (you are, aren't you?!)

People like to be caught up in a larger vision.

The next psychology lesson is this: people like to be caught up in a larger vision. Most people, even the rich and famous, get "stuck" in their daily routines. They get up, go to work, eat meals, play with the kids on the weekends, retire and do some traveling or relaxing, and grow old watching the grandkids play.

Because most people don't like the fact that they get stuck in a "standard" routine, they like to break free by getting caught up in bigger stories and visions. Epic movies, great novels, and a night at the symphony are all ways to escape the humdrum and get caught up in a larger story.

You might not realize it yet, but your non-profit is another great way for people to escape the routine and get caught up in a larger story and vision for the future. What work are you doing? Are you curing cancer? Feeding the hungry? Educating future generations? People *want* to get caught up in your vision... so let them! Cast a big vision, and paint a big picture.

Your cultivation process has to be about engaging people in your vision and allowing them to escape the routine by working with you to meet your common challenges and accomplish your common mission.

People want to be heard.

Finally, it is important to remember that people – all people – want to be heard. Everyone thinks that they have good ideas and good stories to tell. Nothing builds a relationship so much as listening to another person.

Because your non-profit is trying to build relationships with prospects, it is imperative that you listen to them as part of the cultivation process. This means asking them for their input, hearing their ideas, and acknowledging their contribution of time and talent to your organization. Hear your prospects, and they will become your donors.

Now that we know the keys to understanding the cultivation process, it's time to move right into how that process plays out...

Entry Points for New Prospects

As a growing non-profit, it is not enough to simply identify a great group of prospects. You need to begin to *engage* with them. The way you engage with a new prospect is sometimes referred to as an "entry point." This is the activity whereby the prospect enters your organization's orbit. It is the first real relationship-building activity that you carry out with each of your prospects.

Holding a non-ask event is one of the most common entry points for new prospects. Many non-profits hold informational gatherings at their own location, or at a local business or supporter's home, to introduce their mission to a new group of prospects. Tours of your facility also work well for this purpose.

Generally, I like to tell non-profits that they should be holding a non-ask event as an entry point at least once per quarter. Over the course of that quarter, they should be talking with new prospects and inviting them to the event, which should last at least 45 minutes, but no longer than 90. The key to these events is simply motivating people to want to continue along the cultivation path… telling them about your organization, answering their questions, and drawing them closer to your group.

Of course, events are not the only entry points for new prospects. Another great way to start the process is by setting up individual meetings with donors. If you have new major donor prospects (such as those referred by a board member), breaking bread with the prospect over a meal (or simply meeting with them in their office for 30 minutes) can be a great way to kick off a relationship. Phone calls work as well.

If your non-profit offers volunteer opportunities or does community outreach like putting up booths at fairs, these can also serve as great entry points for new prospects.

The key here is to think through your entry points: are you providing good solid non-ask entry points to your prospects? How often? Each time you come across a new prospect, think to yourself, "What would be the best entry point for this person? How can we best start our relationship with this new prospect?"

Ways to Build a Relationship with Your Prospects

Once a prospect has entered your orbit through an entry point, it's time to begin building a relationship with the prospect – ideally a relationship that is constantly growing and strengthening. There is any number of ways to develop a relationship with a prospect. Here are some of the most common strategies used by non-profits:

Communications

Communicating with your prospects on a regular basis is a great way to strengthen your relationship with them. Possibilities include sending out a paper or e-mail newsletter, mailing annual reports, keeping your website updated, doing short e-blasts to your network, etc.

Events

Non-ask events are great cultivation tools. Whether you are hosting a tour of your facility, bringing in a guest speaker, holding a "thank you" coffee at a local business, or doing a roundtable discussion, prospects and donors should be invited to at least one (and preferably more) free events hosted by your organization each year that are directly related to your mission.

Volunteer Opportunities

When people donate their time, it is often a first step towards donating their money. Offer volunteer opportunities so that your prospects can get actively involved without opening up their wallets – it will make them feel like part of your team and put you in a great position to ask for a gift at a later date. Remember, even if you don't currently offer volunteer opportunities, with some creativity, every organization can find something for volunteers to do.

Committee Membership

Placing prospects on a committee that is doing something related to your non-profit is a great way to get someone engaged. For example, you may form a committee of people to look at ways to generate more PR and buzz around your organization, or you could pull together an auction committee that runs a silent auction at your next fundraiser. Getting people working for you, as part of a group, is a great way to keep them engaged.

Public Relations

You may not think about public relations (PR) as a way of cultivating donors, but it is. Each time a prospect sees a story about your non-profit in the local paper or hears about it on the radio, he or she will not only feel great about their association with you, but will also feel the desire to continue getting more involved with your efforts.

Direct Action

Does your non-profit offer opportunities for supporters to write letters to legislators or other influential people about a certain issue? Have you ever held a rally? How about a health clinic (if you're in a health-related non-profit)? Have you encouraged supporters to write letters to the editor of the local newspaper about a particular subject? Getting your prospects involved in direct action on your behalf is a great way to cultivate them and draw them closer to your non-profit.

Participatory Fundraising

While the vast majority of cultivation tactics should be non-ask, non-fundraising strategies, many non-profits have found that holding participatory fundraising events (things like walk-a-thons or silent auctions... where the organization is asking people to fundraise by *doing* something) are a good way to get prospects to get their feet wet in fundraising without feeling pressured to do so. For example, you may have a prospect who isn't ready for an ask yet that *is* ready to walk in a walk-a-thon and raise $250 for your non-profit as part of that effort. Their participation will go a long way to making that person feel like part of your team and prepare them for future asks.

Your best bet for prospecting is to mix-and-match the above tactics, using a number of them over the course of your prospecting cycle. For example, you may send out 4 e-newsletters per year, plus two paper "snail mail" newsletters each year as well as one annual report. In addition, you could hold 4 non-ask events each year and once per year hold a drive to get people to sign a petition focused on your issue. Keep the activity level up, and keep drawing prospects into deeper relationships with your non-profit.

Drawing Prospects through the Funnel

Remember our funnel analogy... as you interact more with your prospects, a number of them will weed themselves out and drop off your radar screen.

Your job as a fundraiser is to slowly draw people through the funnel, drawing them closer to your organization by making an ever stronger connection.

For example, your first contact with a certain prospect may be when they come to a non-ask event. You then follow up and ask the person via a phone call if they have any questions and for their thoughts on a particular issue. You place that person on your mailing list, and send them a copy of your annual report. Then, you ask the prospect if they'd like to serve on a committee you are putting together. At each step, the person is being drawn closer and closer to your organization. By the time they are through the funnel, they know you, they understand your mission, they are on a committee, etc. – of course they will want to support you financially! That's when it's time to make an ask.

Great fundraising organizations get good at walking people down the path and drawing them through the funnel.

Keeping Donors Engaged

Of course, once you do make an ask (that's the topic of the next section) and the person says "yes," you'll need to keep cultivating the donor. Many non-profits forget about this key step... in order to keep donors engaged and keep them giving year after year, campaign after campaign, it is important to keep cultivating them.

This means that your non-profit should set up a cultivation path for current donors that walks them towards their next gift. This "current donor cultivation" funnel should include lots of thank-you's, and lots of opportunities for current donors to take leadership positions on event committees, etc.

Turning Donors into Evangelists

Another key result of continued cultivation of donors, even after they give, is that your non-profit will be able to turn lots of your donors into evangelists for your organization. This is where your "cultivation funnel" becomes a "cultivation circle" – your efforts come full circle as those prospects you worked so hard to cultivate then go out, help you spread the message of your non-profit and open up their own networks to find *new* prospects to connect with your organization.

Chapter 4:
How to Make Successful
Fundraising Asks

There's no doubt about it... making asks can be one of the most intimidating tasks for any fundraiser. The thought of sitting down across the table from someone and asking them to give your organization $5,000 or $50,000 is enough to make many people eschew the profession all together.

Yet, the ability to make a fundraising ask in person and/or on the phone is one of the most essential skills any professional fundraiser can possess. Sure, writing great grants is important, holding seamless events is too... but nothing compares to the ability to make a cogent, non-threatening, inspiring fundraising ask.

Remember, depending on where you live, individual fundraising likely constitutes between 60-80% of the total fundraising revenue for non-profits in your nation. A significant portion of this giving (and a vast majority of the largest gifts) is the result of direct, personal fundraising asks. As a development professional, executive director, board member, or even a manager on the program side of an organization... you need to know how to make a good fundraising ask.

Taking the Fear Out of Fundraising Asks

Making asks can be scary, but it doesn't need to be. The most important advice I can give you to help you take the fear out of making asks is to practice. Not only will practicing asks help you overcome the anxiety that naturally comes from making asks, but it will also make you a better fundraiser... you'll have your spiel down pat, know how to anticipate objections, and know how to craft a customized ask based on the prospect you are approaching.

I always advise new front-line fundraisers and those who are not comfortable making asks to spend time practicing: first by themselves, running through ask scripts, writing out answers to common objections, imagining themselves sitting across from a donor and asking for money. Then, I suggest they practice with other members of their team, either other development staff or some of the program staff, or even with trusted volunteers.

Finally, I encourage them to get out into the field making "real" asks... preferably along with an experienced member of the development staff who can sit in on the asks and help do an analysis after the fact: What went well? What didn't go well?

Remember... asking for money for your non-profit isn't dirty, slimy, or unethical. Your non-profit does good work. You need money to continue to do good work. You need to fundraise. Without making asks, there is no fundraising, and without fundraising, you don't get to continue carrying out your mission.

It's Cultivate, Then Ask... Not the Other Way Around

The success rate for your fundraising asks will increase dramatically if you understand and implement this one basic rule: prospects should be cultivated before they are asked.

Many development professionals, particularly those new to the game, try to "score" big donations quickly by making asks first, before any relationship is built. These folks hope that once the person says "yes" and writes a check, the donor can be cultivated to build an ongoing relationship.

The scenario usually looks something like this: your new development associate meets a potential donor at your annual fundraising event. This prospect came as the guest of another donor to your organization. The development associate does a follow up call the week after the event to thank the prospect for coming, and to set up an in-person visit (so far, so good). At this meeting, after some good conversation, your development staff member makes a big ask for your new capital campaign.

Big mistake.

The development associate is mistaking the fact that the prospect came to an event and knows a current donor for a true relationship with your organization. This is *not* a relationship with your non-profit. It is the *start* of a relationship. Asks like these rarely work, and when they do result in a gift, it is usually a one-time gift without any ongoing support. Don't make this mistake. Cultivation comes first. Then you make your ask.

The Ask Principles

As you plan your asks, keep these key principles in mind:

People Don't Like to Be Sold

Whether it is a used car salesperson, an insurance agent making a cold call, or a non-profit fundraiser making an ask, people don't like feeling as if they are being sold something. That's why the best salespeople use conversations to draw out wants and needs from buyers, and then present them with a product or service that fills their needs. That's why insurance agents make most of their sales through referrals by friends, family, and current customers. And that's why non-profit fundraisers need to cultivate first and ask second.

People don't want to feel as if your non-profit is "selling" them something. They worry that they will make a donation to you and wake up the next day with "donor's remorse." The best way to overcome this fear is to build a relationship with your prospect. Find out what *they* are interested in… what programs or services that you offer are most important to *them*… how *they* want to give. Make your cultivation and your ask about them, not about you.

People Want to Give

While people don't like to be sold, they *do* like to give. People like to give to non-profits. Giving makes them feel good, and provides them with very real psychological and/or spiritual rewards. Make it easy for them to give. Paint a compelling picture. People want to give and be helpful in general, and if you build a relationship with them and paint a big enough vision, they will want to give and be helpful specifically to your organization.

People Don't Give Unless They Are Asked

This is a key point that needs to be driven home for every organization: for the most part, people don't give unless they are asked. Rare indeed is the situation where your non-profit receives a sizeable donation from a person or company without first asking that person or company to donate. People want to give, but they won't give unless you ask them.

Far too many non-profits set up fundraising events and hope for the best, without making any real asks. Sending out invitations to a fundraising event is the weakest possible form of an ask. In fact, it's almost a non-ask. Asking people from your board and support networks to co-host the event and sell 10 tickets each... that is an ask. Asking companies to sponsor the event at $1,000 a pop... that is an ask, too. Just slapping stamps on invitations? Not really an ask.

The other major problem I see with non-profits is the belief that because they are doing good work, if they just get their name out there, get brochures into the right hands, get a couple of good stories in the local paper, and spend some time at events and tours talking about how much money you need to keep operating, that the money will come rolling in. Nothing is further from the truth. Mentioning how much money you need is not an ask. Talking about how much money you need, then directly asking someone (in person or on the phone) to give a certain portion of that amount... that, my friends, is an ask.

Asks are questions. Asks mention specific amounts. Asks are just that... asks. People don't give unless they are asked.

People Want to Understand Where Their Money is Going

Prospects feel much better about saying "yes" to your asks when they understand where their money is going. If you ask someone for $100,000, he or she wants to know what that money will be used for. If you need a host committee member to sell 10 tickets to your event at $100 per ticket, they want to know why you need to raise another $1,000 for your non-profit.

Do you know why you need the money? Does your staff? Can your staff, board, and fundraising volunteers all explain in a succinct and clear manner why you need to raise the money that you are currently trying to raise?

How much does it cost you to serve one more meal, do one more operation, accept one more child into your school, provide one more scholarship? Whatever your non-profit's mission is, break down your program budget into bite sized chunks. If you are approaching a donor who has a heart for serving the poor and asking her to make a $50,000 gift to your soup kitchen, and you can explain that $50,000 will allow you to serve another 25,000 hot meals this coming year, that's far more powerful than simply asking for the cash for general expenses.

Also, be transparent with your donors. Your prospects (particularly your larger donor prospects) will understand that a certain portion of every donated dollar goes to cover overhead expenses. Keep these expenses reasonable, and be willing to share with donors what percent of their donation will go to overhead costs.

People Want to Know that They are Making a Difference

If your non-profit doesn't have a big vision... if you're doing the same thing this year as last year, serving the same number of people, or carrying out the same activities... it's going to be very hard for donors to understand why they should make a big donation to your organization.

Donors want to know that they are making a difference and moving the dial. It's easier to make asks and raise money when your organization has a big vision and can articulate that vision for donors. Allow your prospects to make a big impact by donating to your organization. If you ask them to make a big gift to simply maintain the status quo they will likely donate elsewhere.

People Need to Have Their Objections Answered (Even If They Don't Mention Them)

Just as in sales, your donors *will* have objections when you make asks. And again, just as in sales, they may not always voice those objections. It is your job as a non-profit fundraiser to anticipate those objections based on the relationship you have with the prospect and to answer them quickly and convincingly.

Some of the most common objections donors have are: not thinking that their gift will make a real difference, not trusting that the organization will use the money as they say they will, not thinking the organization will be able to accomplish its mission, worrying that once the organization receives the money, the donor will stop having input at the non-profit, and not understanding the terms and conditions of the gift agreement.

The best thing your development staff can do, if they anticipate an objection in the donor's mind, is bring it out into the open and answer it. For example:

"Mr. Welsh, it seems like you're concerned that you won't have ongoing input into the Help-a-Student Fund at our organization once your $1 million gift is used to establish it. My suggestion would be that we create an advisory board for the fund, and that you chair that board, which will have oversight over the use of the funds. Would that be something you would be interested in?"

Notice that you're not giving Mr. Welsh a seat on your organization's board of directors (though that may be a possibility depending on the size of the gift and the size of your organization). Instead, you are creating an advisory group to oversee the fund being created with Mr. Welsh's sizeable donation.

People Want to Give to Organizations They Trust

It is imperative for your non-profit to establish trust with your prospects and donors. People give to organizations they trust. Nothing is a bigger deal-breaker than a lack of trust. The way to develop trust is through the ongoing cultivation process, as well as being totally open and transparent with your donors.

Offer facility tours… people want to see what goes on in your office. Print up annual reports including full financials… donors want easy access to your financial information. Gather data showing the effects of your work… people want to be sure that your non-profit is making a difference, and the only thing that really proves this is cold, hard numbers.

Last, but not least, be accessible. If a prospect or donor calls your office, and no one answers, and no one calls him or her back for a week, you're going to seem unprofessional and unworthy of a donor's trust.

People Give Based on Relationships

Remember what we said in the cultivation section… fundraising is all about relationships. People give based on relationships, both relationships with your organization as well as relationships with people at your organization. Take the time to build inter-personal relationships with your prospects. Spend time getting to know them. Then make your asks.

Planning the Ask

Before you make any ask of a donor or prospect, be sure to ask yourself the following questions:

1. **Who Am I Asking?** It's important to know your prospect. Who are you asking? What do you know about this person? During your cultivation of this prospect, did you find out what parts of your cause matter most to him or her? Have you crafted an ask tailored to this specific prospect, based on his / her interests and desires?

2. **What am I asking for?** How much money are you asking this person to give to your organization? During the cultivation phase, did you figure out what this person's giving capacity is? (Or, did you at least research their capacity online?) What type of gift are you asking for: Capital campaign? Annual fund? Endowment? Planned giving? Are you asking for a one time gift or a multi-year commitment? What terms and conditions? Do you have a gift agreement prepared?

Also, go into your ask with the following mindset:

Understand That There Will Be "No's": And that's ok! Fundraising is like baseball... even the best and most experienced practitioners receive lots of "no's." Don't let them get you down. No's are simply a (small) part of the fundraising game.

But Expect a Yes: Attitude matters in fundraising. If you go into a fundraising ask assuming you will get a no, you probably will. Remember, your organization's mission matters! Go into every fundraising ask expecting a yes and asking for a yes.

Show People How They Can Make a Concrete Difference or Reach a Concrete Goal: People like to know that their donation is doing something specific and concrete. If at all possible, ask them to contribute to help do something specific, even if it is only to help you reach your own personal fundraising goal. For example, "Would you contribute $50 to pay for 25 meals for the homeless?" or "I'm trying to raise $1,000 for the Boy Scouts. Will you donate $100 to help me reach that goal?"

The Process: Anatomy of an Ask

Great, you say: I've built relationships, I've planned out my ask. Now, tell me... how do I actually make an ask? The best way to make an ask (any ask, whether for money, time, volunteer hours, or anything else) is by following these simple steps:

1. Get the pleasantries out of the way.

Talk about the kids, the family, work, the last time you saw the other person. Get the small talk out of the way first.

2. Make a transition.

Once the small talk is out of the way, make a transition so that people know the topic has changed to something far more serious. Good transitions include, "Listen... I want to talk about something important," "I've got a serious question for you," or, "Jane, I need your help win a very important matter."

3. Make the connection.

Once you've moved into more serious conversation through your transition, remind the prospect of the connection that you personally have with the organization, and that they have with the organization (if they have one). For instance, "Jim, as you know, I've been on the board of the Farmer's Assistance Fund for three years now..." or, "Colleen, you've been to three events at the Rising Sun School now, and have volunteered at our annual community day..."

4. <u>Make them cry.</u>

Maybe that sounds a little over the top… but you want to make sure that the person you are talking to understands the impact of your mission. Remind them what your charity does, and why it is important. Good examples are, "Samuel, every day, hundreds of people are diagnosed with XYZ disease, and each year 2,500 will die because they can't afford the medication they need to treat their affliction" or "Janet, I'm heartbroken when I look into the faces of these former child soldiers. I see such pain, and I can't believe we don't have the resources to help every single one."

5. <u>Make them understand why you need what you are asking for.</u>

This is the background for your specific ask. Why are you asking them to come to an event? ("We're trying to raise our public profile…") Why are you asking them to give $500? ("We want to serve more hungry families" or "We want to provide 40 more scholarships to needy children so that they can get a great education").

6. <u>Make the ask.</u>

Remember to make it a question, and to ask for something concrete and specific.

So, the formula is:

Small-Talk

Transition

Connection

Emotion

Need

Ask

That may seem like a complicated formula, but once you practice it a few times, you'll see that is actually quite natural, and makes for a pleasant experience. Using this formula, your ask may sound like this:

Hi Ruth, how are you? How are the kids? (Pleasantries)

Listen, I've got something important to ask you. (Make the Transition)

You've been working with the free clinic for almost a year now, and I know it's something that is very near and dear to your heart. I love seeing you at our monthly advisory committee meetings! (Make the Connection)

Every time I visit the clinic, I see meet the nicest families, who seem just like mine, only they can't afford even basic medical care for their children. I see kids who have to be admitted because their families couldn't afford antibiotics for a simple infection. It's very sad! We have to do more to help these families in need. (Make Them Cry)

Ruth, right now, we can only serve about 50% of the families who need our help. Our goal is to be able to serve every single family and child that needs medical care at the clinic. We need to raise another $100,000 to make that dream a reality. (Tell Them Why)

Would you be willing to contribute $25,000 to help us reach that goal? (Make the Ask)

Don't be afraid, as part of your planning process, to write out a script for yourself and practice it over and over again so you'll be ready for your ask. And remember, always profusely thank everyone who responds to your ask, and be sure to thank those who say "no" for their time and consideration.

Chapter 5:
Stewardship - How to Turn One-Time Donors into Lifelong Supporters of Your Organization

You've found new prospects. You've approached them to begin a relationship. You've cultivated them, strengthening that relationship and building trust. Finally, you made an ask and the prospect said, "Yes." The check came, and you send a thank-you note. Now, your work is done.

Wait... what?

Your work is far from over! When someone makes a gift and you acknowledge it, that's just the beginning of the rest of your relationship with the donor: the stewardship phase. Far too many non-profits that are great on prospecting, cultivation, and asking are terrible at stewarding. Far too many development directors think, "We got a check! My work here is done... now, on to the next prospect in my cultivation funnel!"

Non-profits that think like that are in for a tough road as they try to grow their development efforts. Great donor stewardship is the key to a successful, prevailing, growing non-profit organization.

What is Stewardship?

I don't often refer to stock definitions but here I will, because I think Wikipedia's definition of "stewardship" is instructive: *"Stewardship is an ethic that embodies responsible planning and management of resources... and is linked to the concept of sustainability."*

As non-profits, we have limited resources and our planning processes are (or should be geared) towards the responsible use of those limited resources for maximum gain... that is, they should be geared to make a maximum impact in the world according to our mission. One of the most precious resources we have is our donors. We must plan and manage our relationship with these donors with an eye towards sustaining the relationship in order to sustain our organization.

Why Does Stewardship Matter?

Stewardship matters because individuals and companies who give to your non-profit once are likely to give again. In fact, a current donor is five times more likely to give to your non-profit than a new prospect is. Can you see why your current donors are "resources" that you need to steward?

Non-profit organizations that don't care for their current donors will lose them. If your idea of stewarding your donors is simply to ask them for money twice per year, they will eventually look for another place to invest their charitable giving dollars. Finding new donors to make up for all of the old donors you lose in this way will be a challenging (if not impossible) task. If you are relying on prospecting for new donors as the long-term base of your fundraising organization, you will not succeed, and if you do, it will only be with far more work, expense and hassle than it otherwise could have been.

If, on the other hand, you are constantly stewarding your donors and treating them like the amazing resources that they are in addition to prospecting for new donors, you will find that your fundraising efforts go much more smoothly… not only because your current donors will form a good and solid foundation for your fundraising efforts each year, but also because your current donors will help you find new prospects from within their own networks. Donor stewardship matters at every non-profit, *including yours!*

The 7 Essential Principles of Donor Stewardship

Having discussed the importance of donor stewardship, let's look at the principles behind a great donor stewardship program:

Stewardship is a Process

It is important to remember that, much like donor cultivation, donor stewardship is a process. The process starts when the donor makes a gift and you send an acknowledgement letter. The relationship-building process that you began in the cultivation phase doesn't end with the gift, it just moves on to a new level. As with cultivation, during the stewardship phase the relationship should continue to grow and strengthen.

Stewardship is not a one-time thing. Sending a thank you note and adding the donor to your mailing list does *not* constitute good stewardship. Your non-profit should have a stewardship plan in place for your donors that specifically spells out what will happen once someone makes a gift. Many non-profits have found it helpful to have two stewardship plans in place: one for smaller donors and one for larger donors. For your biggest donors, you will likely want to have an individualized stewardship plan in place for that person that takes into account their gift size as well as their likes, dislikes, and interests.

Stewardship Requires Communication

At its core, the stewardship process is one of relationship-building. And deep down, building good relationships is all about communication. Your stewardship program relies on communication between your non-profit and your donor. Thus, good stewardship requires good communication.

This means you should always be ready to talk to your donors. Donor calls should get priority from your staff and their letters and e-mails should be answered swiftly. Donors should receive newsletters and other information, be invited to events, and asked for their input. The more you talk to your donors, the healthier your relationship with them will be.

Stewardship Requires Transparency

People give based on emotional response and a relationship of trust. Your mission moves them, and makes them want to give... and they *trust* you to make a difference. Trust requires transparency.

If you want to truly build a relationship of trust with your donors, and draw them ever-closer to your organization, you need to be honest with them about your organization's plans for the future, about your financial situation, and most importantly about where that donor's money is going.

If you can tell a donor exactly where you spent their money and exactly how many people you were able to help because of the donation, do so. If you can send the donor pictures of the difference their donation made, send them. If you can't talk about exactly where the money went, be sure to tell them generally where the money went.

For example, if you run a scholarship program, and a donor gave you $10,000, tell them how many students received scholarships and where those students are going to school. If you can send them thank you notes from each of those students... even better! If, for whatever reason, you can't directly identify the students who received the funds, talk about how many scholarships you gave out in general, where the money is going (how much to each school? How much in each town?) and also how many scholarships the $10,000 provided, on average.

You'll also want to be very transparent with your donors in a broader sense. Send out an annual financial report (or an annual report with a financial section) that tells donors exactly how you are spending their money. How much are you spending on overhead? How much is going to programs? How much money does it cost to serve one person? How many more people could you serve if you raised an additional $1,000? What about an additional $1,000,000?

Don't limit this type of transparency to your annual reports, either. Constantly remind donors how an additional $1,000 could feed one more impoverished village for a month or how $50 can pay for another mosquito tent. Tell your donors when you receive a major new gift, or launch a major new initiative. The more transparent you are, the more your donors will trust your organization.

The Best Donors Give More than Money

If a donor gives a gift, then starts participating on one of your non-profit's committees... or starts writing letters to the editor on your behalf... or starts volunteering for you... they are much more likely to give again than someone who simply gives and then takes no further action.

Simply put... the best donors (the ones who stay excited, give year after year and increase their gift size overtime) give more than just money... they give their time and expertise to your charity.
This means that once someone gives a gift, your staff should make every effort to get that person involved somehow, whether it is through volunteering, serving on your marketing committee, chairing the silent auction, or simply offering their advice on one of your programs. Get them involved, and they will continue to give year after year.

Of course, some people will not be want to (or not be able to) get more involved beyond writing a check, and that's ok. The important thing is that you make the effort so that all of those who *do* want to get involved can do so.

Keep the Process Fresh and Exciting

Nothing kills donor enthusiasm more than getting the same communications and invitations year after year. Most donor stewardship programs look something like this: donor makes a gift and gets a thank you note. Donor gets invited to three events per year, two are fundraising events, one is informational only. Donor gets our annual appeal and annual letter. Donor gets 4 e-newsletters per year.

Don't get me wrong – that's a great start, and more than most non-profits are doing to steward donors in an organized fashion. But after getting the same stuff year after year... donors get tired and bored. When donors get bored, they start looking for other organizations to get involved in that *will* be new and exciting, at least for two or three years. In order to keep your donors engaged and involved, you have to keep the process fresh and exciting.

The best way to accomplish this task is by inserting a couple of new cultivation tactics each year while cycling others out of your rotation. For example one year you could have a well-known guest speaker come to a donors-only event. The next year, you could send out a photo-book to your best donors with photos taken at your facility over the course of the year. Another year, you could form an ad-hoc committee that provides recommendations on some facet of your program, and solicit members from among your donor-base. Whatever you do, keep it fresh and new.

Recognition is Crucial

They don't like to admit it, but donors like to be recognized. That's why most non-profit annual reports include a list of that year's donors, and why offering "naming opportunities" is such a great way to encourage large gifts. Recognition of donors is crucial to your donor stewardship efforts.

In addition to the annual report lists and naming opportunities mentioned above, you can recognize your donors by offering special donor-only events, providing lapel pins and other branded materials to your donors, or creating giving clubs that recognize donors at different levels of participation. Whatever you do, be sure you have a donor recognition program in place at your organization.

Solicit Sparingly – But Do Solicit

There are two extremes when it comes to donor stewardship programs.

Some non-profits solicit too much – their donors feel like they are constantly getting asked for money. If you are asking the same donors for money 4 or 5 times per year (or more) you likely fall into this category (even if those asks are for different things... your donors will still feel like they are being asked all of the time). The exception to this rule is direct mail-only donors – who can usually be safely asked for money multiple times per year without suffering donor fatigue.

On the other extreme, many non-profits who are running otherwise exemplary stewardship programs ask their donors for money too rarely. These organizations worry that if they ask for money more than once per year donors will get turned off. So they rely on their annual appeal or their annual event exclusively to raise money from their stewardship funnel. Unfortunately, many times donors would be happy to give more often than that and in fact some can get turned off by not getting asked more often – figuring that your organization doesn't really need their help.

I have found that for many non-profits, the sweet spot is to make asks 2-3 times per year for donors who have already given once, making sure that each ask is for a different category of giving wherever possible (for example, you may ask for an annual fund gift via letter, an event sponsorship via event invitation, and a capital campaign gift via phone call... or whatever your giving categories are). Of course, your mileage may vary, and this rule of thumb will not apply at every organization. For some, it will be more, for a few, it will be less. The only way you will know is by testing and asking.

9 Ways to Steward Your Donors

Now that we know the basic principles behind donor stewardship, it's time to talk about the actual tactics that non-profits use to steward donors. We talked about several of these methods in the sections above. Here are the nine most popular and successful tactics for stewarding donors throughout the year, in no particular order:

Newsletters / E-Newsletters

Sending out snail mail newsletters and e-newsletters has become one of the most popular arrows in the fundraiser's quiver for a reason: they work. Newsletters (and e-newsletters) are easy to produce and send, and donors love getting them. They are a quick and easy way to keep your entire donor network up to date on what is going on at your non-profit.

If you have a donor list of any size, consider sending out a newsletter by mail or e-mail at least once per quarter, or perhaps once per month.

A Regularly Updated Website

Your website can be a great way to steward your donors if you train them to check back in with your site on a regular basis. Of course the only way that people will want to visit your site regularly is if it (a) is updated regularly and (b) contains entertaining, emotional, or useful information.

Modern website content management systems (such as WordPress and Expression Engine) make it easy even for non-technically inclined staff to manage and update a website. Setup such a system at your charity and keep your website interesting and up to date. Then, spread the word by telling your donors and prospects to check out the site on a regular basis, and include the site's URL in every communication you send out. Also, post special reports and other interesting "one-off" items on the site, and when you do, send out an e-mail blast alerting donors that they can get their own copy by visiting your site. This encourages donors to visit your website more often.

Non-Ask Events

Non-ask events are one of my favorite methods for stewarding donors. A non-ask event is an event held by your non-profit that targets donors (or prospects), but does not include any fundraising ask or cost of admission for attendees. The goal of a non-ask event is to move donors closer to your organization (and eventually, toward even larger gifts and involvement), and to move prospects towards making their first gift.

Non-ask events are an opportunity to tell attendees about your mission, introduce them to your staff, and make them feel like part of your team. While these types of events can take many forms, generally they involve a tour of your office / facility, with time for socializing and a short program, or they can be held at a local restaurant where attendees hear about your mission over cocktails and light appetizers.

As part of these events you will want to give your guests time to eat, drink, and mingle, then put on a short program that introduces your mission: what you do and how you do it. You'll want to come at it from an emotional angle: Why is your mission important? What are the outcomes of your work? Be sure to introduce your staff. Give attendees some time to ask questions, and send them home with some literature. Let them know that someone will be following up with them to see if they have any further questions.

Then, send them home. The most successful non-ask events are short, and the program and speeches don't drag on. Aim to have attendees in and out in 60-90 minutes, with only 10-15 minutes of talking. If you are doing a tour, try to have 10-15 minutes of talking and a 10-15 minute tour, with the rest of the time reserved for socializing and questions.

Another great type of non-ask event is the "special" event, where you bring in a well-known speaker, author, or celebrity for a one-time event talking about the mission of your non-profit.

One-on-One or Small Group Meetings

There's nothing like personal contact to build and maintain relationships. For larger donors, your Executive Director, Board Chair, Development Director, and perhaps other board members should regularly be going out and meeting with them (I recommend breakfast and lunch meetings, or for busier donors, short 15 minute catch-up meetings at their office). The goal of these meetings is to check in, update the donor on the organization, hand them some materials, see if they have any questions, and then move on. While one-on-one meetings can and should be used to make asks, I also recommend that you go out and see your larger donors at least once per year *without asking for money*.

For mid-level donors, you can have small group meetings at your organization's office, at a local restaurant or coffee shop, or at one of the donors' offices for the same purpose: personalized attention, an update, and questions, all without an ask.

Personal Phone Calls

As with one-one-one and small group meetings, personal phone calls can and should be used to make asks. That being said, mid-level and larger donors should also get occasional calls from your non-profit's staff and board with updates and announcements. These non-ask calls strengthen the donor relationship by providing an extra level of personal care and attention to your donor.

Participatory Fundraising Events

Participatory fundraising is the strategy of using dozens, hundreds, or thousands of people, participating in a single even or campaign, to raise money for an organization. Things like walk-a-thons, collecting change (Operation Rice Bowl), and restaurant weeks where a number of eateries all donate a percentage of profits to a charity are all examples of participatory fundraising.

While this is certainly "fundraising," for your current donors you don't need to count an ask for a participatory event (like "walk in our walk-a-thon" or "collect spare change at your child's school") as a ask for purposes of our 2-3 asks per year rule mentioned above. Instead, count this as a stewardship tactic. You'll raise some money, but more importantly, your donors will feel a deeper connection with your organization by participating in these events, which also will help them to feel like part of your "team."

Special Action Campaigns

Letter writing campaigns, rallies, and other "special action" campaigns can likewise help your donors feel like an important part of your team. Ask your donors to participate in campaigns like this, tell them why the campaign is important and then thank them for their action.

Giving Clubs

Donor giving clubs are a great way to steward donors. Giving clubs are usually based on various levels of giving (for example, you may have a giving club for donors who give $1,000-$5,000 per year, one for donors who give $5,000-$25,000 per year, and one for donors who give $25,000+ per year, as well as a "legacy" giving club for donors who remember your organization in their will. Obviously, your levels and the number of clubs you host will depend on your non-profit's specific circumstances).

Giving clubs should offer different benefits to different levels, including exclusive events and newsletters, gifts, tickets to paid events, sponsorship opportunities, public recognition, etc.

Branded Giveaways

Finally, branded giveaways with your organization's name and logo can make great thank-you / stewardship gifts for your donors. Lapel pins are a popular choice, as are pens, calendars, and other ornaments.

How to Effectively Use Giving Societies and Donor Clubs to Steward Donors

Giving societies and donor clubs are groups set up by a non-profit to help cultivate and steward donors, keep them loyal to the organization, and encourage them to give more (and larger) gifts in the future. Generally, non-profits set up various groups at different giving levels, and offer corresponding benefits to group members.

For example, a legal aid society may set up three groups, The Advocates, The Defenders, and The Friends, and offer membership to donors who give at least $25,000, $10,000 and $2,000 respectively. In return, donors get benefits like access to special events, newsletters, lapel pins, etc., with donors at higher levels getting larger benefits.

Please note that we can use the terms "giving society" and "donor club" interchangeably, they both generally refer to the same types of groups.

Giving and benefit levels for donor clubs will vary depending on the organization (e.g. at one organization, a $25,000 donor may qualify as one of the charity's top donors, while at another non-profit that might barely be considered a "major gift"). All non-profits are different.

Types of Societies and Clubs

There are many different types of giving societies that a non-profit can set up, based on its needs. Some of the most common types of groups include:

- Major Donor Groups: Donor clubs focused on major givers

- Mid-Level Donor Groups: Donor clubs focused on mid-level givers

- Minor Donor Groups: Donor clubs focused on small-dollar ($5, $25, $100, etc.) level supporters

- <u>Annual Giving Clubs</u>: Groups comprised of those who make a qualifying-level donation each and every year

- <u>Monthly Giving Clubs</u>: Giving societies centered on those who sign-up for monthly (recurring) credit card giving

- <u>Legacy Societies</u>: Donor club for those who have pledged a bequest or planned gift to the non-profit

- <u>Young Professionals Groups</u>: Focused on those under a certain age who have given a certain amount to the organization

- <u>Affinity Groups</u>: Donor clubs focused on supporters who share one or more "affinities" or traits, such as geographical region, occupation, age, hobby, etc.

Why These Groups Work

Donor clubs and giving societies work to increase donor loyalty and lifetime donor value because they make your donors feel like part of your team. Fundraising is about building relationships with our donors. Giving societies build stronger, deeper relationships with donors because they make your donors feel "special," which they are.

The benefits you offer to your donor club members show them that you appreciate them and that their support matters. Furthermore, the regular communications you send out and events you hold with your society members strengthens that bond and creates the sense that this is "our" organization, one that club members are proud to support and help "lead."

Finally, giving clubs help *systematize* your donor funnel and provide order to the chaotic world of donor cultivation. Giving clubs with various levels and benefit plans force you to think through the donor experience and place it on a schedule, which helps reduce fundraising stress for staff and donors alike.

The Do's and Don'ts of Giving Societies and Donor Clubs

Now that we know what giving societies and donor clubs are, and why they work, let's briefly look at a few fundamental do's and don'ts for utilizing them at your non-profit:

1. DO treat donor club members as individuals.

While donor clubs are a great way to provide structure to your fundraising efforts, remember that every donor is different and that each will require differing amounts of contact and hand-holding. Don't let donor clubs prevent you from treating your supporters like real, individual people.

2. DON'T take giving society members for granted.

Some non-profits make the mistake of thinking that once someone is a member of a giving club, they will continue to give year in, year out, no matter what you do. Nothing could be further from the truth. Your donors aren't ATMs. They are people. They require relationship-building and stewardship.

3. DO start small...

Many non-profits launching giving societies think they have to have 3, 4, or more clubs / levels right out of the gate. You don't – there's nothing wrong with launching your program with just one group / level. In fact, it is usually the smart way to dip your toes into the water. Consider launching just one group next year, and see where it goes from there.

4. DON'T offer lifetime memberships in your clubs.

A few organizations offer "lifetime membership" options for joining their giving societies (e.g. one non-profit I know has a $5,000+ per year minimum for one of its clubs, but for $50,000 you get lifetime membership). I don't like lifetime memberships because they encourage "one and done" philanthropy, where a person will give once and likely never give again, and will do so in good conscience because they are a lifetime member of your giving club. I much prefer ongoing (and on-*growing*) relationships with my donors.

Setting the Giving Levels

The first step in creating well-run donor clubs at your organization is to set the giving level(s) for your club or clubs. As you think through these target levels, you'll want to be sure that you have enough current prospects in each level to make the club worth your time and energy.

For example, if you currently have 100 donors in the $1-$1,000 range 40 donors in the $1,000 – $5,000 range, and 8 donors in the $5,000+ range, you probably don't need a giving club for those giving $25,000 or more per year… at least not yet.

When setting your giving levels, make them large enough that they encompass a wide group of donors / potential donors, but small enough that they still seem exclusive. For the organization above, this might mean having a donor club at the $1,000+ level and another at the $5,000+ level, but not setting up a club for donors $5-$5,000, which is too large a swath of donors to maintain exclusivity.

Defining Benefits

For each donor club / giving level, the organization should offer a range of benefits that serve to both recognize the donor for his or her support as well as to continue cultivating the donor for future gifts. Some common giving society benefits include:

- Invitations to exclusive events
- Member-only newsletters, magazines, and reports

- Special lapel pins or buttons
- Recognition in the annual report, on the website, etc.

The benefits you offer should be related to your organization and to the donor, but you should feel free to be creative about what you give your club members.

Naming the Clubs / Levels

Each giving society / donor club level should have a name. The best types of club names are those that relate to your mission (e.g. for a scholarship fund, you could have groups called Educators, Scholars, Professors, Learning Partners, etc.)

Other popular ways to name donor clubs are using the names of past leaders of the non-profit or founding board members, or using standard naming conventions like "Friend of..." "Chairman's Circle..." etc.)

Launching Your Clubs

When launching your giving clubs, it is important to remember that one of the main goals of these groups is to encourage your donors to stretch a little to reach the next giving level.

When you launch your clubs, my suggestion is that you ask those that are already giving at that level (but who are not close to another, higher level) to become the "Founding Members" or "Charter Members" of that club. Consider appointing an honorary chairperson from among these first members to serve a one year term as the head of that donor club.

Then, approach those donors who are giving slightly below the club level and "invite" them to become members by upgrading their gift. As with all asks, the best way to solicit a giving club gift is to ask in person. The next best way is by phone, followed by a snail mail letter / invitation.

Giving clubs work very well for annual funds and general giving to non-profits, as well as for capital, endowment, and other campaigns. But remember... donor clubs take work. You must constantly be asking prospects to join, cultivating members, and upgrading members to higher levels.

Using Giving Societies and Clubs to Retain and Upgrade Donors

The prime reasons for using giving societies and donor clubs at a non-profit are to (a) retain donors and (b) upgrade them to new levels. If your non-profit isn't doing this as part of its donor club effort, then you're not getting everything you can out of this fundraising tactic.

Use giving societies to retain donors by offering your club members constant cultivation and recognition. Make them feel special and part of your "team" because of their membership. Offer members a dedicated donor representative or a direct line to the Executive Director, particularly at higher giving levels.

Similarly, use donor clubs to upgrade your donors by regularly scouring your club lists to see which donors might be ready to move up a level. Spend extra time cultivating those donors, then make a clear and concrete ask for an upgrade. I have found that giving club members are much more likely to say "yes" to an upgrade ask then non-members, if they have the capacity to give at that level.

If you're not using giving societies and donor clubs at your non-profit, consider adding them to your fundraising mix for the coming year.

Stewardship Phase 2: Leveraging Donors' Networks

As mentioned above, the primary purpose for donor stewardship is to ensure that the donor becomes a lifelong giver to your organization and hopefully that he or she gives at a higher and higher level each year. Once a donor is on board and actively engaged in your stewardship program, "Phase 2" of your efforts is leveraging your donor's networks to find new donors.

As mentioned above in our section on prospecting, one of the best ways to find new donors is by getting your current donors to open up their own networks on your behalf. By asking your donors to introduce you to others who might also be interested in giving, you are leveraging your relationship with the donor to find more prospects as well as building an even stronger relationship with that donor.

In our next section, below, we are going to talk about how to leverage your current donors to build viral fundraising networks that will dramatically increase the reach of your current fundraising operation.

Chapter 6:
Building Donor Fundraising
Networks and Affinity Groups

Building fundraising networks is my favorite topic in fundraising, because it is so very crucial to creating sustainable, vital non-profit organizations. Organizations can grow by focusing on direct mail, or events, or planned giving. They can sustain themselves year to year through silent auctions, fundraising e-mails, and hosted events. But unless we are talking about a major national organization with a wide fundraising base of smaller givers, very few non-profits reach the stage where they are thriving, where they're worried less about where the next dollar will come from and more about how big an impact they can make, without building fundraising networks.

What are "Fundraising Networks?"

A fundraising network is a group of people who have committed to raise money on behalf of an organization or charity. It can be a formal committee, loose group of support, board of directors, or other coalition that is systematically opening up its rolodex on your behalf, introducing you to new prospects who may be interested in giving to your organization.

Some common examples are finance committees, development committees, or young professionals fundraising groups. Many organizations have multiple... or even dozens of... fundraising networks working for them, all of which combine to form one gigantic network that raises a lot of money on behalf of a charity.

There are any number of ways you can grow your own fundraising network "tree," and any number of levels you can progress through. It's a lot like a multi-level marketing company: you start with a group of people who already support you and your organization. You cultivate them, you get them involved. Then, you ask them to introduce you to their friends. You then cultivate their friends and get them involved. You ask them to make a donation, and they do. Then, when the time is right, you ask this new group (who by now has been with your organization for enough time to become supporters) to introduce you to *their* friends, neighbors, colleagues, etc.

It is (or should be) a never-ending cycle of bringing in new groups of prospects, turning them into donors, and then asking them to bring in the next group of prospects. The math is appealing. Let's say you start with your 10 board members, and ask them to introduce your organization to their friends and colleagues. Let's assume that 5 actually do. If those 5 board members each introduce you to five new people, that's 25 new prospects. With your board members' help, you cultivate these prospects and convert 15 of them into donors. Over time, you ask these 15 new donors to help you reach into *their* networks. Let's say that once again, half (7) do. If those 7 each introduce you to five new people, that's 35 new prospects… and so on, and so on.

The place to start, of course, is with your current board, donors, volunteers, and other supporters.

What are "Coalitions" and "Affinity" Groups?

One of the best ways to build fundraising networks is to organize your donors and friends into coalitions or "affinity groups" that form around a common trait or goal, and then work together to increase your fundraising network. The terms "coalition" and "affinity group" are interchangeable, but I prefer affinity groups, so let's use that term. Your affinity groups could be centered on any number of different traits:

Age

For example, you could have a young professionals / young friends of group, a senior citizens group, or if you are a school, alumni groups based on what year someone graduated.

Geography

You could form groups based on what state, county, town, or neighborhood someone lives in.

Industry

Perhaps your organization would benefit from a "doctors for..." group or an "attorneys for..." coalition, or some other industry specific affinity group.

Interests

Would it make sense for you to have a dog lovers group, or a "parents with children" group, or a homeschoolers group? What about other interests that some of your supporters share?

Giving Level / Major Donor Clubs

Many non-profits have found that forming clubs based on how much someone has given to their organization works well. For example, maybe your "Executive Level" club consists of donors who gave $100,000 or more to your non-profit, and your "Silver Level" club consists of donors who gave $25,000 or more to your charity.

Minor Donor Clubs

Another great option is to have minor-donor level clubs for people who give a small amount to your non-profit, particularly if they give a small amount year after year. For example, maybe people who give $50 or more per year can become "members" or "friends of..." your organization, and people who give $250 or more can join your "Boosters" or other level club.

The key with building affinity groups is to make them into interactive "clubs." Hold meetings – send out e-updates and member-only newsletters – give people leadership roles on the committee – in short, make everyone feel like an extra-special part of an extra-special team. This will not only encourage them to donate to your organization, but will make them much more likely to be willing to open up their own network to find new donors for your organization.

Why are Fundraising Networks and Affinity Groups Important?

Fundraising networks are important because they allow you to multiply your fundraising efforts. Instead of asking just one person for just one donation, by building a fundraising network you can ask that one person to fundraise on your behalf, thus turning one ask into several, or even into hundreds, depending on the skill of your network members.

One of the biggest problems faced by non-profits is their ability (or inability) to constantly feed their fundraising funnel with new prospects. How many times have you said to yourself, "Gee, I wish we had more folks to approach for a donation!" or "Wow, I wish we had more prospects for this event..." Building good fundraising networks will allow your organization to have a never-ending supply of leads. Your best bet is to build a combination of fundraising networks at your non-profit: both standard fundraising networks, without affinity group labels, (such as one starting with your board and moving outward from there), as well as branded affinity groups focused on various traits, industries, locales, etc.

How to Build Fundraising Networks for Your Non-Profit

Building a fundraising network may seem intimidating – how are you going to get an ever-increasing number of people to open up their rolodexes to you, so you can cultivate them and make an ask? The truth though, is that this process need not be scary – you can start small, and grow your network and affinity groups over time.

The best place to start is with your board and with your largest current donors. You should *never* approach someone to open up their phonebook to you until you have cultivated them first. Likewise, my suggestion is that your first ask to someone you have cultivated should always be for money – you should always ask them to make a financial investment in your organization's success *before* you ask them to help you build your fundraising network.

Go to your current board and donors, and tell them what you are doing – that you are looking to introduce your organization to new people who may be interested in getting involved. Then make it easy for your board and supporters to help you. You can make it easy by giving them materials on your organization that they can use to talk to others about your non-profit, by giving them sample scripts and talking points, or... my favorite method... by setting up a "non-ask" event that they can invite their friends to where they know that you will *not* ask for money, but will instead simply introduce your mission, your staff, and your work to their contacts (you will, of course, follow up later with those that are interested in getting involved).

In order for people to feel comfortable handing their friends and colleagues over to you, they will need to feel comfortable with your process. I suggest that you explain to them *exactly* the method you will use in cultivating these contacts so that they can get comfortable with it. The best strategy, in my experience, is the following:

First, your donor / supporter invites their contacts to a "non-ask" event to hear about your organization. (Many organizations set up these events several times per year). At this event, their questions are answered and they are given materials on the non-profit, they take a tour of your facility and meet your staff, as well as see the good work that you do.

Then, after the event, someone from your staff calls each person who attended to thank them for getting more involved (you could offer a volunteer opportunity, offer to send more information on a specific program, ask them to join a committee... basically anything that is *not* asking for money).

The results of these calls should be reported back to the person who invited the prospect to the meeting. If the person said "no," meaning they don't want to get more involved, the non-profit should stop calling and only pick up the cultivation if the board member or other donor who brought the contact into your funnel has another conversation and changes the prospect's mind. If the person says "yes," they do want to get more involved, then you can consider them a true prospect and place them directly into your cultivation process.

How to Build Affinity Groups for Your Non-Profit

The plan for starting affinity groups is similar, except that with affinity groups, you'll want to start by finding donors and supporters to help lead the group – the best groups have strong chairmen, co-chairs, or other leaders who are willing to work hard to pull in members, lead the meetings, and otherwise provide leadership and motivation for the group.

Start by approaching people who might want to have leadership roles in the club, then move on to talking with current supporters who might want to be members. Once you have a core group of leaders and members, you can start branching out by asking these core members to reach into their own networks to find *new* members.

One great way to build affinity groups is to start with a non-ask event. Put together a host committee and hold an event that talks about your organization – then transition the host committee into the leadership of the group, and transition the event attendees into the membership if the group. Then, cultivate, cultivate, cultivate.

For example, if you trying to build a young professionals affinity group for your town's hospital, you could start by finding a number of young leaders to form a host committee and hold a non-ask event (maybe a happy hour?) at a popular local pub. During this event, your hospital leadership would put on a short program, talking about the hospital's mission and the good work it does in the community. Then, as a follow up, you would ask the host committee to help you set up a young professionals group for your hospital, and use the guest list from the event to invite young people to join the group as members.

How to Grow Your Fundraising Networks

Many non-profits start putting together fundraising networks only to see the effort peter out. They ask their board to provide contacts, hold a non-ask event, make follow up calls, and then, that's it. They may get one or two donations from the effort, but it never snowballs into the kind of network they originally dreamed of having.

Don't let this happen to you. The reason so many non-profits never build thriving networks is because they never move on to cultivating the second level of prospects and never get to the good stuff of asking them for *their* contacts / colleagues. You see, the real key to *growing* your fundraising network is to move through succeeding levels of prospects. Most non-profits STOP after the first non-ask event. They have the event, make the calls, and then stop. You can't stop – you have to take that group of contacts provided by your key donors or board and cultivate them just as you would any other prospect. Then you need to make an ask for money, followed by asking them to open up their networks to your non-profit. And so on, and so on...

Prospect -- Cultivate -- Ask for money – Cultivate -- Ask for introductions to new prospects. Rinse and repeat.

How to Sustain Your Fundraising Networks

Like a garden, your fundraising networks require care, attention, and cultivation. You'll need to provide motivation and recognition to your network and affinity group members, and you'll need to constantly cultivate them. Once someone provides a donation, or opens their network to you by providing a few new contacts for you to speak with, don't stop the cultivation process. Keep them in the funnel. They will provide you with additional donations and contacts over time, and become true evangelists for your organization.

4 Keys to Successful Fundraising Networks

Here are the 4 keys to building truly successful and sustainable fundraising networks:

#1 – Stay Organized

It can be challenging to keep track of all of the moving parts that go into building fundraising networks – the new contacts, the cultivation points, the event attendees, the funnel... but staying organized is crucial to fundraising network success. You'll need to make sure you have full contact information for every new prospect that comes through the network, including which current donor / supporter referred the person. You'll also need to keep track of things like your affinity groups' leaders and meetings, as well as where each and every prospect currently falls in your network-building program.

#2 – Stay Motivated

There's a lot of excitement for members when they first join a fundraising network or an affinity group – there are new people to meet, new meetings and events to go to, new tasks to perform. But, for most people, the initial excitement wears off and they can find themselves less and less motivated to stay engaged. It is the job of your non-profit to keep people engaged and excited.

There are several ways to accomplish this task. First, keep your members informed – let them know what is going on at your organization and how they can be involved. Second, have lots of activities for them – including some "non-work" events like committee retreats, lunch events, and other social activities. Finally, offer them tons of recognition and thanks (more on that below).

#3 – Recognition and Thanks

Fundraising for a non-profit as a network member or affinity group member can seem like a thankless task. It is imperative for your group's morale that you offer your members a ton of recognition and thanks for all of their hard work.

Similarly, I suggest setting up a "benefits package" and recognition levels for those who are helping you build your network. While people who agree to serve as part of your fundraising network will generally do so because they either believe strongly in the organization or want to support you personally (or both), it is often a good idea to offer a "benefits package" to your committee members, just to let them know how important their work is. Such benefits can include tickets to events, special lapel pins, regular seminars or meetings with community leaders, a special e-mail newsletter, recognition in your organization's annual report, etc.

#4 – Cultivate Before Asking

It should go without saying, but it is rarely a good idea to make an ask before you have properly cultivated a prospect. This means that (a) you shouldn't ask for money before you have cultivated them and (b) you shouldn't ask them to open up their networks to you until you have cultivated them. Cultivate before asking. If you don't, you're unlikely to get people to say "yes," and if they do say yes, it will be a one-time gift.

Start a Fundraising Virus!

"Viral fundraising" is a term I use to describe a fast-spreading, well-designed fundraising campaign that uses, and spreads beyond, your fundraising networks... like a virus. These types of fundraising campaigns are usually but not always spread over the internet, from person to person, many of whom donate money to your non-profit organization.

Perhaps the best way to explain what viral fundraising is would be to provide you with an example:

Let's say your non-profit is providing clean drinking water in Africa. Your goal is to start a campaign that will provide clean drinking water to 10,000 new people, and it will cost $3 per person, for a total campaign goal of $30,000. You have spent a lot of time building a network online – an e-mail newsletter list, social networking, a great website... as well as a number of fundraising networks and affinity groups.

You decide to focus on getting people to give chunks of $100 – you'll need 300 people to give $100 to your organization, and each person that does will be providing clean drinking water for 33 people. You set up a webpage that has the name and picture of the 25 villages that will be served by your effort. Everyone who gives money gets to click on the picture of the village where they want their money to be used. As each village's need is met, the picture turns black and white, with a note that says "We have clean water!" – Your goal is to make this exciting – get people to give by allowing them choice, and allowing them to see the difference they are making. If someone gives $100 (your target amount) or more, their name appears on your site near the village they are helping.

You then e-mail out this webpage (which, of course, has a donation link) to your e-mail list, post it on your website and social network outposts, and send a snail mail letter out to your key supporters noting the new campaign.

Because this is such a unique campaign and because it is so easily understandable, people not only give, but forward the e-mail on to their friends. Many of those friends donate and send out the link to *their* friends, and so on and so on, until you've made more than your $30,000 goal.

That is viral fundraising. The campaign spreads further than your own network, and takes on a life of its own.

While you can't guarantee that one of your fundraising campaigns will go viral, what you can do is make it easier for that to happen by doing the following things:

First, make sure that your campaign is easy to understand. Make it clear who you are helping, how much is required to make a difference, and what each donation will accomplish.

Second, make sure your campaign is unique and appealing. People will want to spread your campaign if they know their friends will be amused, moved, or otherwise enjoy receiving the e-mail.

Third, have a base in place. If you are a new non-profit with no e-mail list, very little social networking presence, and a small donor file, you will find it incredibly hard to get a viral fundraising campaign off the ground. Work on building a base before you try to launch such an effort.

Finally, make your ask bite-sized. It is incredibly hard to do a viral fundraising push asking for $1,000 donations. People simply aren't willing to spread an e-mail with an ask that size, since most people will be reluctant to ask their friends to participate. Make your ask for a campaign like this in the $10-$100 range, to make sure it can spread.

Chapter 7:
How to Write an Amazing Case for Support for Your Non-Profit

Your case for support (sometimes called your "case statement," a term we will use interchangeably in this book) is one of the most important documents you can write for your non-profit. It forms the basis for all of your donor communications and asks, and provides a valuable resource to everyone who is soliciting donations on your behalf.

What is a Case for Support?

A case for support is one of the most important documents in your non-profit's fundraising arsenal. Your case statement:

- Is donor-oriented / donor-facing (written for donors)
- Clearly illustrates your organization's mission and vision for the future
- Tells donors why you need funding and what outcomes you are seeking from their investment
- Offers strong reasons why prospects should make gifts to your organization.

Simply put, your case for support is a 2-7 page document that tells donors who your organization is, what it has accomplished in the past, outlines your vision for the future, tells the donor why your organization's vision matters and why the donor should care, and gives the donor a chance to get involved by making an investment in your non-profit.

If that's still too wordy, I will try to boil it down even further: **Case statements cast a bold vision for a better future, and invite donors to get caught up in that vision.**

Great case statements include a mix of both emotionally compelling stories and descriptions of the work you are doing, as well as cold, hard facts that back up your claim to be a positive force in the world. In a great article in Philanthropy News Digest, Carl Richardson tells us that "effective fundraising is a result of telling your story." Your case for support does just that – it tells your organization's story in a way that leads to more gifts for your non-profit.

What Organizations Need a Case Statement?

Every single non-profit organization needs a case statement. Every. Single. One.

In my view, the case for support should be one of the first things you do when you form your non-profit. Without a strong case for support, you won't be able to raise money. Without the ability to raise money, you won't be able to carry out your mission. In short, neglecting your fundraising is neglecting your mission, and neglecting your case for support is neglecting your fundraising.

People want to give to organizations who cast a compelling vision. As you approach donors, they will want to know why they should care about your non-profit's work. *You* know they should care. The case for support is your opportunity to show *them* why they should care.

If you want to raise money, you need a *written* case for support.

How Do You Use a Case for Support?

The case statement you write will form the basis for all of your non-profit communications. As you write newsletters, direct mail, your website, donor materials, etc., you should constantly be referring back to your case for support both for the logic and language you are using to talk to donors.

You should also create an "external" case for support that is shorter than your overall case for support and drawn from it, and that is suitable for sharing directly with donors.

This modified version of your case statement can serve as a sort of major donor prospectus that you can give to higher level givers that are considering a gift to your non-profit. Many organizations also use the case for support on their websites and in their grant proposals as the rationale for giving. Several charities I have worked with have successfully boiled the case statement down into a one or two page lower-level donor brochure that can be used at events, walk-a-thons and in other donor prospecting.

Every non-profit need a strong case for support, no matter how small or large the organization is or what its fundraising revenues are.

7 Key Items to Include in Your Case Statement

As you lay out a plan to write your case for support, it is important to know which ideas and items should be included in the statement. Here are the 7 key concepts which need to be included in every case:

#1: An Emotional Opening - Donors and prospects will use the first paragraph or two of your case statement to decide whether or not the rest of the document is worth reading.

Use your opening to pack an emotional punch. Avoid the temptation to start with something like, "Our organization was founded in 1942 by…" and instead start with something like, "Michael was hungry, desperate, and alone, until he found us."

#2: Your Mission and Vision – Why does your organization exist? Why should people care? What is your big, bold vision for the future?

#3: History of the Organization – Give a brief summary of the founding of your organization and a short history of its work to date.

#4: Explanation of Your Programs – Tell the reader what programs you are currently running. Give a short explanation of each.

#5: Outcomes and Proof of Impact – Show proof that what you are doing is worthwhile. Use statistics and charts, but more importantly, tell the stories of those you have helped, use testimonials, and then back those up with the numbers.

#6: Financial Needs – How much money does your organization need to raise? Why does it need to raise that amount (what will it be used for?) Why do you need to raise it *now*?

#7: Means of Support – Give your reader different ways to support your efforts. Do you have a leadership giving program? Annual giving campaign? Planned giving opportunities? Briefly spell those out here.

Generally, these parts can be included in any order. Thus, while the emotional opening has to come first, if for some reason you think an explanation of your programs should come before the history of your organization then write it that way. The case statement needs to be coherent and make sense for your organization, so don't get wedded to any one formula.

Likewise, some organizations may find that they need to add additional parts. That's fine too. Just don't go overboard. Your case for support is not a "kitchen sink" document... you don't need to include every little thing in it, just what matters for compelling a donor to get more involved.

The Process of Writing Your Case for Support

Every non-profit I have ever worked with has had a different process for writing its case for support. Some take far too long and set up multiple committees to write and bless the project. Others are far too flippant, and write the case statement almost on a whim. For most organizations, though, I have found the following basic process to be the most effective:

1. Select a Writer – It is important that the organization select one person to "own" the writing process for the case statement. Don't have different people work on different parts, it almost never works in producing a coherent case for support. Select one person (generally from the staff or an outside consultant) to write the case statement.

2. Determine the Stakeholders – Next, figure out which stakeholders are going to have input into the case for support. These are the people the writer will work with to gather information and ideas for the draft statement. Generally, organizations include some staff members, board members, and often some clients of the organization in this category.

3. Gather Information – The write should then talk with each of the stakeholders to (a) get their take on the mission, vision, programs and other key concepts for the case statement, and (b) to collect data that is needed on things like outcomes, financial needs, etc.

4. Write a First Draft – At this point, the writer creates a first draft of the case for support.

5. Revise the Draft – The organization then holds one or more rounds of revisions by circulating the case statement to the stakeholders that were selected to get their thoughts, ideas, and comments. The executive committee of the board should also be involved in the revision rounds.

6. Vote to Approve the Case Statement – It is my strong suggestion that every organization has its board of directors vote to approve the final version of the case for support, to ensure that the entire organization is behind the final document and understands its importance to the organization.

How Long Should Your Case Statement Be?

Generally, your case for support will be between 4-10 pages. That being said, don't worry about going even longer. You can always pare back the amount of information that is included in donor materials. For example, you may write a 14 page case for support and decide to include the entire thing in your major donor portfolio, but pare it down to a 2 page document for minor donor groups.

Don't make your case for support too short, however. If your case statement is only 3 pages long, it is highly likely that you are missing compelling and pertinent information.

How Long Should This Process Take?

I've heard lots of horror stories from non-profits that took 6 months, 12 months, or even longer to craft their case for support. I believe that taking this long to work on the case statement is unnecessary and counterproductive. It stems from the belief that the writers and stakeholders need to walk on egg shells in creating the document because if its importance to the development of the organization.

The case statement *is* important, but it is no good to you if it isn't written. In my view, the entire process of writing your case for support from selecting the writer all the way through approval by the board should take no more than 3 months, and can be completed in as little as 1 month if your non-profit is ambitious.

Remember the Goal of Your Case

The most important thing to remember when creating your case for support is the ultimate goal of the document: to case a vision for prospects that is so compelling that it convinces them to make a gift. If your case statement accomplishes this task, then it is doing its job.

Chapter 8:
How to Get Your Board to Lead Your Fundraising Efforts

I'm a strong proponent of the notion that a non-profit's board of directors should be actively engaged in the organization's fundraising efforts.

This means that the board should not only hold an organized board giving campaign each year, but that the board should also help the non-profit build a fundraising network by opening up their own personal Rolodexes to help the organization grow its prospect list.

That being said, board members don't get involved with non-profits solely to fundraise. And many board members feel that the non-profits they serve ask them to go back to the same people for money again and again, which obviously produces diminishing returns.

And... frankly... many non-charities recruit board members with the notion that fundraising is only a small part of what the board does, only to change course when a consultant tells them that the board should be far more involved in development than it currently is. When this happens, board members feel shell shocked, and often reluctant.

Self-Inflicted Fundraising Wounds

Much of the fear and anxiety that board members feel about fundraising is caused by non-profits themselves. So often, Development Directors and Executive Directors approach board members with what I call "fundraising dictates." These dictates usually sound like this:

"We need you to give us the names of 5 people we can approach for gifts."

"It's annual gala time. Who can you get sponsorships from?"

"I want to set up more fundraising meetings this year. Which of your colleagues can I ask for a gift?"

With an approach like that, it's no wonder a board member would be reluctant to share her friends, family, coworkers and business partners with a non-profit organization. If the charity is that tactless with their own board member, imagine how forward they will be with her contacts!

Board Fundraising Need Not Cause Anxiety

Asking your board to help you raise more money need not cause anxiety or sleepless nights. The board should see fundraising as a *partnership* between the development office and the board, as opposed to a competitive venture where the development staff is constantly trying to trick the board into sharing more names or make more asks.

The best way to reduce anxiety is to stop seeing your board as a source of *revenue*, and start seeing your board as a source of *introductions*. Sure, your board should directly donate to your organization. And yes... your board should occasionally make asks from folks in their network. But for the most part, your board should be introducing their friends and business associates to your non-profit, and your organization should be slowly and respectfully walking these contacts down the cultivation funnel.

A Simple Strategy that Works

Many times, when I work with an organization that wants its board to be more active in fundraising, I tell them to try a simple strategy. It will likely work for your non-profit too:

First, at your next board meeting, tell the board that you are changing tactics. You are no longer asking the board to directly ask for money, unless they feel comfortable doing so. Instead, you are asking the board to make introductions to their network.

Second, walk the board through your cultivation funnel. Tell them that when they refer someone to the organization, all they need to do is make the introduction (preferably in-person). You will take it from there. You won't ask the person for money during the first meeting or call. You won't ask the person for money during the second meeting or call. Instead, you will build a relationship with them. You will cultivate before you ask.

Third, set up a series of non-ask events at your organization. Ask your board members to consider inviting colleagues and associates to these events. Remind your board that you won't ask for money at these events, or during the follow up call. Sure, you will eventually ask for money, but only when the person says they really want to get involved. Build trust with your board.

Time and again, I have seen this strategy work with non-profit boards. Over time (usually 6 months to a year), the board starts to trust the development staff with their friends, family and business associates. They start to make introductions, trusting that the fundraisers won't jump the gun. The non-profit stops begging for introductions, and earns them instead.

Why Your Non-Profit Needs an Organized Board Giving Campaign

While almost every non-profit I have worked with has recognized the need for their board members to lead the overall fundraising effort by making a donation, I have been surprised at just how many schools, churches, and charities fail to implement an organized "board giving campaign."

Instead, these organizations mention that they would like board members to give… they may even include a line item in the budget for "board giving." But instead of relying on a well thought out board giving strategy, their plan is simply to wait around and hope. This is a huge mistake. Every non-profit, no matter how small or large, *needs* to hold an annual board giving campaign to encourage 100% of their board members to make a general fund donation to the cause.

If your organization is not yet running a campaign like this – or are holding a less effective "informal" board giving effort, here are three reasons why your non-profit needs to launch a formal board giving campaign this year:

1. More Board Members Will Give, and Those That Do Will Give More

Do you know why annual fundraising events raise so much money for so many organizations? Because they are formal channels for giving that are well planned and organized. Development teams sit down, decide how much they want an event to raise, develop a plan for sponsors, tickets, silent auctions, etc., set a firm deadline (the date of the event) and publicize both their goal and the results of their efforts. This is a highly organized and planned event that encourages people to give.

Likewise, a formal board giving campaign that is well planned and well organized will encourage your board members to give... and will encourage those who already give to give more. The board will have a concrete goal and a set deadline, along with a formal ask. All three will combine to create a powerful incentive for board members to write a (larger) check.

2. You Will Encourage 100% Participation

Make sure that part of your plan for your board giving campaign is 100% participation (i.e. that every board member gives at least something to the organization). This is important because many donors, most foundations, and almost every major philanthropist will want to know that your board is fully invested in your mission before they themselves make a donation. The best way to show this is to be able to announce that your non-profit has a 100% board giving rate.
A formal board giving campaign is the best way to encourage 100% board participation.

3. It Takes the Pressure Off...

A formal board giving campaign takes the pressure off of your development staff when it comes to board fundraising. The best board giving campaigns involve the chairman of the board of directors making the primary ask of the board (even if this is through a letter). The board knows the goal, and sees progress... Thus, instead of spending all year waiting around dropping hints to the board, a board campaign allows the development staff to work with the chairman to set and publicize a goal, and to encourage board members to meet that goal... ideally, one they all vote to approve at a board meeting, which creates buy-in.

How to Run a Successful Board Giving Campaign

This is a formula that has been put into practice at hundreds of non-profit organizations, and is suitable for any non-profit launching (or re-organizing) its board giving activities.

Step #1 – Get Board Buy-In

The first step for running a successful board giving campaign is to get buy-in from your board of directors. This step is often overlooked by non-profit development staffs, but is crucial to running a smooth and successful effort. Simply put, your board must "own" the board giving campaign if it is to reach its overall goal, which should be ambitious.

The best way to get board buy in is for the chairman and executive committee of the board to present the concept of an organized board giving campaign at a regularly scheduled board meeting. This discussion should occur at least one board meeting prior to the meeting where you launch the effort. Your chairman can explain why your non-profit is holding an organized board giving campaign, why board leadership is so important, and float a financial goal for the effort. The board should then be invited to discuss the campaign and the goal, and to vote to approve the plan.

It is imperative that your board chairman and/or executive committee take the lead in announcing the campaign – so important, in fact, that the success of your effort relies on it. Board giving campaigns should be board-led. Very few board giving efforts are successful when the development director or other development staff are the ones announcing the campaign and doing the solicitations. The primary driver of the board giving campaign must be the chairman and other executive officers of the board.

Equally important is that your board vote on, and approve, an overall goal and timeline for the campaign. Board members must go on record stating their approval of the goal and the deadline by which it should be raised.

Step #2 – Officially Launch the Campaign

At the next board meeting (after the board votes to approve the campaign), your chairman should announce the official launch of the campaign, remind the board of the goal and the deadlines, and set a deadline for every board member to make a pledge. Board members should be invited to fill out a pledge form for their board gift and confidentially transmit it by mail, email, or fax back to the chairman of the board. Be sure to make provisions for board members who want to spread their gift payments out over time, or who want to pledge and pay through the United Way.

Step #3 – Letter from the Chairman

In the month following the official launch of the campaign, every board member should receive a letter from the chairman of the board, along with a blank pledge form, reminding them how important this campaign is to the overall mission of the charity, and reminding the board members to get their pledges back in as soon as possible.

Step #4 – Begin Regular Updates

After a significant number of pledges have been received, the organization should begin sending out monthly e-mail updates to the members of the board letting them know (a) how much has been pledged to date, (b) how much has been received to date, (c) what percentage of board members have made a pledge, and (d) what the average pledge amount is.

Give these numbers only in the aggregate. I have found that the strategy of "name and shame" doesn't work well with board giving campaigns... that is, putting out a list of board members along with the size of their gift, and circulating it regularly, generally does not have the desired effect for board giving efforts.

Step #5 – Follow-Up Calls

Finally, as the deadline for pledges approaches, your board chairman should make follow-up calls to those members of the board who have not yet made their pledge, asking them to do so. Your goal should be 100% board participation in the board giving campaign, as well as successfully meeting the overall fundraising goal for the effort.

Remember... your board should take the lead in your fundraising efforts. Their participation in an organized board giving campaign will send a strong signal to others that this non-profit is well-run, stable, and poised to do great things.

Don't Beg Your Board for Fundraising Contacts – Earn Them!

I can't tell you how many times I have heard this plaintive cry from executive directors, development directors, and even board members themselves, "If only our board would give us more names! I know they know more people... we need them to get us in to see their contacts!"

I'm a believer that non-profit boards should be helping, if not leading, the fundraising charge for their organization. I am also a believer that boards can't do it all, and that organizations should primarily be building fundraising networks, holding non-ask events, and using similar tactics to build new prospect lists.

But let's assume that you're building networks and holding non-ask events, but one of the real weak spots in your fundraising really is the fact that your board members aren't opening up their own personal networks to you. They have great contacts, but they're not letting you get to them. What can you do?

Option #1: You Can Beg

This is probably what you're doing already. I'd say a good 50% of every non-profit I have ever come across asks its board members for new fundraising leads several times per year, and the vast majority of those organizations are constantly frustrated by the lack of board response. So they start begging, and pleading...

"We just need three names from each board member!"

"Please help us meet our annual campaign goal. Use the sheet we are passing around to write down the two people you are willing to contact about the campaign."

"Please forward your list of names for the event invitations no later than Friday. If you don't, the board chair will call you relentlessly until she has them in her hands!"

This type of pleading gets old, fast. Sure, it can work. It won't work *well*, but it can work. Your board members will probably throw you a couple of names here and there during these begging sessions, but it won't be the tidal wave you are hoping for, and that you secretly know they are capable of.

Don't you wish your board members <u>came to you</u> with new leads, instead of you having to <u>beg them for contacts</u>? This brings us to...

Option #2: You Can Earn Them

Your board members are, for the most part, normal, practical people. They are committed to your organization, but they are just as committed to the relationships they have with their friends, colleagues, family, and so on. To demonstrate the impact of these dual commitments on their willingness to put you in touch with their personal contacts, let's take a look at two hypothetical scenarios.

What Begging Looks Like (Scenario #1)

In the first scenario, you are begging your board members, for the fourth time this year, to hand over some names for your annual fundraising letter. You're telling them that if everyone just gave four names, and just one of those names ended up making a mid-sized gift, you'd reach your annual fundraising goal.

How do you think your board members feel about leveraging their personal relationships for you at this point? I'll tell you how they feel... Nervous. Protective. Wary. You're so desperate you're begging them, berating them to put you in touch people to receive a fundraising letter. Of course they are nervous, they're worried you are going to do to their friends what you are doing to them – berating them, until they make a gift.

You have put your board in a terrible position, asking them to choose which relationship they value more, their relationship with your organization or their relationships with their closest friends and colleagues. Generally, this is a fight your non-profit will lose.

What Earning it Looks Like (Scenario #2)

Now, let's look at a second scenario. Your non-profit is holding a major event – for free – to announce a new initiative. The event is being attended by several Hollywood movie stars. As luck would have it, you were able to arrange for each board member to receive 5 free tickets to the event, right up front, with backstage passes for a meet and greet after the announcement, including pictures with the A list celebs. Would any of the board members like to participate, you ask?

How do you think your board members feel now? I'll tell you – they're excited. They're already thinking who they can invite to the event. There's one ticket for them, one for their spouse, and three extra for friends they want to impress. Darn! They have at least 10 people they would love to invite. Hands shoot up around the room... Board members want to know if there's any way they can get more than five tickets?

This scenario might be over the top, but it proves a point – your board members do have more contacts, and they cherish the relationships they have with those contacts (rightly so). If your organization does something to *earn* your way into that relationship, in a way that feels right, is compelling, and shows that you can be trusted with the gift of an introduction, and then your board members will make that introduction and let you into their network.

Of course, most non-profits won't be able to bring in celebrity guests for their next free event, but I guarantee you that every non-profit can earn their way into their board's network *without* having to beg and plead, by holding great non-ask events, putting on seminars and shows, publishing unique reports and books, offering compelling "in the trenches" experiences and hands-on philanthropy, pioneering new methods, and probably several hundred other ways.

Chapter 9:
Supercharging Your Non-Profit Fundraising Events

"Fundraising events." It's a phrase that strikes both joy and terror into the hearts of non-profit professionals, board members and volunteers everywhere. Nearly every non-profit uses events to raise money, and nearly every organization that holds events knows that they could be raising more money – with less effort – at each of their affairs. It's frustrating, because you know that you're spending more time than you need to, while simultaneously raising less than you otherwise could. If this is the case at your non-profit, it's time to change the pattern.

Over the course of section, we're going to look in depth at how organizations of all sizes can dramatically increase their revenue while at the same time implementing *systems* that will allow them to reduce the workload required by each event. I know it can be done, because during the course of my fundraising career I have led organizations through hundreds of fundraising events, and have successfully helped non-profits implement all of the strategies detailed in this section.

Let's start by talking about the basic fundamental concepts need to be understood in order to maximize your fundraising event revenue. Then, we'll walk through supercharged strategies for putting together a host committee, finding event sponsors, selling tickets, managing event logistics, developing invitations and other collateral materials, and adding additional revenue streams to your event.

The Ultimate Goal of Your Fundraising Events

As we launch into this section, the first question we need to ask is, "what is the ultimate goal for your non-profit's fundraising events?" I've asked this question to dozens of organizations who have given me hundreds of answers, ranging from "finding new supporters," to "generating press coverage," to "having a really good time." While all of those answers are respectable goals, none is the primary goal of your events. Simply put, the most important goal for your fundraising events is revenue, plain and simple. If you're holding a *fundraising* event, then *raise funds*, with single-minded determination.

You may assume this goes without saying. You may be thinking, "of course fundraising events should raise money! We know that!" Yet, so many non-profits that think the same way spend so much of their time focused on the incidentals of the event, at the expense of raising money. These organizations spend hours debating the entertainment options and invitation card stock. They send 5 staff members to the food tasting to determine the menu, and hold endless networking events for the host committee. But they only spend a small fraction of that time making calls and doing meetings to find sponsors for the event.

Don't make this mistake. Understand that the primary goal for your fundraising event is to raise <u>as much money as possible</u> for your non-profit organization.

Of course, this isn't to say that your charity should not be holding development events that aren't designed around revenue. I am a big fan of "non-ask" events... events that are held to introduce your non-profit to new prospects or cultivate current prospects and donors. These "non-ask" events are *not* fundraising events. They are cultivation events, and have different goals than your fundraising events. Fundraising events should focus on raising money, plain and simple.

Secondary Goals for Your Fundraising Events

Raising money may be the most important goal for your fundraising events, but you can and should have a number of secondary goals. These goals, while less important that fundraising, can consume a portion (but not the majority) of your event planning time, money and resources. Some laudable secondary goals may include:

- Building rapport and deeper relationships with your donors
- Garnering press coverage for your non-profit
- Reaching out to new prospects who come to the event
- Honoring the work of your staff, partners, volunteers and other supporters
- Providing a fun experience for your donors and team

Why Fundraising Events Work

It is extremely important, as you set out on this path, to understand precisely why events work as a fundraising method and why they are so popular with attendees and organizations alike. Knowing these reasons will help your non-profit run events that appeal to guests and meet the needs and goals of your organization:

1. People Like to Feel Like Part of a Team

Donors love to go to events because it makes them feel like part of a larger team that is working together towards a common goal. They enjoy being with a group of like-minded people, and delight in spending time with their friends in a social setting.

2. People Like to Show-Off

People like to be seen as leaders, as important contributors to society, and as someone who is "in the know." For this reason, if a person is involved with your non-profit as a donor, committee member, board member, or volunteer, they will want to not only attend your event, but often will bring along friends and co-workers. Bringing others makes the event more enjoyable for your supporters not only because it is fun to be social with good friends, but also because the donor who invites others will be seen as a leader and / or knowledgeable about social issues.

This tendency, of course, is good for your non-profit because it will allow you to reach into your donors' networks to reach more prospects through your events.

3. All Hands on Deck Efforts Work

At many non-profits, events are "all hands on deck" efforts. This means that everyone... your staff, your board, your donors, your volunteers... everyone pulls together to meet the fundraising and operational goals for the event. There's something about these types of efforts that just works.

Think about it this way: how many times have you been part of an event that was exhausting and draining... one where everyone was working together, but where there were late nights and nearly-missed deadlines... and where the minute the event was over, you tiredly crashed into bed. But, when you awoke the next morning, you realized that you had hit your fundraising goal for the event? For me, that has happened numerous times.

There's just something about an event that has the ability to pull everyone together, constantly remind them of the goal and keep the deadlines front and center. When everyone is rowing in the same direction, constantly communicating, and has a firm end-date (event day!) in mind, things seem to get done.

How Fundraising Events Make Their Money

Fundraising events make money through a number of different strategies. The most important revenue-producing line items for a non-profit fundraising event are (in descending order of importance):

<u>Sponsorships</u>

Event sponsorships are the most important source of revenue for non-profit fundraising events. If you are holding an event that is raising more through ticket sales or silent auction revenue than through sponsors, I can guarantee that you are leaving money on the table. The only possible exception is events that are in their first year or two of life, where the goal is to throw an annual large event and you started off with a large donor base that is attending the event but you have not yet built rapport with major sponsors. Even in that case, sponsors should overtake ticket sales in a year or two.

Corporate and personal sponsorships are important because your average sponsor gift will be many times larger than your average ticket price. Successfully raising $100,000 through $100 ticket sales will be unbelievably time-consuming and frustrating for most non-profits. Raising the same amount through $5,000 and $10,000 sponsorships, while not necessarily easy, will at least be achievable for more non-profits, and with fewer headaches.

Another benefit to raising money through sponsorships is that companies can generally pay for a sponsorship through either their philanthropic *or* their corporate marketing budgets. Because you will be offering public relations and marketing benefits in return for business sponsorships of your event, most of these companies will be able to legitimately use their advertising and marketing dollars to pay to be sponsors. This is good news for your non-profit because at most companies, the marketing budget exceeds the charitable giving budget by an order of magnitude.

Sponsorships are the most important source of revenue for your non-profit fundraising events.

Ticket Sales

For most events, ticket sales should be the second-highest source of revenue. The possible exceptions to this rule include walk-a-thons and other a-thons, as well as live or silent auctions where it is free to attend, and the revenue streams are limited to sponsorships and auction revenue.

Raffles and Auctions

If your event will include a raffle or auction (either silent or live) this should generally be the third-highest source of revenue, after sponsorships and ticket sales.

Additional Revenue Streams

Other fundraising add-ons such as "sell-a-service" tables, 50/50 drawings, scratch-cards, etc. should, as a rule, be the smallest portion of your non-profit fundraising event revenue.

Later in this book, we're going to be talking about all of these revenue streams in depth, including sponsorships, ticket sales, auctions and other revenue streams, but for now, you should know that if your fundraising events raise more revenue through your auction than through sponsorships, or if you raise more through a 50/50 drawing than from ticket sales, you very well may be leaving money on the table, and should look closely at your event as you read through this book to see if a reconfiguring of your revenue streams may be in order.

Eight Fundamental Concepts for Successful Non-Profit Fundraising Events

As you plan your fundraising events large, small and in-between, there are eight fundamental concepts that you should keep in mind to ensure that you are raising as much as possible:

#1: Fundraising events are still *fundraising*.

Many non-profits focus on the *event* part of fundraising events – they find a great headliner, hire a nice band, find a good venue and print up nice invitations. Then, they expect the money to come flowing in. When the revenue doesn't come, they wonder why.

Fundraising events are still *fundraising*, and all of the rules of fundraising apply. You need to build relationships (with sponsors, auction donors, guests, etc.) You need to cultivate your donors. You need to make asks (even... gasp!... in person and over the phone). The fundamental rules of fundraising don't disappear just because you are raising money through an event.

#2: Who you have on your team matters.

What is your event committee / host committee focusing on? If it's logistics instead of fundraising, you're in trouble. The same goes for your board. If you don't have folks on your team who are committed to fundraising and have large enough personal networks to help raise money, it is unlikely that you will hit your event fundraising goals.

Seek out host committee members and board members who will take ownership of some of the fundraising for the event by selling sponsorships and tickets. Then, provide them with the training and materials they need to do so.

#3: Money saved is money earned.

The revenue goal for your event should be thought of in terms of "net revenue," not "gross revenue." Gross revenue is all of the money you bring in at an event, without regard to event costs. Net revenue is the money you raise at an event minus the event costs. Your non-profit needs money to pay for programs and organizational overhead – the only money that you will be able to spend on those items is the money that is left over from the event after you deduct the event costs. Thus, you should focus on *net revenue*.

Money saved at your event is money earned for your non-profit. Think of it this way: if you hold a nice event for your organization that raises $25,000 and spend $15,000 on the venue, catering, collateral materials, etc., you will end up with $10,000 in net revenue that goes to your organization. On the other hand, perhaps you can get some of your materials donated and go with a slightly less expensive, though still nice menu. In that case, you raise $25,000 and spend $10,000 on the event. This means you end up with $15,000 in net revenue that goes to your organization… that's a 50% increase in fundraising revenue to your bottom line!

Spend most of your time focused on bringing in money for the event, but remember to take a hard look at costs and possible in-kind donations so that you can keep more of the money that the event raises.

#4: Don't get distracted by the sideshow.

There's a lot of "sideshow" with non-profit events. There are color schemes to pick, wine baskets to put together, event favors to package, floral arrangements to choose. Don't get sucked in. What matters for your event is fundraising.

Sure, you should have a nice event. Yes, you should choose a color scheme and floral arrangements. But do you need a committee of 5 spending an hour to do so? Or could you just pick one that looks nice and be done with it? I'd rather have a staff member spend 50 minutes making sponsorship calls and 10 minutes choosing floral arrangements than vice versa.

#5: Sponsorships > Ticket Sales > Added Revenue Streams

Focus on sponsorships. Then focus on ticket sales. Then focus on added revenue streams. In that order. Most of your event efforts should be focused on fundraising, and most of your fundraising efforts should be focused on selling sponsorships. A smaller amount of time should be spent on ticket sales, and even less on added revenue streams.

Use the 80 / 20 rule. Focus 80% of your time on the 20% of activities that will raise the majority of the money for your event.

#6: The year's biggest event requires a year-long effort.

Do you hold a large, all-hands-on-deck fundraising event each year, like a gala or annual dinner? If so, your big annual event requires a year-long effort in order to raise the maximum amount of money.
I once worked at a non-profit that held one major dinner per year. It raised a significant portion of the organization's annual budget. When I arrived at the office the next day, one of my staff members said, "That was a really great event, but I'm glad it's over. It was so much work! When will we have to start working on next year's event? A couple of months?" My answer was, "Enjoy today. We'll start working on next year's event *tomorrow.*"

He though I was exaggerating, but I wasn't. Big annual events require big annual efforts. You need to start cultivating this year's event donors for next year's event. You need to go see them. Thank them. Ask them who else might be interested in sponsoring the event. Stay in touch with them. Steward them. Add new prospects. Build new relationships. All before you make your renewal asks for the event, which should be 4-6 months out from the event. It's a year-long endeavor.

#7: Relationships matter.

Fundraising is all about relationships. Fundraising events are all about relationships too. Many non-profits have corporate sponsors that donate to events year after year, but yet the organization never cultivates a relationship with anyone at the company. Similarly, many charities never reach out to event attendees or silent auction item donors after the event, at least not until it comes time to make an ask for *next* year's event.

The best way to exponentially grow your fundraising event revenue is to start cultivating your event donors in a systemized way. Do meetings. Make phone calls. Add them to your mailing list. Hold a thank-you event for your silent auction item donors. Ask your event guests to join your volunteer committee. Cultivate your event donors and you will grow not only next year's event revenue, but your overall donor base as well.

#8: Event revenue grows over time.

If you are launching an event and hope to make it an annual event (either a large annual gala or a small, simple yearly event) understand that event revenue generally grows year over year, at least until you reach a plateau point. This means that if you hold an event this year that raises $50,000 and do all the right things to grow the event (i.e. the things that we will talk about in this chapter), next year you may raise $60,000... and the following year $75,000... and the fourth year $100,000.

This is because events, when properly run, show a compounding effect. If you hold a great event, your guests will tell their friends and bring them to the event next year. If your silent auction gets press coverage, more businesses will want to be featured in the auction next year. If you treat sponsors really well and cultivate them over the course of the year, they will introduce you to other businesses in their network that may want to sponsor your event. Treat your donors and guests right, and you will see your event revenue grow year after year.

Cost / Benefit: Should You Really Have That Event?

Before wrapping up this look at event fundamentals, there's one final topic we need to tackle. It's a tough topic, but one that needs to be addressed. Simply put, for every event you hold, your organization needs to ask, "Should we really be holding this event?"

While many events do work and result in revenue for a non-profit organization, it doesn't mean that every event is created equal. I can't tell you how many non-profits I have worked with that ran the same event year after year, and each year it took hundreds of hours to pull together only to raise a relatively small amount. Yet, when I approached these organizations about taking the event out of their yearly fundraising plans, they balked. "But we always run this event!" "People love to come to our annual chicken dinner!" "What will the donors say!?"

As a non-profit organization, you can't afford to have any sacred cows in your fundraising plan. Every single line item and every use of time and resources should be scrutinized to see if using your staff or money differently would yield better results for your mission and your programs. This is doubly true of events.

Events take time. Lots and lots of time. And usually, events cost money… often a significant amount of money, depending on the type of event you are holding. Because events take lots of time and a significant amount of money, it is doubly important that you perform a cost / benefit analysis on your fundraising events to see if you should continue to hold them.

The Costs of Holding an Event

First, take a look at the costs of holding the particular event you are thinking about holding. How much money will it cost to run the event? How much time will it take your staff and volunteers to put the event together? How much money could your staff raise doing other things if they were *not* working on this event? How will holding this event impact your donors' ability to give to your other fundraising methods throughout the year?

The Benefits of Holding an Event

Next, take a look at the benefits of holding this particular event. How much money would you like to raise? How likely are you to be able to raise that amount? How many new donors will you acquire by holding this event?

Implied Benefits of Holding an Event

Because large events take time to build up a base of support, you should also take a look at how much the event will be able to raise over the next few years, assuming you want this to be an annual event. For example, if you're starting an annual gala event for your organization, you may think it will raise $10,000 this year, $15,000 next year, and $25,000 the year after that.

I call this future fundraising capacity the "implied benefit" of holding an event. Take this benefit into account when performing your cost/benefit analysis. If you decide not to hold the event this year because it will only raise $10,000... but you are reasonably sure it will make $25,000 the third year you hold it, take this into account before making your decision.

The Number One Question to Ask

In summary, I believe that the number one question you should be asking when doing a cost / benefit analysis for your event is this: *If I spent the exact same amount of money and staff time on a different fundraising tactic, would I raise more or less than I would with this event?* If they answer is yes, then you should consider not holding your event.

For example, let's say that your non-profit holds a cocktail event every year that you spend $3,000 and 50 staff hours to pull together and run. The event raises $7,000 each year, so your net revenue for this event is $4,000. Then, one year, you notice that your staff's personal fundraising asks have really been paying off – you notice that each of your development staff members is raising an average of $5,000 per week making personal asks through meetings and phone calls (this is obviously a simplified example, but you get the point). If you are spending $3,000 and 50 hours to run an event and net $4,000 but your staff could be spending 40 hours to make phone calls and hold meetings and netting $5,000, then you should re-consider whether or not this event is worth the effort.

It is my belief that many non-profits are holding events that they just shouldn't be holding, because they are spending too much money and time for too little return on that investment.

How to Build a Strong Host Committee for Your Event

Because fundraising events take a lot of hard work to plan and execute, I encourage non-profit organizations to focus on the 80/20 principle... 80% of your fundraising revenue from an event will result from just 20% of the efforts you put in and strategies you use. Some things, like flowers and table linen color choices, may make for a nicer event, but will do little to increase the revenue for your event. Other things, like your guest list and your auction items, will have a more discernible effect.

There are two things, though, that will have an overwhelming impact on the fundraising revenue for your events – two things that can mean the difference between comfortably beating your fundraising goal for a gala and barely making enough to cover expenses. The two things I am talking about are your host committee and your event sponsors. If you have a great host committee and get it working right, and spend the year focused on sponsorships, you'll have a great event.

In this section, we're going to be focused on how to build and supercharge your event host committee. In the following section, we'll focus on sponsorships.

What is an event "Host Committee?"

There are many definitions for an event host committee. At some non-profits, this is the group that actually does the planning and implementation work for an event – dealing with vendors, setting up the event, cleaning up, etc. At other organizations, this is an honorary committee listed on invitations and signage and made up of representatives from the event's largest sponsors, who do not do any work as part of committee membership. For the purposes of this chapter, however, the host committee has one purpose and one purpose only: fundraising.

I have found that the most successful fundraising events I have ever run have been successful, in large part, because we were able to gather together a group of supporters with large networks who were willing to sell sponsorships and tickets for the event. I normally call this group the "Host Committee."

If you are running an event that already has a "working host committee" that handles logistics and volunteers at the event, that's fine – keep them doing what they are doing, and keep calling them the host committee. But start a second group that is responsible for fundraising for the event. Call it the "Leadership Committee" or "Event Committee" or whatever you can come up with – but put a fundraising group together. Every non-profit fundraising event, no matter how small or large, needs a group of supporters who take ownership for the fundraising around the event. For the purposes of this chapter, we will call this group the "host committee."

Why is a Host Committee Important?

Host committees are vitally important because they allow you to scale your fundraising efforts around an event using the most effective fundraising technique available: leveraging personal networks.

It's hard to raise amazing amounts of money around a fundraising event by relying simply on your staff, board, and mailed invitations. Yet, that's the event game plan at most non-profits: mail out invitations, have the development staff make a couple of calls to last year's sponsors to ask them to donate again this year, and ask the board to come up with new names for sponsors and invitations. Then, the organization waits to see what shakes out. Non-profits that use this game plan are leaving a significant amount of money on the table.

Putting together a host committee – a real, fundraising-focused host committee – is one of the most few ways you can exponentially raise more money at your events this year than you did last year, and keep dramatically increasing your event goals for years to come. Notice that I said it has to be a fundraising-focused host committee. If you simply put together an event-planning host committee that talks about entertainment options and menu tastings, but only spends 10 minutes per meeting on fundraising, then you will *not* see this type of revenue growth.

Host committees are so powerful because they leverage the fundraising networks of the committee members. Instead of your organization simply reaching out to its own donor base for the event, your host committee members are reaching into their own networks as well – contacting their friends, family, vendors, clients, colleagues, etc. to invite people to the event, find new sponsors, locate auction items, and increase your overall revenue from the event... all through connections that your non-profit would not have been able to make otherwise.

Who Should Be On the Host Committee?

The host committee should be comprised of people who support your mission, are willing to fundraise, and have good-sized networks that they are willing to open up to your organization. Ideally, your event committee will include a chairperson who is super-supportive of your organization and who has a massive network, as well as 5-25 (or more) of your donors and supporters who are ready to raise money for the event.

Seek out people who are "connectors," either in their business or social lives – people who know lots of people, aren't shy about asking for money, and really feel passionate about your non-profit's mission and work.

Building an amazing host committee takes time. It is highly unlikely that you will be able to find 25 people who fit this bill your first time holding an event. That's ok. Find 5 people that would be a great fit, and keep your host committee relatively small. Set a goal of growing the size of your committee each year. You will find that, if you run your host committee well and offer them proper recognition and thanks, most of your members will stay on year after year. Of course, each year a handful will likely drop out because they don't enjoy the work or because they move, retire, or their priorities change. That's ok. Stay alert throughout the entire year, looking for people who might be a great fit for your committee so that you can not only replace those who leave each cycle, but can grow your group each year.

High-Level vs. Low-Level Host Committees

When putting together fundraising-focused host committees, most non-profits face a common question: should they be putting together high-level or low-level host committees?

A high-level host committee is one that is populated with decision makers: executives at companies, partners at law firms, local philanthropists, etc. Unless you are working on an event for one of the top national non-profits or one of the top 5 or 6 charities in a major metropolitan area, it's unlikely that you'll be able to snag a Fortune 500 CEO for your host committee (and even if you do, he or she will likely be so busy professionally that they won't be able to spend much time fundraising for you anyway). But you might be able to get a high-level VP from the same company, or the right-hand executive who "handles" charity work for a major businessperson or philanthropist. That's ok – these folks would also be considered "high-level" for host committee purposes.

A low-level host committee is comprised of associates at law firms, young professionals, middle-managers at large companies, well-off (but not wealthy) retirees, etc.

Obviously, your ultimate goal is to put together a high-level host committee. If your board is already a high-level board, you may be able to put together this type of group right from the get go by having your board work their networks to find great host committee members for the event. That being said, most non-profits hosting events have to start with a lower-level host committee and "work up" to a high-level group. That works, so long as you are constantly on the lookout for higher-level folks to join *and* you make sure that you are choosing lower-level folks who are "up-and-comers," well-regarded at their companies and organizations, and who truly do have wide networks from which to fundraise.

How and When to Build Your Host Committee

There's a simple rule of thumb that holds true most non-profit events – particularly major annual events and galas – that most organizations don't hold to: staging an amazingly profitable fundraising events takes an entire year of preparation.

Sure, you can order the flowers 8 weeks out and send the invitations 6 weeks in advance and finalize the menu two weeks before the event. But the real work of the event – the fundraising work – takes an entire year. This is true for finding sponsors as well as building your host committee. Start building your host committee a full year before the event – this means that if you're holding an annual event, you should be getting good host committee members to renew their membership in the group for the coming year almost as soon as they receive this year's "Thank you for being a host committee member!" letter in the mail.

Here's a simple step-by-step process that I use to put together strong host committees:

1 – Put Together a Prospect List

First, gather your team together to decide which people in your orbit would make excellent prospects for your host committee this year. Remember, in order to be truly great prospects for this committee, people need to (a) have good-sized networks, (b) not be shy, and (c) have an attachment to or affinity for your organization.

At the top of your list should be folks who have served on the host committee for this event before (if it is a yearly event) and who performed well in that role. You should also feel free to add in a couple of board members who are strong supporters for the event, but be sure not to fill the committee with a majority of board members. Next, add in donors who you talk with on a regular basis and who meet the committee criteria listed above. You should also include representatives from companies that strongly support your organization, such as past event sponsors and corporate donors. Volunteers with your organization that have strong networks make great candidates for committee membership, as do donor prospects who have indicated that they are ready to get more involved.

Remember – asking someone to be on the host committee is an ask, and cold asks don't really work. Thus, you shouldn't be listing people as host committee prospects if no one from your organization has ever talked to them before, or if they are "aspirational." So many non-profits spend time saying things like, "oh, this CEO would be great for the host committee... how do we reach her?" and "let's make of local philanthropists we'd like on the host committee and then send them all a letter." This doesn't work. Yes, make those lists and try to figure out a way to reach those people over the coming year, but don't count them as host committee prospects, or prospects of any kind, until you've made contact and started the cultivation process. It's a long road from "we should get to know this person" to "this person is a great host committee prospect."

2 – Develop Promotional Materials

The next step in building a strong host committee is developing some promotional materials for the event and the committee which you can use as you approach the prospects. I recommend that you develop the following:

A flyer about the event – This can be done quickly and easily, listing the theme for this year's event, some details on the location and date (if you have them), a blurb about how well last year's event went (if this is an annual affair) and other tidbits, such as info on the silent auction or raffle (if there will be one), ticket sale information, etc.

A host committee flyer – Again, this can be done simply and easily using a word processing program and your office copier. This flyer should spell out the goals and duties of the host committee, different leadership posts that are open, the free tickets or other recognition levels that will granted to the host committee, and contact information for the person in your office who is handling the event.

3 – Approach Prospects

I recommend approaching prospects for the host committee as early as you can for the event, but not more than one year out. If this is an annual event, my suggestion is that you wait at least 4-8 weeks after this year's event before you approach prospects to serve on the host committee for *next* year's event.

When approaching prospects, you are making an ask ("Will you serve on the host committee for our event this year?") As with all asks, the most successful way to ask prospects to be on your host committee will be to ask them directly, either in person or over the phone. It's much more difficult and much less effective to ask this question through e-mail or a snail mail letter.

If you are pressed for time and this is an annual event, you may want to consider inviting all of your host committee members from *this* year's event to a special thank you event at your office to talk about how successful the event was, present them with a small gift, and ask them to serve on the host committee for the coming year. You can then follow-up through e-mail and phone calls for those who don't respond to your initial ask.

For other prospects, assign someone from your staff or board to approach each person individually, either by having breakfast, lunch, coffee or a meeting with the person or by placing a phone call. A really good host committee member could result in $5,000 or more in new revenue for your event, so don't be shy about allowing your staff to spend $40 taking the prospect out for a meal. Make sure the person doing the asking understands the event and the role of the host committee and has copies of the promotional materials you prepared in step #2.

4 – Find Committee Leadership

Once you start to get yeses and build your committee membership, go over the list to find good candidates for committee leadership posts. At the very minimum, see if you can identify a good chairman or chairwoman (or co-chairs) for the committee. Committee chairs should be super-well connected and very passionate about your organization. They will be tasked with helping to run the committee meetings as well as motivating members through phone calls and e-mails.

If you have a large committee, you can also appoint vice-chairs or you can divide the group into sub-committees and appoint sub-committee chairs along with the overall committee chairman/woman.

5 – Hold First Meeting

Now – you're ready to hold your first committee meeting. Send out a letter or e-mail to the entire committee membership asking them to come to a kick-off meeting for the committee. Make it very social and appealing – perhaps a cocktail hour with a 30 minute committee meeting tucked in, or a short meeting followed by a dessert reception. Be sure to make follow-up calls to get as many committee members to the initial meeting as possible. The chances that committee members will drop off of the committee increase exponentially if they don't attend this first meeting.

The initial meeting should be held well in advance of the event – 8 months out would be a common timeframe, after spending 2 months building the committee and the leadership structure. The first meeting should be light and fun. I like to use the following timetable for the initial meeting:

1. Social Time / Networking (30 minutes)
2. Call to Order and Introductions of Members and Staff (10 minutes)
3. Mission and History of the Organization (5 minutes)
4. History of the Event (if it is an annual event) and Event Fundraising Goals (5 minutes)
5. Purpose and Activities of the Host Committee (10 minutes)
6. Q&A (no more than 10 minutes)

That's it – short and sweet. You want to make sure everyone has fun, gets to know the other people on the committee, feels comfortable, and understands the event and that this is a fundraising committee. That's it. Then let them go home, and you can start the "real work" of the committee at the second meeting.

How to Motivate Your Host Committee

Once you put together your host committee, one of your primary tasks as an organization is to keep your committee motivated and working together for the good of the event. Remember – your committee should be introducing your organization and event to their personal contacts, with the goal of getting those contacts to either sponsor the event or purchase tickets and attend the affair.

There are several things you can do to motivate your committee and help them accomplish these goals:

Hold Regular Meetings

Holding regular host committee meetings will provide accountability and motivation for the group. Aim to hold meetings at least every other month, if not monthly. At these meetings, you can provide social time along with updates on the event, recognition of significant member accomplishments, reports from sub-committees, pep talks, etc.

Hold Non-Ask Events

Because your host committee members will likely be approaching contacts that have never heard of your organization and asking them to consider sponsoring or attending the event, I recommend that your organization hold at least one, if not more "non-ask" events for your host committee members.

These non-ask events are simply open houses at your facility or receptions at a board member's office that provide an opportunity for people to learn about your mission, meet your staff and perhaps hear from someone you have helped, if appropriate. Put out hors devours and drinks, limit the events to 60-90 minutes in length, make them free to attend, and ask host committee members to each bring 2 or 3 people to the function who they think might be good prospects for your fundraising event.

Provide Appropriate Materials

Make sure that your host committee members have all of the materials they need to successfully raise money on your behalf, including event invitations, raffle tickets, call scripts, brochures, sponsorship letters, etc.

Track Results

It is important that you track the results of individual committee members so you can offer additional support and help to those who need it, recognize those who are putting in lots of effort, and know who to retain for the following year's host committee.

You should track individual progress with "light touch," meaning you don't want to call people out or embarrass them. Instead, call members who aren't meeting their goals to ask if they need help, and figure out a way to let them graciously drop off of the committee if it turns out that fundraising just isn't their thing (perhaps they can be part of the set-up and tear-down committee for the event, or work the registration table instead of being on the host committee).

Set Up Mini Goals

Establishing short-term mini goals for your host committee is an effective way to get everyone moving in the same direction and ensure that everything seems "doable." Telling your committee that the goal for your annual event is $500,000 may be intimidating for them. Instead, tell them the overall goal, but also tell them that the goal for the host committee is to help raise $100,000 through sponsorships and $50,000 through ticket sales, and that the current goal is to sell $15,000 in sponsorships before the next meeting. This is a much more seemingly "doable" goal.

Committee Leadership

It is important to note that even if your host committee has a leadership structure in place (chairs, sub-committee chairs, etc.) it is up to your staff members to drive the committee forward, run the meetings, track progress, gather materials, etc. Don't rely on your volunteer members to lead the committee, no matter how committed they are. Be sure that a staff member is always available to lead and motivate.

Recognizing and Thanking the Host Committee

Remember that your host committee members are volunteers. They passionately support your work, but they are still volunteers who are taking time away from their families, jobs, hobbies, and work with other organizations in order to help lead the fundraising efforts for your event. It is important to recognize and thank your host committee often, both because they deserve it as well as because you will want them to agree to help in subsequent years as well.

Some great ways to recognize your host committee include listing their names on your event invitations and on your website, inviting them to stand and be recognized at the actual event, printing signage with their names for the event, and of course, sending personalized thank you notes once the event is over.

Dealing with Host Committee Pitfalls

As with all fundraising activities and tactics, non-profits dealing with host committees can face some common pitfalls:

Committee Members that Want to Work on Logistics

Often times, you will update your committee members on event logistics (venue, menu, entertainment, flowers, invitation printing, etc.) and find that one or two members just want to focus on those items. No matter how much you talk about fundraising, these members call and e-mail with ideas on logistics, requests to attend menu tastings and help pick out the flowers, etc.

These members have good intentions, but their activities can become problematic if they turn away from the fundraising activities that are the purpose of the group. I always suggest that you let committee members who are interested in logistics help out in some small way (e.g. participating in the menu tasting), but also have a conversation with them gently nudging them to fulfill the fundraising requirements of their membership. If they fail to do so, the following year you can suggest that they join the volunteer group that helps out with the event, instead of the fundraising-focused host committee.

Inappropriate Host Committee Ideas

You want your host committee to feel "ownership" for the event. You want the members to feel like they are truly part of your team. For that reason, it is imperative that you listen to member ideas about both the fundraising and logistics of your event. If they ideas are good, you can consider implementing them. If they are not so good, well, you are under no obligation to do anything other than say, "thank you for your idea" and then move on.

Of course, once in a while, you'll come across a host committee member that has an "amazing idea" that they just can't stop talking about, but which is inappropriate for the event at hand. This member may be so sure about their idea that they try to dominate committee meetings (and your Executive Director's e-mail inbox) with pleas to implement their suggestion.

Don't let members like this drain time and energy from your staff or committee. Hold a private conversation with the member telling them how much you appreciate their work and their idea, but that you just don't feel it is appropriate for this event. Promise to keep it in mind for future events. In worse case scenarios, be willing to ask the member to step off of the committee if they continue to disrupt the group after you hold a one-on-one meeting with them. Better to lose one member than to distract the entire group from its overall goals.

Relying Too Much on Your Host Committee

No matter how great your event committee is, never rely on them 100%. Once, I watched as a non-profit (against my advice) relied entirely on its event committee to fundraise for an event. The staff handled the event hall, catering, and invitation printing, but the event committee, led by the event chair, was supposedly handling all of the sponsorship and ticket sales. Three weeks before the event, the Executive Director of the organization finally realized his mistake, when he found out that only $1,500 in sponsorships had been sold (against a $10,000 sponsorship goal). Thankfully, the staff took over ticket sales, and by working the phones and holding a coordinated series of meetings with large corporate donors, the team was able to sell out the event and beat the ticket sales goal, which partially made up for the sponsorship debacle.

You want (and need) to put together a phenomenal event committee for your next affair. You want them to set big goals and raise a lot of money. But your staff should also be working on the event by contacting your donors and selling sponsorships, as well as tracking the progress of the committee.

How to Find Sponsors for Your Fundraising Event

In the previous section, we talked about the first pillar of a strong fundraising event: recruiting a stellar host committee. In this section, we're talking about the second pillar: finding and recruiting sponsors for your event.

As we mentioned earlier in this book, the majority of the money for your fundraising events should be raised through sponsorships. Without a strong focus on sponsors, your event will not reach its true potential. If you are setting an ambitious fundraising goal for your event, it will be far easier to reach that goal if you can raise 50%+ of the revenue from large sponsors than if you are trying to raise 100% through individual ticket sales.

What is a Sponsor?

First, let's talk for a minute about what we mean by "sponsor." Sponsors are donors who make a significant contribution to an event (normally in the $250-$100,000 range, depending on the non-profit and the size of the event), often in return for marketing benefits such as signage at the event, premium seating, and including in press opportunities. Sponsors are normally businesses, but can also be individuals, couples / families, government entities or other non-profits.

Because sponsorships usually come with marketing and advertising benefits, relying heavily on sponsors for your events has an additional benefit: it allows you to access an additional pot of dollars for your organization. Corporate charitable giving generally comes from a limited philanthropic budget. Event sponsorships, on the other hand, often come from a much more expansive marketing budget. Thus, businesses and large corporations that might not be able to fit your organization into their charitable giving budget for the year may nonetheless be able to afford a major sponsorship for your annual event.

Developing a Sponsorship Plan

When creating a plan for your event, it is imperative that you include a plan for generating sponsorship dollars. It is also important that you start the prospecting process for sponsors well in advance of the event. Basically, once you have chosen a date, venue and theme, you should start soliciting sponsors. Selling sponsorships takes time – many companies require multiple levels of approvals for marketing expenditures and/or want to include major sponsorships in their overall budget approvals for the year. Thus, reaching out to companies as early as 10 months before an event is not uncommon.

Define Sponsorship Levels and Benefits

The first step to selling sponsorships for you event is to define your sponsorship levels and what benefits are included for each sponsoring company / individual. In defining sponsorship levels, be ambitious but realistic. Look at your donor file and the businesses you are thinking of contacting to understand what levels you can realistically expect to fill. If, for example, you are holding an event for the first time and your largest annual donor gives you $25,000 per year, don't set up a title sponsorship for your event at the $500,000 level... you're not going to get it. On the other hand, many organizations that do have large donors will hold annual galas and price their top sponsorship at $1,000 or $2,500 thus underselling what could be a very lucrative avenue for additional revenue.

When setting sponsorship levels, look at your overall event goal. Assume that you will raise at least 50% of your overall fundraising goal through sponsorships (if not more). Thus, if you want to raise $100,000 from your event, your sponsorship goal should be in the $50,000+ range. Set your sponsor levels accordingly. In this case, you'd want to have a top sponsorship slot of at least $15,000 - $20,000 in order to reach your overall sponsor goal.

Name your sponsorship levels in a way that highlights either your event theme or your organization's work. For example, if you are holding an event to raise money for a school, you could name your sponsor levels: Scholar, Essayist, Author, Contributor, Friend. If you are holding an event with a garden theme your sponsorship levels could be: Rose, Tulip, Petunia, Daffodil, Daisy. If you can't come up with anything that ties into your organization or event, you can also use naming conventions like: Platinum, Gold, Silver, Bronze.

Each sponsor level should include a distinct group of benefits for the sponsoring company, individual, organization or family. These benefits can include:

Marketing Opportunities - What marketing and advertising opportunities can you offer your sponsors in return for their sponsorship?

- Event and pre-event naming opportunities
- Inclusion in press releases and event programs
- Signage at the event
- Recognition by event speakers from the podium
- Press availabilities
- Recognition on the organization's website

Event Benefits - What event benefits can you offer your sponsors in return for their sponsorship?

- Tickets to the event and to any VIP receptions at the event
- Reserved tables at the event
- Inclusion of a sponsor representative as an event chair or co-chair

Be creative in planning your sponsor benefits. Not every sponsor will receive all of the benefits outlined above, and obviously the higher a sponsor's donation is, the more benefits the company or individual will receive. Here are two examples of sponsor benefits flyers that I created for organizations I was working with (organization names have been changed):

St. James School Scholarship Dinner
Levels of Participation

Presenting Sponsor   **$250,000**
Funds Scholarships for 250 Students
- Premium signage at event, premium placement for logo on St. James website
- Opportunity for promotional materials to be given to event attendees
- Up to 4 tables (40 attendees) at dinner & full page ad in program book

Platinum Sponsor   **$100,000**
Funds Scholarships for 100 Students
- Premium signage at event, premium placement for logo on St. James website
- Up to 3 tables (30 attendees) at dinner & full page ad in program book

Patron's Circle   **$50,000**
Funds Scholarships for 50 Students
- Listed on all event materials and on St. James website
- Up to 3 tables (30 attendees) at dinner & full page ad in program book

Benefactor   **$25,000**
Funds Scholarships for 25 Students
- Listed on all event materials and on St. James website
- Up to 2 tables (20 attendees) at dinner & full page ad in program book

Advisor   **$10,000**
Funds Scholarships for 10 Students
- Listed on all event materials and on St. James website
- 1 table (10 attendees) at dinner, if you desire one & full page ad in program book

Advocate   **$5,000**
Funds Scholarships for 5 Students
- Listed on all event materials and on St. James website
- Up to 6 tickets to scholarship dinner & half page ad in program book

Friend   **$1,000**
Funds Scholarship for 1 Student
- 2 tickets to scholarship dinner & half page ad in program book

Individual Supporter   **$250**
A portion of the ticket price supports the scholarship fund
- 1 ticket to scholarship dinner

47th Annual Baltimore Trading Company
Black Tie Gala
Supporting the Columbia Family Shelter

Title Sponsor: Thank you Baltimore Trading Company!

VIP Auction Preview Sponsor: $10,000
- Naming rights for VIP auction preview reception
- Inside back cover of ad calendar, and display advertising at event
- Featured in newspaper and billboard advertising for event
- Logo featured on website for one year on event invitations and materials
- 10 tickets to event and VIP auction preview

Presenting Sponsor(s): $5,000
- Full page ad in ad calendar and display advertising at event
- Featured in newspaper and billboard advertising for event
- Logo featured on website for one year and on invitations and event materials
- 10 tickets to event, 6 tickets to VIP auction preview

Team Excellence Award Sponsors: $2,500
- Naming rights for one of this year's Columbia Excellence Awards, presented at the event
- ½ page ad in ad calendar and display advertising at event
- Featured in newspaper and billboard advertising for event
- Name listed on event invitations and logo featured on website for six months
- 6 tickets to event, 2 tickets to VIP auction preview

Silver Sponsor: $1,000
- ½ page ad in ad calendar and display advertising at event
- Featured in newspaper advertising for event
- Name listed on event invitations and logo featured on website for six months
- 4 tickets to event, 2 tickets to VIP auction preview

Bronze Sponsor: $500
- ¼ page ad in ad calendar and logo featured on website for six months
- 2 tickets to event, 2 tickets to VIP auction preview

Partner Sponsor: $300
- Listing in ad calendar and on website for three months
- 2 tickets to event

Sponsor Renewal

If you are holding an annual event (one that your organization holds each year), the first step in signing up sponsors for the event is sponsor renewal – the best sponsor prospects for your event are those companies and individuals who have previously sponsored the event. I highly recommend that you try to upgrade your sponsors each year until you reach the point where they cannot go any higher based on their financial ability.

For example, if someone sponsored your event at the $2,500 level last year, ask them to consider the $5,000 level this year. They can always say no and stay at the $2,500 level, but it is rare that a sponsor will talk you up to the $5,000 level if you ask her to donate at the $2,500 level.

I use a multi-step process for sponsor renewals:

#1 – Assigning Levels

First, I build a list of all of the companies, organizations and individuals who have sponsored the event in the past three years, and assign target sponsorship levels to each of them. This is how much we are going to ask them for this year.

#2 – The Sponsor Renewal Letter

Then, I send out a sponsor renewal letter to each of the past sponsors asking them to consider renewing or upgrading their sponsorship for this year's event. I like to send this letter out 6-8 months prior to this year's event to give the donors time to get the necessary company approvals, etc., as well as to build a base of financial support for the event well in advance of the time when vendor payments will be due.

As part of this letter, I thank the sponsors for their past support of the event, let them know our ambitious goals for this coming event, and make a direct ask for sponsorship renewal. I ask the donors make a sponsorship pledge, with the option of paying now or receiving an invoice from the organization one month prior to the event. Depending on the organization, we sometimes also offer additional benefits for early renewal, such as extra signage at the event, extra VIP tickets, etc.

A sample sponsorship renewal letter appears on the following pages. This is an actual letter that we successfully used to renew over 75% of the past year's sponsors for an annual gala event prior to our early renewal deadline. The name and identifying characteristics of the organization have been changed:

Rockledge Hospital

Name
Address
City, State, ZIP
October, 2000

Dear Samantha,

It's hard to believe, but this year is the 10th anniversary of our signature annual event, the Purple Tie Ball!

Over the past ten years, the Purple Ball has grown from small gathering of just under 50 people at the Seaport Inn to last year's 400 person reception and silent auction at the Wannamaker Estate. Thanks to supporters like you, this fantastic event has provided much needed revenue to the Hospital, and enabled us to offer free and reduced cost medical care to over 10,000 patients last year.

In honor of this anniversary, our goal is to make the **10th Annual Purple Tie Ball** our biggest and best event ever. This coming year, we will be opening a new wing and dramatically expanding our ability to serve indigent patients.

This year's Ball will provide a significant portion of the revenue we need to complete this expansion.

Over the years, you have been a generous supporter of the Hospital, and of this event. I am writing to ask you to consider renewing your sponsorship by sponsoring the 10th Annual Purple Tie Ball, which will be held on April 29, 2001 at the Wanamaker Estate in downtown Rockledge.

It may seem early to start thinking about next year's event, but April is just around the corner, and with the ambitious growth plan the Hospital has laid out, we need your support now, more than ever.

Your renewal will let us know that we can push ahead with our expansion, and in turn, will be directly responsible for our greatest accomplishment ever: being able to offer free medical services to every patient who can't afford care in the tri-county area.

Would you be willing to sponsor the 10th Annual Purple Tie Ball at the $2,500 or $5,000 level?

Please take a moment to fill out the enclosed sponsor renewal form and send it to my attention in the envelope provided. You may choose to either send a check now with your form, or can request that we send you a bill next year. Either way, your pledge now is crucial to our ability to move forward.

To show our appreciation for your early pledge, we will be displaying special "10th Annual Purple Tie Ball Charter Sponsor" signage at the event which will list all sponsors who make their pledges before December 15, 2000.

Thank you for your continued support!

Peter Marcinkus, MD
Chief Executive Officer

P.S. The 10th Annual Purple Tie Ball is just around the corner! **Will you help us expand our capacity to serve those in need** by serving as a sponsor once again this year?

#3 - Follow Up Calls

Approximately 3 weeks after the letters are sent out, I gather together a team of staff, board members and/or volunteers (depending on the resources of the organization) to make follow up calls to every past sponsor who has not yet sent in their renewal form for the coming year. Most non-profits who use sponsor letters skip this step, yet making personal phone calls is one of the most effective tactics you can use to secure sponsors for your event.
The call script generally goes something like this:

"Hi, Regina, this is Jim calling from Rockledge Hospital, how are you? I'm calling to see if your received our letter about the 10th Annual Purple Tie Ball. Did you receive it? Good. We're so grateful for your continued support of the hospital and the poorest families in our community. This year is our 10th anniversary ball, and we'd like to make it our biggest and best ever. Would you be willing to serve as a sponsor again this year at the $5,000 level?"

Be sure that your calls include definite, concrete asks. Once you make your ask, wait for the person to respond. Give them the time they need to think through their answer, and resist the urge to keep talking to fill the silence.

#4 – The Event Invitation

I always include sponsorship options on the event invitations for the events I am coordinating, and I always include all previous sponsors on the mailing list for our invitations. This means that if someone did not renew their sponsorship through our renewal mailing or the follow-up calls, they have one last opportunity to do so through the event mailing. For sponsors that *have* renewed, we generally still send them an official invitation but include a note inside confirming that they have already reserved a sponsorship and that either (a) their payment has been received or (b) their payment is now due.

Don't be shy about reaching out to sponsors who have made pledges but have not sent in a check as the event approaches. In many cases, businesspeople will have gotten caught up in their work and simply forgotten about sending in the check. Reach out to them by phone to remind them to do so.

Finding New Sponsors

Renewing sponsors is extremely important for your event success, but what will really push you over your fundraising goal is constantly adding a new stream of sponsors to your events each year. For each event you hold, spend some time outlining a list of new sponsorship prospects and approaching them to support your event.

Utilizing Your Network

The first step in finding new prospects for your event should be utilizing your existing network. Ask board members, staff, current donors and volunteers to introduce your organization to people and companies they know who may be interested in sponsoring your event.

Start this process early so that you don't have to "strong-arm" the relationship. If a board member introduces you to a sponsor prospect 8 months before the event, you will have time to gently build a relationship with that person. If the introduction isn't made until 3 weeks before the event, then the board member will either have to call in a favor to secure the sponsorship or wait until future events to make an ask so that you'll have time to build a proper relationship with the prospective donor.

Warm Prospects

One great source of event sponsors that is often overlooked by organizations is your current donor file. Take some time to review your donor list with your team. What people have given to you in the past year that also work for companies that could afford to sponsor your event? Consider calling these donors, telling them how important the event is to your organization and asking them to help you approach their companies for a sponsorship. In many cases, the person will not have ever thought of doing this and will be unsure how to proceed. Have one of your staff members explain the sponsorship process, discuss who to approach at the company, and prepare a letter or script they can use, if necessary.

Cold Prospects

In addition to those sponsors recommended by your network and the warm prospects generated by reviewing your donor file, you should also develop a list of cold prospects for the event. These are companies and organizations that might have an affinity for your cause or be supporters of many non-profit organizations in your community, who might be interested in sponsoring your event.

Prepare this list well in advance so that you have time to cultivate these donors. One of my basic rules of thumb for fundraising is that you have to cultivate a prospect before you ask him or her for money. This is as true for event sponsorships as it is for every other type of fundraising. Resist the urge to compile a list of prospective donors, do a cold mailing to them, and then wonder why no one responded.

Instead, develop your list and spend 6-8 months setting up meetings with these companies, introducing your non-profit to them, building relationships with them and then asking them to support your event. It's much more time consuming than simply mailing out a letter, but it's also much more effective.

The Importance of Year-Round Cultivation for Your Event

It is crucial that you view sponsor cultivation for your events as a year-round activity. Many non-profits only start to think about sponsors in the 2 or 3 months immediately prior to an event. By that point, it is generally too late to find and cultivate new sponsors for the event.

Instead, spend all year on the lookout for great sponsors for your organization's events. Meet with current donors and sponsors and ask them for referrals to new prospective sponsors. Work with your board, staff and volunteers to identify companies that may be interested in sponsoring your event, and then build a relationship with these companies. Remember, generating sponsorships is still *fundraising*. Like all fundraising it is about building relationships, and that takes time.

Filling the Room: How to Sell More Tickets than Ever Before

You're holding a brand new fundraising event for your organization. You've sold lots of sponsorships, sourced some nice auction items, and convinced the town's most popular newscaster to emcee the event. The planning for the event went far better than you ever could have hoped. You're walking on cloud nine.

You arrive at the event venue excited and ready for a great night. You open the doors and feel... heartbroken. Tables are empty, seats unfilled. The hall, which can hold 300 people, looks bare with just 50 supporters in attendance. You hold out hope that more will show up. You spend the rest of the night waiting, looking out the window at the parking lot, praying that 20 more... 10 more... 5 more people might show up. It's the nightmare of event planners everywhere.

Now picture another scenario. You did the same great planning and found the same great sponsors, auction items and emcee. This time, you walk into the room and it is packed. Standing room only. The aisles are filled with people craning their necks to look at your auction items. There are lines at the bars and food stations. The room is full of energy, conversation and laughter. You spend your time greeting supporters and worrying where you're going to fit the people who are still streaming through the door.

Obviously, we'd all prefer to walk into the second, full room instead of the first. The question is... how? How can you make sure to fill your events with happy, paying attendees?

Why Full Events are Important

Holding "full" events makes the event planner and development team feel good, but beyond that, there are three important reasons that organizations strive to fill the room at their functions:

Raise More Money

The first and more important reason to fill your events is to raise more money. Most of the events you hold will have a ticket price or cost to attend. The more tickets you sell, the more money you will raise. If you have event add-ons like auctions or raffles, the more people you have in the room, the higher your auction or raffle revenue will be.

Of course, this brings up an interesting point that I have discussed many times with many different organizations... how should you price your tickets? Should you be using your tickets simply to recoup the costs of the event, while making your revenue from sponsors and add-ons like auctions? Or should you be trying to make a "profit" on each ticket that can go to your organization's bottom line?

My recommendation is that you take a hybrid approach. You shouldn't overprice your tickets, and thus drive people away from the event. The vast majority of your event revenue should come from selling sponsorships, not from tickets. That being said, I am of the mindset that you should make a small profit on every ticket sold. This adds to your overall revenue, obviously... but it also helps you avoid the situation (which I have seen at many organizations who price their tickets "at cost") where additional attendees become a hassle after a certain point. I really dislike hearing organizations say, "Ugh! We sold 5 more tickets! Now I have to add another table. I don't know how to fit it!" Far better to make a profit on every ticket and say, "Yeah! We sold another ticket! Who knows where we'll fit everybody!!!?"

Build Buzz and Excitement

Filling the room at your event also helps to build buzz and excitement around the event for your donors and their guests. Full events are more enjoyable and more exciting than half-full events. If this is an annual event, having a full room will make your attendees more likely to attend next year, because they remember what a great time the event was this year.

More buzz and excitement will also encourage your donors to help sell tickets and sponsorships for the event next year, because they can honestly tell their friends and colleagues what a great function it is.

Impress Sponsors and Press

Finally, a full room helps to impress your event sponsors as well as any members of the press that you were able to convince to cover the event.

For sponsors, a full event will make them feel like they made a wise investment by sponsoring the affair. Companies will like that their name and logo are in front of lots of people and that they are associated with such a successful event.

For the press, a full room shows that people care about and are interested in both the non-profit and the event, and suggests that this is an event and an organization worthy of press coverage.

The Two Ways to Ensure a Full Room

There are two main ways to ensure a full room. You can either get more people to come to the event, or hold it in a smaller room. I prefer the former. Think big about your events, and for annual events, see if you can grow the event attendance year after year.

Of course, that's not to say that room size isn't a concern. It is. You should be realistic about what you really will be able to accomplish in terms of attendance. It's better to have a slightly smaller room that's bursting at the seams with people than a cavernous hall that looks empty. Choose a room size that fits your event, then work hard to pack the space with supporters.

5 Keys to Selling Lots of Tickets for Your Next Event

As you plan your next fundraising event, remember these five keys to successfully selling lots of tickets to your affair:

#1: Start Early

Many non-profits think that they have to wait until the invitations get mailed in order to start selling tickets. This is simply not true, and thinking like this forces organizations to leave lots of money on the table.

Start your ticket selling process early. Get your host committee to start selling to their network early. Get your online ticket-selling platform launched as early as you can. When you send out your save the date cards, allow people to purchase tickets at an early-bird discount on your event webpage. The more tickets you sell early to your "regulars", the more you'll be able to focus on bringing new supporters in to the event as it nears.

#2: Utilize Your Supporters' Networks

This is crucial to maximizing your event revenue. For every event you hold (and particularly annual dinners or galas) you should be utilizing your supporters' networks to sell tickets. This means getting your supporters, donors, and friends to go out and sell tickets to their friends, colleagues, partners and associates on your behalf.

Start by getting everyone on your board and your event host committee to commit to sell a certain number of tickets for the event. This can start early, well in advance of the invitations being mailed. Create a flyer or other handout that they can use to take ticket orders. Then, approach some of your key volunteers and donors and ask them to take a leadership role in the event's success by selling tickets within their networks. The more networks you can reach in to, the more tickets your organization will sell.

#3: Follow-Up on Invitations

Every non-profit sends out invitations to its fundraising events, but very few follow up those invitations with a phone call. Having your staff, board, or well-trained volunteers call each invitee in the 2 weeks following your invitation mailing can significantly increase your response rate. The call doesn't have to be a hard sell. I usually use something like this:

Hi Jim, this is Steve from the 5th Street Women's Shelter. I'm calling to make sure that you received the invitation to our 30th annual white tie gala. Did you get your copy in the mail?

[If No] I'm sorry to hear that. I'd love to send you another copy by e-mail. What is the best e-mail address to send it to?

[If Yes] Great! Do you know if you will be able to attend?

It's that simple, and it works wonders.

#4: Sell to Groups

Your organization is likely already making group ticket sales through sponsorships – offering sponsors whole tables (or more) of tickets in return for major donations. Carry this one step further by offering discounted tickets for bulk purchases by supportive organizations or groups.

For example, you may be running an event that is $50 per person. Why not approach your big sponsors (who are already getting some free tickets with their sponsorships) and ask if they'd like to bring their whole company to the event, at a rate of $500 for 15 additional tickets? Or, approach local fraternal or religious organizations and ask if they'd like to support the event by buying 10 tickets for their members at $40/ticket.

This strategy won't work for every event, but it's a great strategy for some events, particularly mid-level events.

#5: Add Pizzazz

The more excited people are about an event, the more likely they are to attend and to encourage their friends and colleagues to do the same. There are any number of ways you can add pizzazz and get people excited about the event, including:

- Find a local celebrity to serve as the headliner for the event
- Partner with a local professional or well-known college sports team to have the coaches and players attend the event
- Feature a well-known local band
- Find amazing items for your live or silent auction or raffle
- Have a fun theme, like "Taste of San Diego" featuring popular local chefs

To Comp or Not to Comp?

This is another question that often comes up when planning non-profit fundraising events. Who, if anyone, should we comp by giving them free tickets to the event? Here are some thoughts:

Board Members

My position is that board members should buy tickets to your events. There are exceptions to this rule, of course (e.g. one abuse shelter I know reserves two spots on its board for former clients, many of whom are poor. These board members are comped for all events). But, for the most part, board members have a responsibility to support the organization and one way they can do so, and provide leadership, is by purchasing tickets for events.

Host Committee Members

Again, except in very rare circumstances, my belief is that event host committee members should buy tickets for the event. The purpose of the host committee is to fundraise. Purchasing tickets shows leadership and helps the event reach its goals. Some non-profits have successfully offered discounted host committee tickets, but I am in favor of full-priced tickets for committee members.

Volunteers

When it comes to comping volunteers, my rule of thumb is, if you have the room, go for it. Many non-profits use free event tickets as rewards for loyal volunteers, and this has the added benefit of helping you fill the room. I like to wait until the week or two before the event to give free tickets to select volunteers in order to (a) make sure we have space and (b) allow those volunteers with the means to purchase tickets to do so. Also, I don't recommend giving free tickets to *all* of your volunteers, unless you desperately need to fill seats. Instead, use the tickets as a reward for volunteers who have been particularly helpful.

VIPs

Most VIPs can afford to pay for their own tickets, but many will still expect free tickets in order to attend. (VIPs can include local politicians, professional athletes, local celebs, etc.) Keep this in mind when approaching local VIPs to attend. Those that do attend will likely want to be comped. If having the VIPs at your event will increase attendance, add prestige for sponsors or build excitement and buzz, then there's nothing wrong with inviting... and comping... VIP guests.

"Fill the Room" Comps

As you get closer to your event date, most non-profits find that they need more people to come in order to really fill the room. This often happens because sponsors pay for an event, but only send a couple of people, or because you've sold a ton of tickets but are still short of really packing the place. When that happens, it's time to hand out some comps to fill the room.

Remember, comped tickets usually cost you money because of per-person catering and bar charges, so be careful how many people you comp under this regime, but it's important to fill your room... comps are particularly ok if you sold lots of sponsorships, and the sponsors aren't using all of their free seats.

Make a list of comp prospects and send out a letter telling those people that you'd like to honor their support of your organization by giving them 2 free tickets to the event. Mail these letters out at least 10 days before the event. Tell the recipients that in order to receive their tickets, they need to call or e-mail you by the day before the event (or whenever your seating chart deadline is). Mail these letters to your volunteers, former board members, clients, or anyone else who might be interested in coming to the event with a complimentary ticket.

Tickets vs. Guestlists

Over the course of this section, I have constantly been referring to "selling tickets." Yet, many organizations don't use paper tickets, and instead use guestlists of people who paid for admittance. Which is better?

The answer is, "it depends." Generally, I think it is better for the organization to use a guest list instead of tickets. Tickets can be a pain to track, people lose them, and you'll still need to keep a guestlist denoting who paid and who didn't, who took tickets to "sell" but never returned the cash and unused tickets, etc. Thus, I like to use guestlists for my events. You can send out invitations and use event handouts for your board and host committee to use in selling the event, but maintain a guestlist of who paid and who didn't.

That being said, for some organizations, using actual paper tickets is the right choice. This is often the case at non-profits with lots of senior citizen attendees or that have traditionally used tickets and now would have a problem switching away from them. In general, use the strategy that will help you raise the most money. If all things are equal, then use a guestlist instead of paper tickets, because it is an easier strategy for the organization.

Selling Tickets Online

While you might not need online ticket sales capacity for smaller events in supporter's homes, etc., for larger events like annual dinners, galas, large silent auctions, etc., every non-profit should be using an online component for selling tickets.

Online Sales Infrastructure

Setting up a webpage for selling event tickets should be relatively easy for most organizations. First, set up a dedicated webpage that talks about your event and is linked from the homepage of your website. Use this event page to "sell" the affair, and include a "Buy Tickets Today!" button that people can click to purchase tickets.

When that button is clicked, send people to a simple, one page checkout form where they can enter their credit card information, select sponsorship levels, enter the number of tickets and the attendee names, etc. Your webmaster should be able to set this page up easily in conjunction with your credit card payment processor. Be sure to use a secure (https://) page to inspire confidence in your visitors.

Using Your Ticket URL

Once your sales and payment pages have been set up, you can include your online ticket sales URL (webpage) information on your paper invitations and in all of your written communications regarding the event (including your paper newsletters, direct mail, etc.) For this reason, I advise making your ticket URL easy to remember and spell. It's far easier for people to remember and correctly type in:

www.PhillyShelter/tickets

than it is to have them type in:

www.PhillyShelter/events/2013blacktieball/payments739283.php

Make your ticket URL as easy to remember and as simple as possible. Have the URL you promote link to the sales page (that explains and sells the event and includes the "Buy Your Tickets Today!" button) instead of the actual payment page, which should be as simple and clean as possible.

Promoting the Event Online
You should also be promoting your event online fairly aggressively using all of the avenues available to you. Send out multiple promotions to your e-mail list touting your event, and use your social media networks to drive people to the ticket page. Ask your host committee, board, and other supporters who are active online to do the same.
Unique Ticket Ideas for Your Next Event

Before we close this section, I wanted to take a look at three unique ticket ideas that I have seen in action at non-profit fundraising events over the past few years. Would any of these unique ideas work for you?

Bring-A-Friend Tickets

One organization used "Bring-A-Friend" tickets. These were perforated three-part tickets: one section was kept by the non-profit when it sold the ticket, one section was kept by the purchaser and allowed them and their spouse or a guest to come to the event, and the third section could be ripped off and given to a friend who could then come to the event with a spouse or guest. This was a fairly low dollar event ($40) and the goal was to fill the room in a rally-like atmosphere. The event also featured a local celebrity speaker who supported the organization.

It was unique and it worked – the ballroom was overflowing.

Tiered Tickets

While many organizations use different event tiers (e.g. a VIP pre-reception for $500, dinner for $100), one non-profit I came in contact with took tiers to a new level by offering "seating tiers" for an event featuring a famous singer from the 60's as the entertainment at a black-tie gala.

Tables in the front row cost $500/ticket. Tables in the next 3 rows cost $350/ticket, and tables in the back 5 rows cost $275/ticket.

Sponsored Tickets

I love this idea and have used it myself to great effect. Let's say you've been very successful in selling sponsorships to an event, but still need to fill the room. You decide that you want to either allow some clients of the organization to attend the event, or that you want to introduce new people to the event by having them come for free. What's your solution? How about sponsored tickets?

Approach some of your sponsors (or your large annual donors who are not sponsoring this event) and tell them that you want to give away 100 tickets to the people your organization has helped… or that you want to give away 100 tickets to promising young professionals who can't afford the ticket price but will likely be the future donors to the organization. Ask the donor to sponsor the tickets by paying for a certain number of the ones you are giving away. Stamp those tickets with the message, "This ticket sponsored by XYZ Company" and recognize the sponsor at the event for their extra support.

How to Minimize Cost and Maximize Revenue at Your Next Event

We've talked about supercharging your host committee, maximizing sponsorships and selling tickets to the event. Now it's time to turn our attention to something that most non-profits spend lots of time on, but in the *wrong* way: event logistics.

I say that most non-profits spend time on logistics in the wrong way because most organizations don't think of event logistics as a profit center. Instead, they worry about flowers, menu items and fancy papers for gala invitations. I like to think of event logistics as the fourth leg of the revenue picture (along with sponsorships, ticket sales and the host committee). I think of logistics in this way not only because cutting costs helps your bottom line, but because when an event goes smoothly, people enjoy themselves and want to come back year after year.

In this section, we're going to take a look at how you can use event logistics to bolster fundraising events at your organization. Note that while some of the points we will be making will seem to apply mostly to larger events, the truth is that the majority of these strategies can and should be used for events of all sizes.

The 5 Principles of Successful Fundraising Event Logistics

First, let's take a look at the five principles which guide our understanding of why focusing on event logistics is so important:

#1 – Costs Matter

So many non-profits focus solely on event revenue (how much can we raise from this event?) without thinking about event costs. Your event bottom line... the amount generated from the event that you'll be able to spend on your programs and services... is determined by *both* gross revenue and event costs. Every dollar you save in holding an event is a dollar you can spend on furthering your mission.

Of course, many organizations that do think about costs go overboard with them. While you don't want to lose sight of potential cost savings for your event, you also don't want to keep ROI (return on investment) in mind. If you can save $2,000 on your event costs by not adding extra room for your silent auction and instead keeping the auction items closer together, that might be a good idea... unless adding that extra room will allow people to get a better look at your auction items and bid more, resulting in $3,000 in extra bids. In that case, you'd actually make $1,000 *profit* by spending $2,000 on the extra space.

Costs matter, but keep ROI in mind.

#2 – Time is Money

Dollars spent are not the only costs you should be watching as you prepare for your event. You should also keep a close eye on how much time you, your staff, board and volunteers are spending preparing for the event. Events can be *very* time consuming, if you let them be.

Remember that there is a money cost to your time. If your Development Director spends 100 hours preparing for your annual gala over the course of a few months, and raises $50,000... but could have raised $100,000 if she spent the same 100 hours on major donor fundraising... then you either need to rethink your event or figure out a way for your Development Director to spend less time on the event (perhaps by using other staff and volunteers or by systemizing the process so she can get more done in less time).

Fundraising time comes down to a series of choices… if your event is taking up too much time in preparation, execution and follow-up, you need to streamline it or consider dumping it in favor of other fundraising activities. Don't get sentimental about your events. Your focus should be on doing whatever you can to raise as much money as possible to carry out your non-profit's mission.

#3 – Great Event Flow = Happy Guests = More Revenue

Spend some time thinking through the best possible flow for every event you hold. This includes how people register and pay for an event, what they do see and hear while they are there, and how you follow-up with them after the event is over.

We'll be talking more about each of those items later in this book, but for now know that making your event flow really well is important. Why? Because when your event flows well, your guests and sponsors will be happy. They will enjoy the event more. When they enjoy the event more, it will make them want to spend more money at the event (if you are holding an auction, raffle, etc.), attend the event again next year (if it is an annual event), and they will be left with really good feelings about your organization that will help you continuing to cultivate and steward them and raise their lifetime donor value for your non-profit.

#4 – People Get Bored, Fast

Did you ever notice how kindergarten teachers switch activities with their classes every 10-15 minutes? It's because kids get bored with things fast. They lose attention and focus. And when they get bored, things go haywire. We like to think that as adults, we have longer attention spans and can stay focused for as long as we want. Sadly, nothing could be further from the truth.

People (including adults) get bored fast. When they get bored, they lose focus. Did you ever notice that when an event drags on, people start to hold conversations with each other, and the din starts to drown out the speakers? People leave events early, play on their smartphones or tablets, or just generally zone out and miss all of the important things you are telling them…

Plan your event flow with this in mind. Keep your speeches and event program short. Provide lots to do and see. Know that after 10-15 minutes of doing the same thing, people will start to lose focus.

#5 – Annual Events Build Annually

One final reason why event flow is so important is because events build on themselves – if you are holding the same event every year (such as your yearly silent auction or annual gala) and it goes really great this year, people will want to come back next year and will be more willing to invite their friends and family to come along with them. If people have fun this year, they'll come back next year. If the event was frustrating, long and boring this year, they won't want to come back next year.

Annual events build annually. Focus on logistics and make sure people have a great experience, and they'll come back year after year. The same is true for sponsors... if an event goes well this year, they'll be more likely to sponsor your function again next year.

The Search for In-Kind Event Goods and Services

One of the most common ways to keep event costs low is to find companies that are willing to donate goods and services in-kind for the event, or who are willing to lower their prices so that a portion of the items/services are given in-kind. Over the course of my career, I have worked with organizations that have received some or all of the following items free for their events:

- Venue / Event Space
- Food / Catering
- Beer / Wine / Alcohol
- Flowers / Balloons / Decorations
- Entertainment / Band / Performers
- Printing
- Tables / Chairs / Linens
- Audio / Visual

The best way to approach vendors for in-kind donations is to so with a personal visit or call. Create a list of all of the things your organization will be spending money on for your coming event. Then, generate a list of 2 or 3 potential vendors for each line item. Also, circulate this list to your board, volunteers, event host committee and staff to see if any of them have friends, relatives or acquaintances who might be able to provide any of those items free or at low cost. I have found that for almost every event where I have followed this strategy, several staff and board members have contacts that developed into free or reduced goods/services for the event.

For any company where you have a "warm" lead (i.e. they already do business with your non-profit or you or someone you are affiliated with has a connection at that business), call the company up directly and see if you can set up a meeting or at least have a phone conversation to explain your non-profit, your mission and this event, and make an ask. Remember – this *is* an ask, so all of the usual rules apply – be clear, concise, and make a concrete ask. It's best to make the ask in person, but over the phone can work as well.

For companies where you don't have a warm contact, start by sending them a letter explaining your organization, your mission and this event, and telling them that you'll be contacting them over the next week to discuss partnering with them on the event. Then, make the follow-up calls and try to either set up meetings or have the ask conversation on the phone.

When approaching a company for an in-kind event donation, you want to focus on two things: your mission, and the marketing benefits you are offering to the company. Your mission is important because most businesses will want to donate to non-profits that are making a difference and can explain that difference in a compelling way.

Of course, some of the companies you approach will primarily be interested in getting the positive press and marketing benefits that you are offering, so outline these as well. Count in-kind donors as sponsors, and offer them the same sponsorship levels that you give to donors who give cash for the event. Provide signage, tickets, etc. to those who give in-kind donations for your events.

Also, be prepared for companies who offer significant reductions in price but do not offer completely free items for your event. (For example, I have seen wineries offer 70% off bottles for events, catering companies reduce their prices by 50%, and venues ask you to pay for the catering and staff but waive hall rental fees, etc.). Reduced prices can be a huge help, so if a company says they can't give you the items or services for free, ask them for a major reduction in price.

I like to count 50% of a company's reduction as a sponsorship benefit. Thus, if your caterer was going to charge you $5,000 but agrees to slash the price to $2,500 as an in-kind donation, I would give them the benefits for 50% of the $2,500 reduction ($1,250) as a sponsorship package. On the other hand, when companies are willing to donate the entire cost, I give them the sponsorship benefits commensurate with 100% of their reduced prices.

Putting Together an Effective Volunteer Team

Many organizations could not pull together their events without the help of volunteers. Great volunteers can be a significant blessing to a non-profit event, but poorly trained and mismanaged volunteers can turn out to be a real problem.

For the purposes of this section, we are talking about working volunteers (those who help set-up, run and clean-up after an event), not fundraising volunteers who sit on your event host committee or are responsible solely for selling tickets, finding sponsors, etc. It is important that you use your volunteers and event staff as effectively as possible. Here's how:

First, it is incredibly important to recruit your event team as early as possible. This means defining who on your non-profit's staff will be involved with the event, and identifying volunteers that will help.

Second, you should clearly define roles, tasks and deadlines for everyone on your team, including staff and volunteers. Fundraising events can be extremely complex affairs. It's essential that everyone on the team knows what they are expected to do, and what the deadlines are for that activity. This is doubly important for volunteers.

The best way to go about this is to define the roles you will need to fill before you solicit volunteers. For each role, you'll want to answer the following questions:

- What is the role?
- How many people do I need in this role?
- What are the responsibilities of this role?
- What are the deadlines for this role?
- What skill sets should I be looking for in someone to fill this role?
- What is this role's estimated time commitment?

For example, you may decide that you need three people to run the registration table at your event, and that the responsibilities of this role include welcoming people to the event, checking them in, taking payment if they haven't already paid, keeping track of who comes to the event, and answering any questions they have about the auction process.

The deadlines might include coming to training on a certain day, then being at the event for a certain number of hours. The skill sets you are looking for would be a friendly demeanor and attention to detail. The time commitment would be one hour training and four hours at the event.

Once you have all of your roles detailed, you'll know how many people you need to work the event. Then, take a look at your staff who will be working the event, and slip them into roles. (Often, staff will fill supervisory roles, with volunteers filling in event staff roles). Then, start recruiting volunteers to fill the other roles that are essential to the success of your event.

In order to make sure your staff and volunteers complete the tasks that you need from them, you have to spell out those tasks and deadlines clearly and early in the event cycle. I've seen many, many non-profit events fail and/or be more frustrating for the event leadership than they need to be because the non-profit did not spell out volunteer tasks clearly enough.

Once you clearly define roles and deadlines, stay on top of your team. Provide them the training and support they need to succeed, and track their progress.

Volunteer Training

In my mind, nothing is more important to running an effective volunteer team than providing appropriate training. For every non-profit event I hold, I ask our volunteers to come to a short 30-45 minute training session, either immediately prior to the event or at a separate time one or two days before the event is to be held. At these training sessions, I do the following:

1. Introduce the staff and volunteer team to ensure that everyone knows everyone else (5 minutes)

2. Make sure everyone knows the mission of the organization and the importance of this event (5 minutes)

3. Thank the volunteers profusely and make sure they know just how important they are to making this event work, and thus how important they are to our organization and to our mission (2 minutes)

4. Explain the different volunteer jobs at the event, and divide the volunteers up into teams to perform each role (5 minutes)

5. Have your staff work separately with each team to explain the particular job they will be doing at the event (5-10 minutes)

Thanking Volunteers

It is extremely important that your volunteers know how appreciative you are of their efforts. There are several ways to accomplish this:

First, every volunteer for your events should receive a thank-you letter in the week or two after the event. Send out volunteer thank you letters at the same time you are sending out your thank you notes to your event donors.

Second, I like to make sure that every volunteer who works an even has some time to actually enjoy the event. If your event is a sit-down dinner, this could mean having one or two tables for the volunteers to sit at and rotating shifts throughout the night so that every volunteer has a chance to eat and relax. If you're running a silent auction, consider diving the night into three shifts and making sure that each volunteer gets one shift off to walk through and bid on items, etc.

Third, consider having an annual volunteer appreciation breakfast, dinner, or cocktail hour to thank all of your volunteers (including your event volunteers) for their support.

Roving Volunteers

For larger events, I like to have a team of roving volunteers that is stationed around the room simply to point people towards the restrooms, answer questions, help senior citizens up from their seats, etc. Be sure that these volunteers are either wearing event shirts or nametags that clearly identify them as part of the event team.

Mapping Your Event

One of the major pieces to ensuring a positive experience is mapping out your event space to provide a great flow. Doing so is an art, and takes practice. When mapping out your event space, you'll want to make sure that people have enough room to move around and not be cramped, while at the same time having people be close enough together to make the room look full and to promote conversations and merriment.

If you are having a silent auction, consider placing the auction items around the room in a way that forces people to move around to see all of the items, and which encourages them to move all in the same direction as they look through the tables. This can be done by placing the items around the room in a semi-circle, outside of the tables, or by placing the tables in the center of the room in a snaking or concentric circles fashion.

If you're holding a raffle or other contest, place the tables for those in the center or front of the room, so that people will be forced to move around and move through the room in order to participate, instead of congregating in the back near the doors.

Making Event Registration a Positive Experience

Would you be surprised to hear me say that your event registration table is one of the most important pieces of your non-profit fundraising event? Well... I think it is. Here's why: Your event registration table is the first thing your guests see when they arrive at your event. If they have a bad experience at registration, it will set a bad mood for them for the entire event.

You should use your registration table to capture the name and contact information of *every single person* who attends your event. This means asking guests who didn't buy tickets but are coming with another guest or are attending as part of a sponsored table to fill out registration cards in addition to the paying guests. Why is this important? Because it allows you to follow-up with those attendees to cultivate them, build relationships with them and move them along your donor funnel. Most non-profits only capture the names of those who are actually buying the tickets… this leaves money on the table.

How can you make event registration a positive experience? Keep it moving! Nothing is worse than showing up to an event and finding a long, slow-moving line at check-in, when all you want to do is go into the event and get some appetizers.

In order to keep your event check-in moving, make sure you have enough people working the registration tables and that you are only collecting the minimum amount of information from attendees: name, address, phone number and e-mail address. Also, be sure that you are prepared to accept checks, cash and credit cards and that your team is well trained and understands the giving / sponsorship levels, how many tickets each pre-paid guest is entitled to, etc.

When holding large events like annual dinners or gala balls, I have found that having one registration table clearly marked "Pre-Paid Ticket Check-In" and the other marked "Ticket Payments" works well – this way, everyone who has already paid can simply go up and sign-in, while those who have not yet paid can write out checks or swipe their credit cards and fill-out registration cards, etc.

One final tip for large events: consider having an "ambassador" – a volunteer or staff member who stands by the doors and welcomes people to the event, while at the same time pointing them in the direction of the different registration tables and answering any questions they might have. This is a nice touch and helps improve the flow when you're holding events with hundreds of guests.

Add-On Logistics: Raffles

Your goal with raffles should be to make sure that as many people as possible purchase tickets. There are several ways you can accomplish this.

First, accept credit cards. I know this is something that you don't see very often at non-profit events, but I have found that when our raffle table accepts credit cards and checks (as opposed to just cash), people buy far more tickets.

Second, have volunteers going from table to table to sell raffle tickets and highlight the items that are available to be won. Teach your volunteers how to "sell" the raffle and get people jazzed to buy. Also, be sure your event emcee mentions the raffle numerous times from the podium.

Third, consider selling raffle tickets right on your event invitations. Many non-profits have had success sending out event invitations that include a small check-off box that says something like

_____ *Add (1) (2) (3) raffle tickets to my event ticket purchase at $20 per ticket (3 for $50)*

This works particularly well when you are raffling off big-ticket items that can be highlighted right on the event invitation.

Fourth, be sure that your raffle table is impossible to miss as people enter the event hall. I like to place the raffle table right smack in the middle of the room about 50 feet after people enter the doors, with huge signage and a volunteer directing them to the table. This way, they can't miss it.

Add-On Logistics: Silent Auction Checkouts

It is imperative that if you are holding a silent auction, you set-up your checkout process to move smoothly. If checkout takes forever or is full of glitches, people will be far less willing to bid on items the next time they come to one of your events.

I have found that, for auctions with more than 25 items, the best way to set up checkout is by having two separate areas: one for payments, and one for picking up gift cards. Remember, as you are setting up your items, you are *not* leaving gift cards and gift certificates out with the bid sheets. Instead, you should place a display (on a regular sized piece of paper) with the gift car / certificate details out on auction tables, and then use an accordion folder or a binder with clear plastic insert pages to keep your gift cards and certificates in numerical order by item number.

Then, set up two distinct areas right next to each other for checkout. The "payments" section is where people can go to make auction payment by credit card, cash, or check. If someone makes a payment for a gift card or gift certificate, your auction staff should give them a slip that shows they paid for the item, and lists the item number, and then direct them over to the "gift card" table to pick up the cards / certificates they paid for. This avoids having people have to wait in line to pay while your staff finds the gift cards, and keeps the whole check out procedure moving. Note that you'll need staff / volunteers at the gift card table than you do at the payments table. Assuming you are accepting credit cards, you can break down your payments table even further by having one line that is "cash or check" only, and one or more lines that are "credit card, cash, or check."

If you are having a very large auction, you may event want to place stanchions and velvet rope (rope lines) out to create separate lines at your auction checkout tables, to help create a more orderly system, and keep the lines together and moving.

The goal of all of this is to keep your checkout space organized and moving smoothly. Nothing is worse than running a great, fun, and profitable event, but having people only remember how they waited in line for 30 minutes to checkout, and when they go up to the front, your staff couldn't find their gift card, and it had to be mailed to them later. Chances are that person won't come back next year, and if they do, they won't bid on anything because they won't want to wait in line. Better to have a system in place that allows your guests to check out with as much ease as possible.

Signage Matters

One of the keys to making your checkout system work is *signage*. Simply having your guests know where they are going and what they are doing will work wonders in keeping things moving along. At the very least, you should have large, clear signs directing auction winners to the AUCTION CHECKOUT. If you are separating out payments from gift card pick-up, you should also have large signs pointing the way: PAY HERE and GIFT CARD PICK-UP. Similarly, if you have a cash / check only payment line, you should have signage announcing CASH / CHECKS ONLY and CREDIT CARDS / CASH / CHECKS.

If you have a very large auction, you may also want to have a "traffic cop" – a volunteer who stands out in front of the checkout area and helps people decide which queue to get into.

Where to Place Your Checkout?

The final question you will need to decide on in relation to your auction check out is where to place the checkout at the event location. There are three primary considerations you will need to make as you finalize your checkout:

First, you need to have enough room for your auction checkout tables, your staff, and the lines of people that will be waiting to check out.

Second, if you are offering credit card payments, you will need power outlets to plug in your card readers and/or laptops.

Third, the best place to locate your auction checkout is near the exit from the event room or venue. You want people to see the checkout on their way out... that way, if they won an item, they won't forget to come over and pay for it. Place your checkout near the door on the way out, and place big signs so people see them as they leave.

The Program Portion of the Event: How to Make Sure Your Guests Have a Good Time

The vast majority of your event should be social time – a chance for people to meet, mingle, eat, drink, and bid / buy (if appropriate). That being said, of course you will want to have an event program prepared that will allow you to introduce your mission to anyone in the audience is not already familiar with your work as well as to thank your sponsors and those who made the event a success.

I recommend that if you are running a 2 hour event, no more than 15-20 minutes be taken up by the program. For a 3 hour event, this can expand to 25-30 minutes if necessary. Going any longer could make your guests feel like your event is dragging.

Also, no speaker should talk for more than 5 or 6 minutes. Much as with our kindergarten example, event guests get bored quickly with speakers who go on and on. Unless one of your speakers is unbelievably entertaining (think: a local Bill Clinton or Conan O'Brien), then give them each 5 minute speaking slots.

Whatever you do, be sure that someone gets up to speak specifically about your mission: why your organization matters, the compelling work you do, and why you need funding. If possible, have one or more people who were helped by the organization get up and speak as well. Use this opportunity to really tell your story and present your case for support. Remember, some of the people there as guests may never have really heard about your non-profit. Use this opportunity to cultivate them.

Database Entries and Other Uses for the Data You Collected

After your event, be sure to enter the data you collected at the event into your donor database. You *did* get contact information for everyone who attended as part of your registration process, didn't you? Now – stay in touch with those folks. If someone is new to your organization, follow-up. Send thank you letters to everyone who attended, even if they didn't pay or make a donation. Hold a thank you event for your silent auction and raffle item sponsors. Be creative!

I like to have a development team member look over each of the silent auction bid sheets to see if there were new people (not in our database) who were bidding on lots of items or who were bidding on some high-end / expensive items. If so, consider setting up meetings or doing phone calls with those people to see if they might be good prospects for a future ask for your organization.

Creating Amazing Invitations, Web Pages, and Other Collateral Materials for Your Events

Did you know that designing your invitations, event web presence, and other collateral materials the right way can add a significant percentage to your overall event revenue? In this section we're going to look at the ways you can supercharge these items to make sure your raising as much money as possible from each and every event.

The Goal for Your Invitations and Web Presence

Many organizations have misguided ideas about the purposes and goals for their event invitations and web presence. They think that their materials should be expertly designed, cutting edge and expensive to show off the quality and professionalism of the non-profit. They spend a lot of money designing and creating invitations and event websites that look great, but don't convert very well. This is a mistake.

Don't get me wrong – there's nothing inherently bad about designing great looking invitations or websites. But the primary purpose of your event materials is not to impress people, it's to sell. Your invitations and event web pages should convert well. They should result in more tickets being sold, more sponsorships being purchased, and more people coming to your event.

In order to accomplish this task, they have to be easy to use. If someone can't figure out how to buy a sponsorship on your website, then chances are they are *not* going to call your office to figure it out. If a supporter wants to buy a table for your event, but can't figure out how to use their credit card with your event invitation, they may just opt to send a check for two tickets instead, rather than go through the hassle of figuring out how to pay on their card. The end result in both cases is that your non-profit loses money.

One word about event invitations – they don't need to cost an arm and a leg. I have seen non-profits spend exorbitant amounts of money on invitation design and printing, and make the same amount as they would have with a simple and traditional design. When creating and printing invitations, think return on investment. If your board wants to do fancy expensive invitations for your event, go ahead and give it a try. But test the result. If you spend an extra $2,000 on invitations but bring in an additional $3,500 because of the better quality invites, then by all means keep doing it. If, on the other hand, you spend an extra $2,000 but only bring in an extra $500, nix the expensive invites and go back to the cheaper version.

The Goal for Your Other Event Collateral Materials

When we talk about "other collateral materials" for your event, we're really talking about those things that you print up to hand out at the event itself... things like program books, ad calendars, silent auction books, and other materials that are given away at the function.

The goal for these materials is two-fold:

First, these materials should present your mission, vision, and organization in a positive light. I always encourage non-profits to use things like event programs to present a mini case for support, and if appropriate, testimonials or stories from those your non-profit has helped. This is your chance to get your message out to event attendees who don't know your organization very well. Think about it – you have a captive audience. How many times have you attended an event and while you were at your table waiting for the next course to be served found yourself reading the adbook or flipping through the program? Use this time and space to present your case!

Second, these event materials should make your events easier to participate in and navigate. What can you include that will make the event more enjoyable for your guests? Examples of things you can include that fulfill this goal include seating charts, silent auction listings or floor plans, lists of cocktails the bar can prepare, etc.

Be creative. I once saw a non-profit include a page of tear-out raffle coupons in their program booklet, with pens at every table. In addition to buying raffle tickets at the raffle table, people could fill out the tickets and tear them off while they ate, and place them (along with payment for the tickets) into the baskets being carried around by staff members before dessert was served. Raffle sales increased that year by over 25%!

5 Ways to Supercharge Your Invitations

For most non-profits, the event invitation is the primary way they will be selling tickets to the event. Here are 5 ways to squeeze more revenue out of your event invitations:

1 – Make Them Simple

No one likes opening an invitation and then having to spend time figuring out the who, what, when, where and why of the event. There's a reason that most fundraising event invitations follow a similar format:

Please come to the twenty-third annual
Black and White Ball
Thursday, the twenty-fourth of October
7 o'clock in the evening
The Crystal Tea Room
at The Wannamaker Building
Philadelphia, PA

All proceeds will fund the
Adult Learning Center

Black and white attire
Cocktails 6:30 pm
Dinner 7:30 pm

Now obviously, they don't all follow that exact format, and yours doesn't have to either… but what *will* help you is keeping it simple. Tell people about the event, ask them to come, and give them the necessary details.

2 – Have a Compelling and Concrete Reply Card

The invitation itself isn't a "hard ask." Generally, there's no question posed on the invitation, just a soft sell like "Please come…" or "You are cordially invited…" The reply card, though, can be a stronger sell.

I advise non-profits to create compelling reply cards for their events that include a bit of your mission on them. I also suggest using a concrete statement or question that serves as a sort of "ask" for the event, right on the reply card. Some examples of this include:

____ Yes, I will help save our local wildlife by attending the 5th Annual Wildlife Affair

____ Yes, I will stand up for abused children by attending the Red Tie Gala

Will you attend the Scholarship Dinner and help educate those who can't afford a quality education? ____ Yes! ____ No.

The reply card is the only place on the invitation where you can really make an ask or "sell" your mission.

3 -- Include Contact Information

Always include contact information for your non-profit somewhere in your invitation package. This is normally done on the reply card, but can also be tastefully done on the invitation itself. Include a contact person's name, phone number and e-mail address. You can do it in a format like this:

If you have any questions about the event, please contact Julian Narita at (123) 456-7890 or drjulian@hopeforsws.org

This way, if people are getting the invitation and want to know more details, have questions about how to pay, want to purchase sponsorships or multiple tickets, or have any other questions, they can easily figure out who to call. If you don't include contact information, many of those who have questions will set the invitation aside, figuring that they will look up the contact information and call at another time... and will never get around to it.

4 – Sell the Theme, Entertainment and Hosts

If you have a unique theme, band, performer, or other compelling and fun reason to come to the event, be sure to mention it (sell it!) on the invitation. People like to come to fun events. For example, if you're having a Mardi Gras themed event, don't just "plop" it in, like this:

Please come to our annual dinner
Thursday, the twenty-fourth of October
7 o'clock in the evening
Wayne Manor
Gotham

Mardi Gras Theme
Dinner 7:30 pm

If you do that, you're telling people about the theme, but not really benefitting from it the way you could. Instead, try to build excitement for the event, like this:

Break Out Your Masks and Dancing Shoes for Our
33rd Annual Mardi Gras Masquerade Ball

Thursday, the twenty-fourth of October
7 o'clock in the evening
Wayne Manor
Gotham

Will YOU Be Named the King or Queen of
This Year's Mardi Gras Ball?

Black Tie Masquerade Attire
Dinner 7:30 pm

Similarly, if you have an impressive host committee or a committee comprised of members that people will know (or comprised of members from companies and businesses that people will know) then be sure to include a host committee list on your invitation or on a separate card inserted into your invitation. This will encourage people to attend.

5 – Clearly Show who Benefits

Finally, some organizations, when holding a named event (The 24th Annual Big Game Bash or The Yellow Tie Ball), will forget to put who benefits from the event on the invitation. This is a mistake. Putting a note on the front of the invitation reminding the recipient of which non-profit benefits from the event encourages people to have a heart for that mission to take an extra-long look at the invitation to decide whether or not to attend. Thus, in the examples above, I would add a line to each of the invitations that says something like:

Event benefits the Oakmark Hospital Foundation

5 Ways to Supercharge Your Event Web Presence

Over the past decade and a half, the internet has become a key resource to non-profits in selling tickets and sponsorships to fundraising events. Here are 5 ways to supercharge your event web presence to guarantee more revenue:

1 – Have a Dedicated Event Web Page

When setting up your events, create a dedicated web page on your site that talks exclusively about your event. Give the page a unique and easy to remember URL, something like newyorkshelter.org/gala or something similar. Then, include this URL on your event invitations, in your newsletters, and everywhere else you can think of.

Be sure that this page includes not only information about the event, but also a bright big button people can press to purchase tickets (or a form they can fill out, with credit card information, righty on the page).

2 – Sell!

In designing the event page on your website, you need to think like a marketer – your goal is to get people to buy... to click on that big BUY NOW button to purchase tickets for your event. So, on your event page, you have to sell!

Include some compelling and emotional information about your mission and vision on this page. Tell people how important this event is to your organization's overall success. And, most importantly, use a concrete ask (e.g. "Will you help us by purchasing a ticket today? Use the button below to get your tickets now").

3- Use a 1 or 2 Page Sales Process

Have you ever gone to a non-profit's website and clicked onto their event page, and decided to purchase tickets? Then when you clicked on Buy Now, you went to another page to fill in the number of tickets and the guest names, and then... you clicked on Continue, and came to another page that asked for your name, address, phone number and e-mail address, and then... you clicked on Continue, and came to another page to enter in your credit card information, and then... you clicked a Purchase Tickets Now button and then... you got a page with all of your details and the ticket details and had to click a button to Confirm... just to buy a couple of tickets to an event?

I have seen far too many non-profits with ticket purchase mechanisms like this. And it drives people away from your site. They abandon the process midway through because they get bored, or think twice about buying tickets, or just get frustrated.

Don't frustrate your donors! Use either a 1 or 2 page sales process on your event webpage. If you use a 1 page sales process, this means that you include information about the event at the top of the page, and then instead of people having to click on a button to buy tickets, you make your ask and they can simply fill out the form, including ALL of the information you need (even credit card information) right on that page and click Buy. Then they're done.

If you use a 2 page sales process, you have one event page that talks about the event and your mission and makes the ask, and people click on the Buy Tickets Now button and are taken to a page where they can fill out all of their information (including credit card information) right on that page and click Buy. Then they're done.

1 and 2 page sales processes work. Any more than 2 pages, and you're losing donors.

4 – Send Out E-Mail and Social Media Invitations

Once you have your event webpage set up, don't be shy about using your online resources to sell tickets and drive people to the page. Send out an e-mail invitation and regular e-mail blasts encouraging people to buy tickets and sponsorships. Use your social media networks to do the same. Keep your event (and the corresponding event page) front and center for your supporters and friends.

5 – Put Your Event on Your Homepage

If you have an event page set up for an upcoming event, showcase it on your organization's homepage. Don't hide your fundraising events under your "Events" tab on the navigation bar for your site. Put it front and center. Many people visiting your site through other pages (such as program pages) will click on your homepage just to see what you have to offer. Make sure they see information about your event and a link to your event page.

5 Ways to Supercharge Your Other Event Collateral Materials

As mentioned above, "other event collateral materials" include your event program, silent auction books, adbooks, and any other printed materials you hand out at the event. Remember, your two goals for these items are to educate attendees about your mission and to make your event easier to navigate. Here are 5 strategies for supercharging these materials:

1 – Be Mission-Centered

One of the main goals for event collateral materials is to make your case and educate about your mission. Thus, you need to keep your collateral materials mission-centered. Include as much information as you can about what your organization does, why people should care, why you need money, and why the need is urgent. Also include testimonials from clients or stories from people you have helped and, if appropriate, pictures of your work.

Even if you are putting together an adbook that is mostly marketing materials from sponsors, you should still strive to keep it mission-focused by interspersing information and pictures of your work throughout the book.

2 – Make Them Keepable / Shareable

Most non-profit event collateral materials are tossed in the trash before the guests even walk out the door... what a waste! If appropriate for your event, consider finding ways to make your event programs and other handouts valuable enough to keep around after the event, or even worthy of being shared with other people. This gives more people more time to read about your work and see the good that your organization is doing in the world.

For example, if you are holding a lower end event, what about including coupons or free passes to other events in your program book? For higher end events, maybe the auction program can be redeemed for a free meal at a local restaurant or free sports tickets from a team that supports your organization. Or what if your event program also had a portion of a novel in the back of it, courtesy of a local author? Or maybe a map showing the 25 best places to eat in town? Be creative!

3 – Cross-Sell

Use your event collateral materials to cross sell other fundraising events you will be holding or to push other fundraising opportunities for you non-profit. Holding an annual dinner? Push the upcoming golf tournament in your program book. Preparing for your walk-a-thon? Tell everyone that if they bring their number (running bib) to your fundraising bbq they will get 50% off admission.

4 – Recognize Sponsors and Hosts

Event collateral materials are the perfect place to recognize and thank your sponsors, host committee and event volunteers. Include a page or two to thank everyone who helped – by name. Do this even if your sponsors are getting ad space in the same book as part of their sponsorship. A personal thank you to the host committee or sponsors written from the Executive Director or Board Chair is a nice way to show your supporters that you value their help and support.

5 – Use Them to Follow Up

What to do with your event programs and auction books after the event is over? Here's an idea – use them to follow up with sponsors and donors! Why not send one of each of the collateral materials to each sponsor along with your thank you note, so that they can have them in their office to show off to colleagues?

You can also send the auction books and programs to businesses and supporters who donate silent auction items to the event to show them what a successful event they were involved with. For the most part, businesses that donate silent auction items to an event don't come to the affair. Sending them a copy of the auction book and program along with a thank you note is a great way to start building a deeper relationship with the these companies.

Adding Auctions, Raffles, and Other Revenue Streams to Your Events

In this section, we're going to add a final piece to your fundraising event pie: auctions, raffles, and other add-ons.

The Role of Revenue Add-Ons for Non-Profit Events

As you think about adding auctions and other add-ons for your fundraising event, it's important to remember that they are, well, *add-ons*. These additional revenue streams can add lots of fun and sometimes, lots of revenue to your events, but they should never be the prime fundraising method for your non-profit events.

Every non-profit fundraising event, even large silent auctions, should raise the majority of its money through sponsorships. Earlier in this book, we talked about sponsorships and how important they are for fundraising events. I can guarantee you that if you are raising most of the money at one of your events from a silent auction or raffle, you are leaving money on the table.

Likewise, for most fundraising events, ticket sales should raise more than add-ons. This is not universally true, but the events where raffles or auctions can and should raise more than ticket sales are the exception, not the rule.

For an example of an event where the raffle should raise more than ticket sales, think about the new car raffles that used to be popular at parish churches a decade or two ago. At these events, it may have cost $5 to come in the door to the big event, which included a live band, pay-as-you go food and drink, and games for the kids, but the majority of the money was raised from $25 or $50 per chance contests to win a lower-end new car. The goal for these events was to get a car dealer to donate the car, and then sell 500 $50 chances, while also making money at the door and on food sales, etc.

For most events, though, the primary revenue driver should be sponsorships, followed by ticket sales, and then add-ons.

This doesn't mean that add-ons aren't worth it, though. Live and silent auctions, raffles, and other event add-ons can provide a significant boost to the bottom line and also make an event more enjoyable for the guests, which in turn drives ticket sales. Let's take a look at the most popular types of add-ons to see what you can do to maximize your revenue from each.

But First... A Cautionary Word About Resources

As you plan your fundraising events, remember, that many event add-ons are *a lot* of work. They are time and manpower intensive. They can bring added stress and uncertainty to your events. So you'll want to do a cost / benefit analysis for each add-on you are thinking of launching for your event.

Think about it... if you decide to hold a silent auction, you're going to need to find great items to auction off. You're going to need to track the items that are donated, find extra volunteers to work the event, and collect payment for anywhere from 10-200 items that are auctioned off. In short, running a silent auction takes a real commitment from your organization.

Silent auctions are time and manpower intensive. Raffles are less so, but still require extra time and personnel. Be sure that your organization is ready to commit the time it takes to make your add-on a success. You can run your event with staff or volunteers, or a combination of the two, but either way, it's going to take a significant marshaling of resources from your school, church, or charity.

Silent Auctions for Fun and Fundraising

Without a doubt, silent auctions are the most popular fundraising event add-on for non-profit organizations. I have personally managed a number of silent auctions that raised five and six figures for their organizations, and can attest to the revenue and fun they bring to events. Here are some key concepts to keep in mind as you plan your silent auction event:

Organization = Success

Silent auctions (and live auctions, for that matter) can seem overwhelming. In addition to all of the hoopla that goes on with holding an event (invitations, catering, space planning, coat check, follow up calls), auctions add the additional tasks of finding, tracking, and accepting payment for dozens or hundreds of auction items.

If you're holding a silent auction, and you're not organized, you are sunk. Great silent auctions are based on great organization. As you will find out over the course of your event planning, auctions have lots of moving parts. The best auctions I have been a part of have had plans in place, before the first item was solicited, for how the items would be collected, categorized, and stored.

My suggestion is to create a master auction spreadsheet and have one (and only one) person responsible for entering all of the information on each item into the spreadsheet as the donated auction items come in. Stay organized, otherwise you'll end up with a room or rooms full of stacked auction items, and have no idea what they are, where they came from, who to thank, or how to sell them.

It's Fundraising, so You Have to ASK

Many silent auction event organizers forget one key fact about the events they are planning... these events are, by their very nature, *fundraising*. Fundraising requires making asks. This is true for any type of fundraising event, including silent auctions.

It's not enough to simply hire a caterer, rent out a hall, and announce that you are having a silent auction on such and such a date. In order to hold a successful event, your team is going to have to get on the phones, set up meetings, send out letters, and make actual fundraising asks to businesses, donors, and attendees.

First, you will need to *ask* businesses and friends to donate items for the auction. This will usually mean sending out letters, making follow up calls, and visiting stores and companies in person.

Then, you will need to *ask* people to attend the event. This will usually mean finding people to serve on a host committee and motivating them to invite their friends, as well as sending out invitations, making follow up calls, and sometimes asking in person.

Finally, at the event, you will need to *ask* people to bid on items, encourage them to bid higher, and create a sense of urgency in your audience.

As you can see, event logistics are only a small part of holding a successful event. Hitting your fundraising goal at an auction will require shoe leather and a willingness to make fundraising calls. You will need a significant portion of your team and volunteers to hit the streets and pick up the phones. This is where many organizations falter: they don't realize that making asks is the most important factor in whether or not your event succeeds.

Know Your Audience

As with any fundraising activity, it is important to know your audience for a silent auction event. What connections to do you have? Who is on your board? Who is on your host committee? What does the charity's donor list look like?

The answers to these questions will determine what types of auction items you will be able to get donated for the event, and also what type of attendees will be coming. Why do these answers matter? Simply because you will need to line up your event expectations with the reality of your audience situation.

Is your organization small, with a relatively modest donor base of lower paid professionals, middle class two family households, and young professionals? Then it is unlikely that you will be able to auction off very many high-end items at your event. Is your organization well matured, with a donor base and board composed of the leading businesspeople in your city? Then while you will probably be able to auction off high-end items, it is unlikely that gift baskets made up of dollar-store type items will sell well.

Similarly, your audience matters for soliciting auction items. Are you a well-known charity with a well-known event? Then you should be shooting for larger items, celebrity items, and "experiences" donated by sports teams and large companies. Are you a small charity known by your core group, but not enjoying widespread notoriety? Stick with local restaurants, friends of friends, and nice gift baskets. Then, as you grow, add larger items each year.

Remember, It's an Event

It's important to remember that your silent auction event is just that... an event. As you plan, think of it in those terms. What makes events appealing? What will make *this* event appealing to *my audience*?

Because your silent auction will be held as part of an event, it is important that you hold the auction in a location that lends itself to this type of event. There has to be ample parking available, <u>plenty of space for the auction items</u> and the food and drink, plus the registration area. You'll need to decorate the space to add an appropriate atmosphere.

Some organizations get so caught up in finding and tracking items and finding and tracking attendees that they forget to focus on basic event fundamentals. Ultimately, this is an event, and people will only want to come back next year if they have a great time. Most people you solicit next year won't remember most of the details of the auction itself, but will remember what a great time it was, which is directly influenced by food, drink, and décor.

Silent Auction Events Improve with Time

The first year you hold your event, you may be a little disappointed. You may not receive all of the auction items you had hoped would be donated, or only 100 people may show up when you were hoping for 200. Don't despair! A basic rule of thumb is that silent auction events improve with time.

Most major silent auction events started very small. I recently worked on a major silent auction that started ten years ago with forty people attending, bidding on five items. Now, the event has snowballed into a major event, raising well over six-figures every year. This silent auction, like countless others, has improved over time.

Why do silent auction events become better with age? Two reasons: first, retailers, restaurants, and other supporters who donate auction items this year are likely to do so again next year. Many of these donors will get into a rhythm of donating to your cause year after year. The first year, it may have taken an in-person visit to get that $100 gift certificate from a local steak restaurant. The next year, it may only take a call. The third year, you may only need to send a letter in order to get the donation. This means that you'll have plenty of extra time to solicit new donors. As your event ages, more and more donors will be giving, year after year, meaning more items for your auction and more revenue for your charity.

The second reason auctions become better with age is your donors / audience. As time goes on, more and more people will come to anticipate your silent auction event. If you hold an annual silent auction event around the same time each year, and the events turn out to be a great time, your donors and their friends will start marking the event on their calendars and will become regular attendees. This will allow you to focus on bringing in new donors and guests. Just as with silent auction items, your event attendance will snowball over time. An event that starts with ten items and fifty guests may well see twenty five items and eighty guests the next year, and three times that many in five years.

Holding a Live Auction

Live auctions can be a fun and profitable add-on for your fundraising events, either in conjunction with a silent auction or without a silent component.

Live auctions, as the name implies, are when a live auctioneer gets up and opens up public bidding on a handful of (normally high-end) items. In my experience, live auctions should only be used if the following conditions *all* exist:

<u>Your Event is at Least Three Years Old</u> – Fundraising events build up steam over time. The first three years will be spent getting the kinks out, building up a base of donors and attendees, and getting used to the process. Unless your event has been held successfully for at least three years, or you somehow know you will have a large and wealthy crowd in attendance, it may be too early to add a live auction component to your silent auction event.

<u>You Have the Right Attendees</u> – Live auctions take a certain type of attendee… people who have enough money to spend to purchase high end items, and aren't afraid that everyone knows that they are bidding. In fact, live auctions work best when your guests try to show each other up by outbidding other bidders. Don't add a live auction component unless your guests are wealthy enough to afford the items and don't mind showing off a little bit.

<u>You Have the Right Items</u> – Live auctions take time and attention away from other activities at your event. During the live auction, people will stop bidding on silent auction items so that they can keep an eye on the live auction spectacle. Make sure you have items that are high-end enough (expensive enough!) to justify taking this time away from silent bidding, raffles, and networking opportunities. Likewise, your live items need to be spectacular enough that they make people want to outbid each other.

<u>You Have the Right Emcee / Auctioneer</u> – There's an art behind getting the bidding going (and keeping it going) with a live auction. Make sure you have an emcee or auctioneer who can talk up the items and whip the crowd into a bidding frenzy. This may be a local celebrity or simply a gifted auctioneer.

Using a Raffle to Raise More at Your Event

A raffle can be a nice boost to the bottom line for your fundraising event. Raffles make particular sense at silent auctions because people come with money to spend, and often wait around until the raffle winner is announced, meaning they will have more time to view and bid on items. They can also be used at low and mid-level fundraising events and dinners, but normally are not appropriate for high-dollar balls and galas.

Before adding a raffle to your event, double check that raffles are legal for non-profits in your area. If they are, choose attractive items that get donated for the event to use in the raffle, or purchase them at a reasonable price. I have found it works best to have at least two raffle prizes (a grand prize and a first prize) or, better yet, three prizes (grand prize, first prize, second prize).

Try to find items for the raffle that are large enough that you can sell raffle tickets for at least $5 / ea. I like to be able to offer tickets for either $5 each / 3 for $12, or $10 each / 3 for $25. Some high-end raffles may feature tickets in the $25 - $100 range.

Here are four tips for increasing the revenue you bring in with your raffle add-on:

#1: Accept Cash, Checks and Credit Cards

I suggest that your non-profit be prepared to accept cash, checks and credit cards as payment for raffle tickets. In my personal experience, raffles that accept major credit cards sell 10-20% more raffle tickets as people who left their cash at home can easily take a chance on winning. Make sure to advertise the fact that you are accepting credit cards at the raffle table through signage and announcements from the podium.

#2: Display the Items, When Possible

Nothing gets people salivating over the possibility of winning an item more than being able to see the item right in front of them as they purchase chances. Whenever possible, create a nice display with the items that may be won so that event attendees can easily see them.

#3: Be Visible

I've seen far too many non-profits that hold fundraising events, add a raffle, tuck the raffle table out of the way in a corner of the event venue and then wonder why they didn't sell as many chances as they thought they would. Don't make this mistake. If you're going to be holding a raffle, you might as well try to sell as many tickets as possible. Place your raffle table front and center as people are coming in to the event hall. Have huge signs printed up touting the raffle and noting the prizes. Be sure people can find your raffle table easily.

#4: Sell!

This goes hand in hand with being visible. In order to raise as much as possible, train your staff and volunteers to really *sell* the tickets. This means encouraging guests who are only buying one ticket to buy two or three, sending staff members roving from table to table selling tickets, and ensuring that the emcee makes several announcements about the raffle from the podium. Don't be pushy, but do sell.

Other Revenue Streams for Your Fundraising Events

I have seen dozens of other revenue streams that non-profits have added to events over the years. While I can't include them all in this book, I did want to mention two of my favorite event add-ons, both of which I have successfully used over the years. Bear in mind that in order to be successful, these need to be used at the "right" event with the "right" organization.

Super Events

Super events are a fundraising tactic that some non-profits have started borrowing from political fundraisers. With these events, you recruit lots of event hosts to hold a small fundraising event on behalf of your charity on the same night, and all around the same theme. The events are often tied together by a conference call with the non-profit's key supporters, board chair, or executive director, or by a live Internet event or video call to the "main event" hosted by the board of directors.

Super events work because they leverage your efforts... in many cases, the amount of time you would spend on supporting hosts who want to hold small ($500-$5,000 net) fundraising events may not be worth the return. However, using super events, you can support a network of hosts who are each raising money for your group, with much higher returns.

For example, you may hold a super event to launch your new fundraising campaign where 10 event hosts each hold an event and raise an average of $2,000 for your organization. If each host held a separate event scattered throughout the year, your staff may spend a total of 30 hours supporting these events (3 hours spent X 10 events). With a super event, your staff may only spend 10 hours supporting the whole effort, and raise the same amount. In fact, super events normally raise more money than individual events, because of the increased buzz around the effort.

Buy-a-Service Tables

I like to set up a "Buy a Service" tables right by the exit doors of silent auction and mid-level fundraising events. As people leave, ask them to buy a service for one of your clients... Offer numerous levels of services that the donor can "purchase" on a client's behalf. This isn't done in an auction setting, but is designed to allow people who have money to spend to donate the money to your non-profit in a creative way.

For example, if you are running a sports program for underprivileged youth, you could offer donors the chance to "buy" a set of baseballs for you for $10, a uniform for a child for $20, or cover the fees you have to pay to use the field for one day for $50.

To pull this off, first, figure out what services your organization provides. Try to figure out at least three distinct services, and no more than five. Be sure that the services you select include both smaller and larger items, in terms of cost.

For example, a homeless shelter may come up with "providing meals, providing a place to sleep, and providing pro-bono medical care." A church may come up with "offering adult education classes, providing child care during services, and sponsoring mission trips."

Then, come up with a ballpark amount for how much it costs you to provide that service to one person (round the number off for simplicity). For the homeless shelter example, this may look like: feeding one person for one day, $10; proving a place to sleep for one person for one night, $25; providing basic medical care for one homeless client, $100.

Set up a table with signage announcing the services that your guests can purchase / sponsor, and come up with a nice handout to give each person who donates in this way. Be sure to promote this opportunity from the podium as well as by having staff members roving from table to table explaining the process.

Chapter 10:
Supercharging Your
Direct Mail Fundraising

Fundraising through the mail is a mainstay of non-profit development. In this section, we are going to discuss everything you need to really supercharge your organization's direct mail fundraising efforts, including building your list, writing great letters, designing mail packages, and more.

What is "Direct Mail?"

Let's start at the beginning. What exactly do we mean when we say, "direct mail?"

As you can see from the phrase itself, direct mail is two things: first, it is mail, in that it is sent through the postal system to someone's home or office. Second, it is direct, in that it is sent to a specific person or group of people, as opposed to simply being something like a circular from the supermarket that is delivered to every door in the neighborhood. When we use the term "direct mail," we are also usually referring only to commercial or non-profit mail, and not to personal letters sent between family or friends (yes, some people still send personal letters!)

So, at its simplest, "direct mail" is a business or non-profit communication sent though the "snail mail" postal system to a designated recipient.

Of course, that's the clinical definition of direct mail. The more cynical among you may think of direct mail as "junk mail," but one of the many goals of this chapter is to show you how to make sure your donors and prospects don't see your direct mail as anything less than a valued communication from an organization they support, or are inclined to start supporting.

The Direct Mail Debate: Does it Still Work?

One of the biggest current debates among businesses and non-profits regarding marketing and fundraising is whether or not direct mail still works. We'll get to the statistics in a minute, but first, let's look at the pros and cons of using direct mail as a means of fundraising:

Pros of Direct Mail

One of the biggest reasons to use direct mail is because it allows you to directly target those you want to target, without wasting money communicating with those who aren't likely to contribute to your organization. This isn't true of TV, radio, magazine, newspaper, or almost any other type of mass communication. Direct mail is highly targetable.

Another reason to use direct mail is that it is relatively cheap. You can launch a direct mail campaign for just a few thousand dollars, which is an exponentially lower cost than any other type of mass media.

Finally, direct mail is completely track-able. We'll talk more about metrics in a little bit, but know that you can easily track your returns from direct mail to see which pieces are working, and which aren't... and, you can make changes quickly and cheaply. This is less true in mediums like TV or even online communications.

Cons of Direct Mail

Of course, there are lots of problems and concerns that organizations have with using direct mail. First and foremost among them is the fact that people just don't use the mail like they used to. Now, people do most of their personal communications online, over the phone, through text-messages, etc. Thus, it is easier for people to say things like, "all I get are bills and junk mail," and treat your direct mail letter accordingly.

Second, while direct mail is cheap compared to TV and radio appeals, it is much more expensive than using things like e-mail appeals and website fundraising.

Finally, direct mail takes time – you have to write the letters, hone the list, track responses, remove people from your list, change addresses, etc. This requires staff or volunteer time which could be used on other projects within your organization.

The Verdict on Direct Mail

The final verdict on direct mail, of course, is that it *does* still work. Otherwise, this would be a very short course, wouldn't it?

Direct mail fundraising is still a very effective way to raise money for non-profit organizations for all of the "pro" reasons above. Even more importantly, statistics show that it still works:

- In a 2010 non-profit fundraising study called *Heart of the Donor*, 61% of all people who said they donated to charity in the past year reported making at least one of those gifts through direct mail.

- *Deliver*, a United States Postal Service industry trade magazine, recently cited a study they did that showed that consumer purchasing in response to direct mailings was actually trending slightly up, in terms of the number of consumers who purchase things through direct mailings.

- The 2010 *Campbell Rinker Donor Confidence Survey* showed that 37% of people who gave to charities online did so because they received a direct mail letter from the charity, looked them up online, and made a donation on the non-profit's website.

In short – direct mail still works, both for businesses and non-profits. The only question is, how can you make it work in a time- and cost-effective manner for your non-profit organization?

Understanding Your Audience

One of the most fundamental aspects to successful direct mail fundraising is to understand your audience. You need to step into the shoes of your intended mail recipients and look at it from their perspective – how do they feel about mail they are receiving?

Most people are busy. They work, they raise a family, they have community obligations, bills to pay, things to do. They don't have a ton of time to read your letter. In fact, most people *are* constantly on the lookout for junk mail... meaning that when they pick up their mail, most people sort through it quickly to see what is important and what isn't, often on their way to the trash can to throw out or recycle those items that they don't intend to read. Sadly, most people go through their mail assuming that the vast majority of it will be junk.

What does this mean for your non-profit? It means that you need to design your mail with this fact in mind. We'll talk about this in far more depth later in this book, but for now, just remember that when it comes to your direct mail, you are basically designing for three distinct audiences:

- The 10 Second Club – The vast majority of readers fall into this category. These are the folks that look at your piece and walk it to the trash can – they have your piece in their hands for approximately 10 seconds.

- The Skimmers – A far smaller number of readers are skimmers – people who look through your mail piece on the way to trash can, reading headlines and looking at pictures. They will generally have your piece in their hands for 20-30 seconds, maybe more if something catches their eye (hint!) These people are usually somewhat interested in your mission, and thus more likely to donate, or are just people who like to skim everything before they throw it out so as to not miss anything.

- The Readers – Few and far between, these people actually take the time to read your mail piece. They generally will look through your piece for 1-2 minutes, reading the headlines and drilling down into the text. These people are either very interested in your particular issue or non-profit, or tend to be older, retired folks who enjoy receiving and reading direct mail.

The key is to design your direct mail with the knowledge that most people will hold it in their hands for 30 seconds or less... the key is to use tried and true methods to make your mail more successful and memorable – to design fundraising direct mail *that works*. More on that later in the book.

Housefile & Prospecting Mail: What's the Difference?

The second fundamental thing to understand as we jump into the direct mail waters is the difference between housefile and prospecting mail:

Housefile Mailings

Letters sent to your current list of donors (or recent donors) are called housefile mailings. These letters are mailed to your "housefile" (or a segment thereof) which is composed of people who have already contributed money to your non-profit. With a well-designed letter, these mailings are always profitable, because people who give you money once are likely to do so again. You know they support you, and have the capacity to give, because they have done so already.

Prospecting Mailings

Letters that are mailed to borrowed, created, or purchased lists of people who have never given to your organization before are called prospecting mailings. These letters are sent to a list of prospects in the hope that some portion (anywhere from .25-3%) of the recipients will give, and then those people who do will be moved into the housefile list for future mailings.

Prospecting is both an art and a science, and even the best direct mail fundraisers in the business are shooting for mailings that break-even, or slightly better. Because you are mailing to a brand new list, your goal for these mailings is to simply make your money back – but in addition to making your money back, you get something very, very valuable: a group of people who support your mission and are willing to contribute to your non-profit, and who you can re-solicit over and over again.

As you can see, the real money with prospecting mailings are in the follow-up. You (hopefully) break-even on the first mailing, but then re-mail those who do give over and over again as part of follow-up or housefile mailings.

A strong direct mail fundraising operation will use a mix of housefile and prospecting mailings to raise money while constantly growing the housefile list, which will in turn allow you to raise more money with each mailing. It's a wonderful cycle when done right.

The Importance of Testing & Metrics

One of the beautiful things about direct mail fundraising is that, for the most part, it is completely track-able and knowable. You can see what is working for your organization and what isn't, make changes, and test, test, test till you get the results you are looking for. Of course, none of this will happen if you are not actually measuring your response rates and testing new letters and lists.

It's important to track your housefile mailings, but even more important to test and track your prospecting mailings. In fact, as you'll see later on in our prospecting section, most of the time you will want to send out a test mailing to a portion of a list before you mail the entire list. This way, you'll know what your response rates and average gifts are, and will know whether a mailing to the entire list is going to be profitable.

Testing and measuring results need not be overly burdensome, even for the smallest of non-profits. Any non-profit, even a one-person shop, can keep records on response rate and average gift for mailings with relative ease by using a spreadsheet. The important thing is to remember that if something doesn't work *this time* (whether it is a letter or a list), it is unlikely to work in the future, and vice versa. Do what works, drop the rest.

Understanding List Segmentation

One other important concept in direct mail success is the concept of "list segmentation." As your direct mail housefile grows, you'll want to start segmenting your list into different categories so that you can send them category-appropriate mail when the time is right. The simplest segments are based on giving capacity. You may have small, medium and large donors, or you may have even more giving levels listed. Other possible segments are based on geography, affinity groups (young professionals, retirees, lawyers, etc.) or responses on a donor survey.

Of course, if you're just launching a direct mail program for the first time and your donor file is very small, you'll likely be sending out the same letter to every donor, but as you grow, keep in mind that segmentation will allow you to more closely tailor your letters and asks to the donors that are receiving them.

Where Does Direct Mail Fit In?

Before wrapping up this section, I want to spend a minute talking a little about where direct mail fundraising fits in to your overall development strategy.

Remember, direct mail fundraising is just one arrow in your development quiver. No matter how successful you are with direct mail, you still need to develop other fundraising tactics, be they major giving, planned giving, events, online fundraising, etc. Similarly, if you've had some failures with direct mail fundraising in the past, that's ok – remember, direct mail works, and there's a good chance that it could work for you as one of your many fundraising tactics, if you do it the right way.

Here are some other thoughts on how direct mail fits in to your overall development strategy:

You Need a Long-Term Strategy

Direct mail success requires a long-term strategy. Let's break that phrase apart and look at both components.

First, *direct mail success requires a strategy*. Far too many non-profits go into direct mail with the idea that they'll just throw some letters out there to see what sticks. These organizations don't have a plan for their housefile and prospecting letters, don't keep great databases, don't think about testing and tracking their response rates. This is a huge mistake. By the time you are done this course, you will have all of the information you need to sit down with your team (or yourself, if you're a team of one) and develop a direct mail fundraisings strategy for the next 12 months.

Second, *direct mail success requires a commitment to the long-term*. Just as gala fundraising events usually grow and get better over time, as the even becomes a staple in the local social calendar, so too does direct mail fundraising get better over time.

With your housefile, you will raise more and more money as your donors get used to getting mail communications from you, hearing updates via direct mail, and making donations through the post office.

With your prospecting mail, you will get better over time – you will learn what works for your organization and what doesn't, understand what types of lists work, and have a stable of reliable direct mail letters you can use to fundraise year in, year out to different lists.

Plus – as you engage in prospecting mail, your housefile will grow, as you add new donors to the list, and you will raise money from these donors year in, year out.

Thus, when you jump into direct mail fundraising, expect to see it through the long-term. That's where the money is – in the follow-up, in the housefile, in the repeated mailings, in the ever-growing list.

Your Donor Communications Calendar

Every organization needs a donor communications calendar. Yours is no different. You need a calendar that lays out all of the communications you are going to send out over the course of the year to your donors, including direct mail, e-mail, newsletters, updates, invitations, annual reports, phone campaigns, the works.

Why is a donor communications calendar important for direct mail fundraising? Because direct mail fundraising letters are just one of many donor communications you will be doing over the course of the year. It is important that your communications calendar lays out where the fundraising letters fit into the overall picture. It will allow you to ask questions like, "How often should we send out non-fundraising mail as opposed to fundraising mail?" and "If we send out an e-newsletter on June 3rd, does it help or hurt our ability to drop a housefile mailing on June 5th?"

Your Development Budget

Finally, as with all things in fundraising, your direct mail program is going to be impacted by your development budget.

If you've read any of my other books or my website, you may have heard me rant about the fact that non-profits, as a rule, don't invest enough money into their development programs. I won't rehash that argument here.

What I will say is that direct mail programs take money – it takes money to write the letters (either in staff time or payments to a consultant), print them, mail them, and track the returns. Set aside the money in your development budget to give your direct mail program a real shot to succeed. Don't drop one mailing and then declare, "It doesn't work!" Put the money aside to see it through.

Remember – if you're doing housefile mailings to your own donor list, and that donor list is accurate, up-to-date, and not full of lapsed donors, it is highly, highly likely that your mailing will be profitable. If you're doing prospecting mailing, you'll be shooting to break even, though either making or losing some money is certainly possible. But... you'll gain new donors and make money in the follow-ups as your housefile grows.

Set aside the money you need to really "do" direct mail fundraising.

How to Write Effective Direct Mail Fundraising Letters

There are three main elements to direct mail that determine how effective it will be for fundraising: writing, design, and the list. In this section, we're going to talk about direct mail copywriting – how to write direct mail that works. In the next two sessions, we'll talk about how to design great mail packages and how to build your list.

Why Your Copy Matters

Some people think they have such a great list that they can slap any old drivel down on a page, mail it out, and they'll get a great response. I've never seen prove true. Sure, some organizations have such loyal supporters that they will turn a profit sending out a letter to their housefile, regardless of the strength of their writing, but I can guarantee you that a well-written letter would have pulled in more money for the organization.

Other organizations think that if they spend a great deal of time and money on the design of the letter / package, including full-color printing, expensive paper stock, attractive envelopes, etc., then people will be so blown away, they will give money even though the letter's writing (or "copy," as we call it in the direct marketing trade) is poorly crafted, so long as it doesn't have any typos. Again, you may reap a profit on a poorly-written but well-designed letter, but not nearly what you could have raised with a letter that was well-designed *and* well-written.

This is doubly true for prospecting letters, where the audience doesn't know your organization or hasn't yet given to your non-profit. In this case, a poorly-written fundraising letter will likely lead to losing a significant amount of money on the mailing.

Oddly enough, however, I have often seen the *opposite* happen for non-profits: they send out an amazingly well-written letter, with some basic design work (like using headlines and short paragraphs), but they send out the letter on cheap black-and-white copied letterhead, using cheap paper, cheap envelopes and no advanced packaging or inserts, and the letter pulls amazingly well. Such is the power of great direct mail copy.

Successful direct mail copywriters are often paid thousands of dollars per letter for a reason – because direct mail copy matters – it matters as much as the list and more than the design. Learn to write great direct mail letters, and your organization will enjoy the benefits for years (or decades) to come.

Remembering Your Audience

As you sit down to write your letter, it is important to remember your audience... remember what we said in earlier in the book: most people won't read through the entire letter. Most people will skim the letter on the way to the trash can. This means that your copy will need to be strong enough that in that short 10-second window, you draw enough people in to read the letter that the letter becomes profitable for your organization.

We'll talk much more about how to do that in the next section of this book, but remember: you've got a short amount of time to get people to read your letter. The only way to do that is through amazing copy.

There's a maxim in direct mail writing that goes something like this:

The headlines you use are an advertisement for people to read the first sentence of your letter. Write great headlines and you "sell" people on reading that first sentence...

Your <u>first sentence</u> is an advertisement for people to read the entire first paragraph of your letter. Write a great first sentence and you "sell" people on reading the whole first paragraph of your letter.

The <u>first paragraph</u> of your letter is an advertisement for people to read the second paragraph of your letter. Write a great first paragraph and people will read the second paragraph of your letter.

And so on...

Does this mean you should only focus on writing strong headlines and a strong first and second paragraph, but not worry about the nitty-gritty writing on page 4? Not at all! Remember... your most committed supporters and those most interested in the mission of your organization will be the ones who read all the way through. They will be interested in your headlines, interested in your first paragraph and interested in reading all the way to the end. Then, they will likely give to your organization – do you want them to lose interest 2/3 of the way through your letter? No way! Write a strong letter from beginning to end.

What People Read First & What it Means for Your Letter

Studies have shown that when scanning your letter, people will read certain key items first, and use those items as an indicator as to whether or not they should read the rest of the letter. Those items are:

- The main headline of your letter
- The sub-headlines of your letter
- The pictures / picture captions
- Pull-quotes in the letter
- The P.S. (and P.S.S., etc.) at the bottom of your letter
- Bolded, underlined and italicized words
- The first paragraph of your letter

What does this mean for you, as you write the letter? It means that, first and foremost, you need to include these items in your letter – you may not normally write P.S.'s in your personal letters, but when you are writing a fundraising letter, you absolutely have to have one. The same goes for using bolded words, headlines, etc.

Second, it means that these items – the ones people read first – need to be exceptionally strong. Remember – people are reading the headlines, the P.S., the captions, etc. to see if they want to read the rest of your letter. These items are, in a sense, "ads" for the rest of your letter. If you succeed in getting people interested they will read through more of the letter. If not, they will continue on with their day and your letter will end up in the trash can. This means that you should spend extra time to make sure that these items are exceptionally strong and well-written.

What Do We Mean by "Well-Written?"

It might make sense to pause here for a second to discuss what I mean when I say that a letter, or a section of a letter, is "well-written." Do I mean that the section is grammatically correct? That everything is spelled correctly? That your sentence doesn't start with a preposition? No!

For our purposes, when something is well-written it means that it does its job: it holds your interest and makes it more likely that you will make a donation to the organization that sent the letter. That's it – when a direct mail letter generates lots of revenue for your organization, I call it "well-written," even if it doesn't follow all of the laws of proper English (or whichever language the letter was written in).

The 7 Principles of Writing Effective Direct Mail

Let's a take a look at the seven most important principles of writing effective direct mail:

#1 – Write for Your Readers, not Your High School English Teacher

We touched on this a little above, but it bears repeating: great direct mail fundraising letters needn't be perfect, they just need to "work." And fundraising letters that work are written in a conversational tone that is easily understood by the vast majority of people who are reading them.

This means no high-brow language! No acronyms that people don't understand. No sentences that start, "Our multi-disciplinary team-based approach to forensic interviewing…" (I'm looking at you, Children's Advocacy Centers!)

Direct mail studies have shown that the best letters are written on about a sixth-grade level. Great letters feel conversational… they sound like someone is talking to you. Letters like this are easier to read. If people feel like your letter is difficult to read or understand, guess what? They'll stop reading it! It's ok to use sentence fragments or extra punctuation, and to start sentences with prepositions if doing these things makes your letter easier to read.

Of course, your letter still needs to look like it was written by a professional, so typos are out, as is sloppy writing. You want your letter to be conversational, but not sloppy.

#2 – Let Your Letter be as Long as it Needs to Be

Don't set artificial rules about how long your letters can be. Don't decide that letters from your organization can only be 2 pages (or… gasp! 1 page) long. Take the time to state your case. Take the space you need to write a great letter and make a great ask.

Most non-profit fundraising letters are at least 3 pages long. Many are longer. I've seen organizations successfully use 7 and even 10 page letters in the past. Whatever the length of your letter, just make sure you follow the design rules we will discuss later in this book… including headlines, bolded phrases, etc.

Of course, you don't want to make your letters longer than they need to be. If it really takes you 8 pages to state your case well, do it. But it you could tighten it up to just 4 or 5 pages, do that instead. Readers can and will get mad and stop reading if you try to get them to read 8 pages but repeat yourself and use circuitous language along the way.

One other consideration is postage: use your postage meter (or one at the local post office) to see how many pages you can include in a letter (using the envelopes and paper you are planning to use) for the price of one stamp (or one postal unit). Be extra careful about adding a piece of paper beyond that limit.

For example, if you can send 3 pages in an envelope with a reply envelope for $.45, and your letter is 3 ½ pages long, ask yourself if you can trim off that extra ½ page of copy to save the extra postage charges. Of course, if your letter is 6 pages long, that's a different story, and you're likely going to need to pay the extra postage no matter how much editing you do, assuming your letter was fairly well-written to begin with.

#3 – Appeal to Your Reader's Emotions

Direct mail fundraising letters should be emotional. The best of them appeal to readers' deepest feelings and desires, things like their faith, their worldview and beliefs about humanity, their hope for a better world for their children, their sense of justice and fairness, etc. People give when you touch their soul. Sound over the top? It's not… it's what works. The best letters appeal to emotion without feeling sappy or contrived. Use stories. Use pictures, if appropriate. Show the concrete difference your organization is making in the world. Connect people with your mission and your results. Make them *feel* what you are saying, instead of just reading what you are saying.

Does this mean you shouldn't clearly explain the need or use facts, figures and statistics? No, not at all – use them to make your case. What it does mean, though, is that your letter should lean more towards the emotional side and less towards the clinical side.

#4 – Build to a Crescendo

Great direct mail fundraising letters are like great movies – they have a strong story arc that draws the reader deeper and deeper into the letter. They have a crescendo or climax, a point where the emotion and sense of purpose of the letter come together... then they have the ask, which immediately follows the crescendo.

For example, let's say you are writing a fundraising letter for an abused woman's shelter. You start the letter with a mention of a particular client named Maria (name changed, obviously) who came to the shelter after being abused by her husband. That story is compelling, and initially draws people into the letter.

Then, you talk about what a problem spousal abuse is in your area... readers see a bigger picture, and they get concerned.

After that, your letter talks about the shortage of shelters for abused women in your area, which triggers alarm in your readers. You then talk about the danger for women who are abused and then have to return to their homes because of a lack of shelter beds... this raises further alarm and compassion in your readers.

Then you tie the problem back into Maria, the story you led with... you talk about the problems she would face if she were forced to leave your shelter, and how you can only guarantee a space for each client for 3 nights, because of a lack of space. Readers are hooked, and wondering how they can help you change this by providing more beds / rooms.

You briefly present your plan to open a new wing and talk about how that wing will help save dozens of women like Maria...

Then, you make your ask....

#5 – Make a Concrete Ask

Direct mail letters need concrete asks. Wishy-washy asks just don't work. Whenever a non-profit shows me a letter that they want to send out and it says something like, "Please make a donation today!" or "Please give whatever you can to help us make this dream a reality!" I know the letter is destined to fail. People don't give to generic, wishy-washy asks and when they do, they don't give much.

Instead, ask for "$50, $100, or whatever you can afford," or "your most generous donation of $100, $500, or $1,000 today!" Ask for a concrete number and people will give... and they will give more than if you ask for a generic donation.

Wait! You're probably thinking... how much should I ask for? Well, that depends on two factors:

Capacity: what is the capacity of this donor? How much could they afford to give and/or be willing to give through the mail? If you are tracking your donors well and have a good direct mail system, you can set it up so that the ask amounts are different for each donor and are based on the information you have stored about that donor in your donor database. Otherwise, you can generalize based on the average giving capacity of your entire list, or the entire prospect list you are using.

The Letter – You should also tie the ask in to your letter. If your letter talks about how it costs you $50 to feed one family for one week, then an ask for "$20, $40, or whatever you can afford," doesn't make much sense. But, an ask for your reader to feed 1, 5, or 10 families by giving "$50, $250, $500, or your most generous donation today..." makes a whole lot of sense. People are more likely to give when you tie your ask back into the concrete mission and projects you discussed in your letter.

#6 – Edit Your Letters at Least Twice

The first draft of your fundraising letter is likely to be bloated... that is, it is likely to use too many words to convey each point, it may go over the same thing two or more times, and it will probably not explain everything or tell every story as succinctly as possible. People are busy, and don't want to read fluff.

Thus, every letter you send out should be edited at least twice after the initial draft. Look for typos as well as phrases and sentences that don't make sense; cut the fluff; tighten up your prose; check the overall story arc to make sure it all ties together and reaches the necessary crescendo.

#7 – Use "You" A Lot

Your letters should be written from a first person perspective, meaning you talk about "I" and "we" instead of "the organization," or "the charity." But – and this is super important for writing successful letters – mostly what you should be saying is "you," meaning "you, the donor." Your letters should focus on your work, yes, but really should focus on the donor you are writing to.
This means talking about "your past support," "your concern for the poor," "your assistance with this project," "the difference *you* can make."

"You" is one of the most important words in a direct mail fundraiser's lexicon.

Sample Successful Direct Mail Fundraising Letter

Before we move on, I want to give you the example of an extremely successful direct mail letter to see how another organization put these concepts into practice. Below, I'm presenting a letter I wrote for a fairly small organization that became their most successful direct mail appeal of all time. Here's the story of that letter:

Several years ago, while working for a mid-sized non-profit in a consulting capacity, the organization received a significant piece of good news concerning approval of a new program the charity wanted to launch in conjunction with a local college, but which needed approval from the city government, a process which normally took months, if not years. The non-profit was shocked when, after just three weeks, the approvals came in.

Everything was in place, except the final piece of funding needed to launch the effort... the college wanted to launch the effort ASAP, because of the school's academic calendar. If we could not launch the initiative in the next six weeks, we would have to wait for another year, something the non-profit definitely didn't want to do. We needed to raise an additional $250,000 in order to launch the effort, but weren't sure where the money would come from.

Then, just as we were debating our options, our largest individual donor came to us with an amazing offer: he and his wife would donate $125,000 to the effort *if we could raise the other $125,000 within that six week time frame.* They didn't want us to have to wait another year, and were putting their money up to make sure we wouldn't have to.

We had to raise $125,000 within the next six weeks... at an organization with lots of mid-level donors, but not many high-level donors, and no full-time development staff member. We decided that it was time to send out a major-donor fundraising letter to our mid- and high-level donors
.

We crafted a letter that talked about the program we wanted to launch, gave an overview of the time crunch we faced, and presented the amazing matching gift challenge that was in play. We were frank with our donors: we need to raise $125,000, now... if not, we may never have the opportunity for a matching gift like this again.

We wanted to make sure donors knew this was a special mailing that was going just to our best donors, and which was extremely important and time sensitive. We decided that the best way to do that was to spend the extra dollar and change per letter to send the mailing out by USPS Certified Mail. This was slightly risky, because of the increased costs, but would insure that the letters were opened and would highlight the very real importance of the solicitation.

To our delight, the letter worked. Over the course of the next three weeks, well over $125,000 came in through the mailing, with several donors actually dropping their $1,000 and $2,000 checks off to us to make sure they beat the deadline for the matching grant. The outpouring of support was amazing, and allowed us to launch the new project without delay.

On the following pages, you can see the actual fundraising letter we used to raise six figures in the above scenario. The name and identifying characteristics of the organization have been changed to protect confidentiality.

Rockland Performing Arts Center
P.O. Box 8927 - Rockland, HI

Mr. John Sample
123 Sample Street
Sampletown, HI 12345

Dear Mr. Sample:

I have some amazing news.

For the past two years, RPAC has been working with Rockland University on *The Access to The Arts Initiative*, a project which would send professors and students from the University into our city's public schools to teach art, music and dance, at no cost to the schools or the students.

As you know, this Initiative is so important because of the successive cuts to the arts programs in our city's schools that have left over half of our children without any arts enrichment classes at all! The Access to The Arts Initiative will insure that *every child in our public schools has at least one arts class each week.*

I am happy to report that the City of Rockland has approved our program, and we can begin in September!

This is amazing news, and shows the confidence the city has in our programs. But… in order to launch this coming school year, we need your help!

The Access to The Arts Initiative is a massive undertaking. This coming year, we will be:

- Offering 45 different arts courses across 12 different public elementary schools
- Launching 8 arts courses at Rockland High School
- Fostering a love and appreciation for art, music, and dance in over 10,000 students

After completing our budget, we realized that we still needed to raise an additional $250,000 in order to launch this program *this year.* We were worried that we wouldn't be able to raise that much, which would mean not launching this year…

…but **how could we not launch this year**, and leave so many children without arts education for another school year?

(con't…)

Then, an amazing anonymous donor stepped forward to announce that if we are able to raise $125,000 by June 1st, **he will match it with a $125,000 donation** to the program.

That's why I am writing to you today, and why we need your help. We may never have the opportunity for a matching gift like this again. <u>If we don't hit our goal, we will not be able to launch The Access to The Arts Initiative this year.</u>

John, you have been an amazing supporter of the Rockland Performing Arts Center over the years. You know the value of art, music and dance in our lives, and particularly in the lives of young people.

<u>Will you join us in this effort by making a generous donation of $250, $500, $1000 or whatever you can afford today?</u>

Every dollar you donate will help us reach our goal, and **insure that we are able to receive the full $125,000 matching grant.** You can use the enclosed envelope to send back your check or credit card information, but please do so as soon as possible. Remember, only donations received prior to June 1st will qualify for the matching gift challenge.

Please, help us launch this important initiative and change the lives of thousands of children in our city *this year*!

With gratitude,

Jean Heatherington
Executive Director

P.S. **We have received an amazing $125,000 matching gift challenge**, and need your help to reach our goal. Your gift of $250, $500, $1000 or whatever you can afford will help us reach this goal and make sure that we can launch *The Access to The Arts Initiative* this year! <u>Please make your most generous contribution today!</u>

If you'd like to take a look at a "hall of fame" of sorts highlighting unique and successful direct mail fundraising letters throughout history, then be sure to check out the Showcase of Fundraising Innovation and Inspiration's (SOFII) Direct Mail Showcase at www.SOFII.org - They've got lots of great stuff that's sure to give you a ton of ideas.

Designing Successful Direct Mail Fundraising Packages

In the previous section, we talked at length about the *content* of your direct mail fundraising letters... the words you should use and the stories you should tell. In this section, we're going to be turning our attention to the *design* of your direct mail.

Two Types of Direct Mail Design

When we talk about "direct mail design," we're really talking about two different concepts, both of which will be covered in this direct mail chapter.

First, we're talking about the design of your actual letter – designing a letter layout that will result in maximum revenue for your non-profit.

Second, we're also talking about the design of your entire direct mail "package," meaning everything that gets put in the mail as part of your letter, ranging from the envelopes right down to the stamp.

Let's get started:

Fundamental Concepts for Designing Direct Mail Letters that Work

First, let's turn our attention to the actual letter itself. Again, we're not talking right now about the text content of the letter... instead, we're talking about the *design* of the letter.

What are the goals of direct mail letter design? Are they to make your letter as outlandish and crazy as possible? Or perhaps to show-off your organization's design skills or fancy new color printer? Certainly not! In reality, you only have two main goals for the design of your direct mail letter:

Main Goal #1: To Make Your Letter Look as Interesting and Readable as Possible

Your first goal is to make your letter appealing to the recipient. So appealing, in fact, that they can't help but skim it, or even read the whole thing through. How do you make your letter look appealing? In order to make your letter appealing, it has to look interesting... it has to catch the recipient's attention and make them either wonder what the rest of the letter says, or make them feel intrigued by the stories or projects you are talking about.

Your letter also has to look readable... it has to make the recipient feel like it is going to be an easy read, not something they are going to have to slog through or spend too much time thinking about. Interesting and readable – these are the two design ingredients that convince people to actually read your fundraising letter.

5 Ways to Make Your Letters Look Interesting to Recipients

Use a Headline – Using a compelling headline on your letter can grab people's attention and get them to continue reading the rest of the text. As we mentioned above, a headline is like an "advertisement" for the rest of your letter. If it is interesting enough, people will "buy" and read the next paragraph. Of course, if your headline isn't interesting or compelling, it will actually dissuade people from reading, so make it good!

<u>Use a Compelling, Bolded First Line</u> – Headlines aren't right for all letters. If you're writing a letter and want it to feel more personal, you probably won't use a headline. Instead, write an extremely compelling first line, bold it, and make it a one sentence paragraph. This will encourage people to read that first line, because it will really stand out. Imagine you get a letter from an organization you support and the first line simply says, "**I need your help.**" Or "**Brenda Johnson is dying. Her kids need your help, and so do I.**"

<u>Use a Graphic</u> – Using a picture or graph in your letter makes it look interesting, if that picture or graph is compelling. As they skim, people will look at your graphics… make sure they are so interesting that people will want to read the text around them to find out more information about the story the graphic is telling.

<u>Tell a Story With Your Headlines and P.S.</u> – Earlier in this chapter, you learned that as people skim your letter to decide whether to read it, some of the things they usually look at are the headlines / section headings and the P.S. One of the best ways to make your letter look interesting is to use those headlines and P.S. to tell a consistent story. For example, the five headlines throughout your letter could read something like:

Jimmy's Mom Died When He was 5, and Now His Dad is Out of Work

Thousands of Single Parents in Our City are Struggling to Make Ends Meet

Your Generosity Saved Jimmy and His Family Last Year

This Year, We've Had to Turn Away Over 250 Families Who Need Our Help

Help Us Never to Have to Say "No" Again

These headlines tell a story so that if someone is only skimming through the headlines, they will still understand the gist of your letter, and perhaps be interested enough to read more… Then your P.S. can summarize the story and also contain a summary of the ask, so that if people only read the headlines and P.S. they still get "the ask."

Use Color – Depending on the size and financial resources of your organization, you may or may not be able to afford to use color in your letters, but if you can afford it, using color generally makes a letter seem more interesting and appealing to your readers. You can use color in your letterhead / masthead, on your headings, in your pictures, etc. But don't use anything garish, or else you will actually turn off recipients and they will stop reading the letter.

5 Ways to Make Your Letters Look Readable to Recipients

Use Whitespace – Using lots of "whitespace," (areas where there is no text or graphic) is the primary way to make your letter look readable. You can leave whitespace by increasing the size of the header or footer, by making the margins larger, by adding space between paragraphs, using pull quotes set aside by blank page, and even through your writing style. For example, if you write one sentence like this:

We have lots of work to do…
                    …but we can't do it without your help.

Then you are painlessly using extra whitespace in your letter.

Use a Large Enough Font Size- Some organizations try to fit more content into fewer pages (thus saving on printing and postage) by using a smaller font size. This is a dangerous game. Which paragraph below would you rather read?

This paragraph is written in Times New Roman size 9. I have seen several organizations send out letters using this font and font size.

This paragraph is written in Times New Roman size 12. I have seen several organizations send out letters using this font and font size.

Clearly, the paragraph in font size 12 is easier to read. When a person is presented with a letter in small font, they are much less likely to read the letter than if it is in a readable font size. My preference for fundraising letter is to use an 11 or 12 size font, depending on the particular font we are using.

Use Numbers Sparingly – Using numbers, statistics, and percentages can help you tell your story and get your point across, but don't weigh your letter down with tons of numbers – it makes people think that your letter is going to be difficult to read, and thus they are much less likely to do so.

Include a Facsimile Signature – You may not have thought so, but including a black and white or color facsimile signature on your letter makes your letter seem more readable, because it makes your letter look like it came from a person (and thus people will think it is likely to be more conversational in tone) and not from a faceless, bureaucratic organization (and thus be boilerplate and written-by-committee). Don't make the mistake of putting a name down for the letter writer but not doing a signature as well.

Be Consistent – Don't indent some paragraphs but not others. Don't use different font sizes or different fonts in different parts of the letter (with the exception of headlines and sub-heads, which can be larger or even a different color). Be consistent, which makes your letter look much more readable.

Main Goal #2: To Convince the Recipient to Give to Your Organization

The second main goal of your design is, in fact, the main goal of all of your fundraising work: to get people to make a donation. The main portion of your design work that will encourage people to give is the design that you create for your direct mail packages as a whole, as opposed to your letter, where the text matters more in terms of getting people to give.

However, there are several things you can do with your design that will help convince people to make a donation... for example, always use emotional graphics – words aren't the only thing than can convey emotion. Your pictures and other graphics can convey emotion just as (if not more) effectively. Thus, when sending out your direct mail, don't include a picture of your office... include a picture of the slums your clients live in. Don't include a picture of your Executive Director... include a picture of someone who received a transplant at your hospital.

Fundamental Concepts for Designing Direct Mail Packages that Work

Now that we've talked about the design of your *letter*, let's move on to the design of your direct mail package as a whole.

What is a Direct Mail "Package" and What Should it Include?

Your direct mail "package" is everything you send in the mail with your fundraising letter. At the very least, it needs to include the letter itself, a reply device (which allows you to collect information from people who respond with a donation), a reply envelope and an outer envelope.

I have also seen some non-profits experiment with a self-mailer or all-in-one mailer where the letter is printed on light cardstock along with a tear-off envelope, all of which is then folded upon itself with an address and postage on the outside. I have not had lots of success with this method outside of political fundraising.

The design of your direct mail package matters. Many organizations will spend hours and hours perfecting their fundraising letter, only to spend two minutes thinking about the rest of the items that will go with it. This is a huge mistake.

Think about it – when someone receives your fundraising letter in the mail, what do they see? Not your letter, not the pictures and headlines and P.S. you worked so hard on... they see your envelope. That's it. Many people will use the envelope – and only the envelope – to decide whether or not to open and read the letter. Shouldn't you put as much thought into your envelope as you do into your letter?

The same thing goes for your reply device... many (if not most) organizations have a standard reply card that they use with all of their mailings. In my opinion, this is a mistake. Your reply card is one last chance to make your ask, one last chance to influence people's decision, one last chance to get people to give more than they would otherwise. Shouldn't you design it to tie into your letter? Shouldn't you spend some time thinking it through, and testing what works and what doesn't?

The design of your direct mail package matters. Spend time on the design, and you'll reap extra financial rewards for your organization.

Designing Your Reply Device

The purpose of your reply device is to (a) get more people to give, and (b) get the people who do give to give more. Thus, your reply device should be designed with these goals in mind.

Make sure your reply device is easy to understand. If people think that it is complicated or is asking for too much information, they may not give, since they don't want to fill out that card or envelope. Think through exactly how much information you need to collect on the card. Cut out what isn't necessary, and if your card still looks crowded with just the necessary information, make the card (or envelope) larger.

I also suggest that you include one last ask on the reply device – at the top, you can include something as simple as, "We need your help. Will you make a donation today to help us fight cancer tomorrow?"

Always tie your reply device into your letter. The ask and the giving levels should tie into the letter that is included with the reply device. For example, if your letter talks about how it costs $25 to send a child to a good school for one day, the giving levels on your reply device should be multiples of $25. That's why I recommend that you never just use "standard" reply cards for all of your letters. When you do, you are apt to send out a letter saying $25 covers the cost of one day for one child along with a reply device that asks for gifts of "$10, $30, $75 or whatever you can afford."

I also suggest always including lines so that people can pay by credit card instead of check. This will definitely increase your response rate.

Designing Your Reply Envelope

Your reply envelope is the envelope that donors will use to return the reply device along with their check or credit card information in order to make a donation. (You can also combine the two, by having a reply envelope with a large fold-over flap that has spaces for people to fill in information. These work well for many organizations).

The purpose of your reply envelope is to make it simple for people to return their donation. Thus, keep it simple. Use a standard size envelope and include your return address in a simple and easy to read font.

The biggest question on reply envelopes is whether or not you should use BRE's (postage-paid business reply envelopes) in order to cover postage for your donors. The conventional wisdom years ago was that doing so would increase your donation rate. Current studies, however, have shown that this is much less true than previously thought. Those studies have shown that for housefile mailings to your own donors, using BRE's has no real effect, and for prospect mailings it is only a very marginal effect.

The only mailings where BRE's were shown to have a more significant (but still relatively moderate) effect were for organizations that did lots of prospecting to low dollar donors (donors that give $1-$25). If you do lots of low dollar prospecting, I would suggest *testing* the use of BRE's (but don't use them unless they test better than simple non-postage-paid envelopes). Otherwise, don't use them.

Designing Your Outer Envelope

The outer envelope is the envelope that the entire package comes in – the one that has your organization's return address and the address of the intended recipient.

There are really two ways you can go about designing your outer envelope. On the one hand, you can simply include your non-profit's logo and return address, along with the recipient address, and postage. On the other hand, you can do an outer envelope that includes all of that information plus a "teaser," or a short phrase or sentence that does something to encourage people to open the letter. Some consultants say that you should use the first kind of envelope for housefile mailings, where the donors already know you, and reserve teasers for prospecting mailings. While this sentiment has some validity, I prefer to use teasers on all of my outer envelopes. The teasers will up the open rate more dramatically for prospecting letters than for housefile mailings, but in general, a well-crafted teaser will help no matter who is receiving the letter.

Of course, as I said, in order to help your open rates, the teaser has to be well-crafted. As the name suggests, well-crafted teasers *tease*. They include some notion of what you are writing about, but also leave the person guessing enough to want to open the letter. Some examples of successful teasers I have used include:

We want to honor YOU at this year's gala...

ATTENTION! This letter is your chance to save someone's life.

This is the craziest thing I have ever done...

Your Leadership Survey is enclosed

As you can see, each of these teasers gives away some information, but leaves the person wanting to open the envelope. **None** of these teasers are asks. The outer envelope should not contain an ask. If your teaser is an ask, your open rates will drop significantly

What Type of Postage Should I Use?

There are three types of postage you can use: first class stamps, non-profit rate stamps, and printed indicia (either pre-printed by your printer or applied by a postage meter).

In general, people are more likely to open your letter if it has a "live" stamp, with open rates going up slightly with first class stamps over non-profit rate stamps. The thinking is that postage with stamps looks much more personal than postage printed on the envelope.
The truth is that the only way to know what will work best for your organization is to test. I have found that first class stamps work great on letters without teasers, but their effectiveness over letters with live non-profit rate stamps wanes when you have a teaser. Of course, first class stamps are also much more expensive than non-profit rate stamps.

For most mailings, your best bet is likely live non-profit rate stamps, but if you are planning a direct mail effort of significant scale, definitely test.

A Word about Premiums and Tchotchkes

One of the questions I get asked the most is whether organizations should include premiums and tchotchkes in their mailings... you know, thinks like labels with people's names on them, etc.

In my experience, the answer for most organizations is "no." When you send a premium in your mailing, people are slightly more likely to send back a donation, but the donations they send back in are much smaller... in short, they are paying you for the premium, and that's it – they are *not* investing in your organization, and thus they don't respond as well when you start sending them regular housefile mailings.

Of course, there are hundreds of organizations that do quite well with sending out premiums. These organizations are normally non-profits that are seeking out lots of smaller donations. If this description fits your organization, and you ready to heavily invest in your direct mail prospecting program, then by all means test out using premiums, they may work for you.

Using Direct Mail Prospecting to Find New Donors for Your Organization

If you're going to relying on direct mail for any sizable portion of your fundraising revenue, you've got to constantly grow your housefile list. Relying on current donors over and over again without trying to grow the list is like holding an annual fundraising event and inviting the same people each year, without every trying to recruit new host committee members or expand your guest list.
Successful direct mail fundraising requires that you constantly grow your list. The best way to do this is through *prospecting*.

What is Direct Mail Prospecting?

Letters that are mailed to borrowed, created, or purchased lists of people who have never given to your organization before are called prospecting mailings. These letters are sent to a list of prospects in the hope that some portion (anywhere from .25-3%) of the recipients will give, and then those people who do will be moved into the housefile list for future mailings.

Prospecting is both an art and a science, and even the best non-profit direct mail consultants in the business are shooting for mailings that break-even, or slightly better. Because you are mailing to a brand new list, your goal for these mailings is to simply make your money back – but in addition to making your money back, you get something very, very valuable: a group of people who are willing to contribute to your organization, and who you can re-solicit over and over again.

What is the Goal of Direct Mail Prospecting?

The goal of your direct mail prospecting is simple: you want to add new donors to your list in a cost effective manner. Let's take a look at those two components individually:

First, you want to add new donors to your list. Remember that the biggest indicator as to whether someone will give to your non-profit through direct mail is whether or not they have done so in the past. If someone makes a donation to you through the mail, it is highly likely that they will do so again. Thus, using direct mail prospecting, you will steadily grow your housefile list, and thus increase the money you raise from your housefile mailings.

To see the compounding effects of using prospecting mailings in conjunction with your housefile mailings and annual appeal letters, take a look at the following direct mail plan for a hypothetical non-profit:

Letter:	Housefile Size:	Mailed to:	Net Profit:	New Housefile Size:
Housefile 1	2,000	2,000	$12,000	2,000
Prospecting 1	2,000	5,000	$0	2,050
Prospecting 2	2,050	7,500	$0	2,125
Housefile 2	2,125	2,125	$14,250	2,125
Prospecting 3	2,125	10,000	$0	2,225
Prospecting 4	2,225	10,000	$0	2,325
Housefile 3	2,325	2,325	$16,000	2,325

This would be a pretty typical 12 month direct mail cycle for a relatively small non-profit – 3 housefile mailings in the year with 4 prospecting mailings going out. As you can see from the above example, in just one year, the organization was able to increase the size of its direct mail housefile by 14% and increase the net profit from each of its housefile mailings by a respectable 25%, all without cost, by using direct mail prospecting. These new donors could be expected to give again and again, as long as the organization keeps growing the relationship and does not abuse its list by over-mailing it.

Testing, Testing, Testing

It is extremely important that every organization embarking on direct mail prospecting tests the letter and the list prior to doing a large mailing.

In the example above, I am assuming that the organization is sending the same letter for each of the prospecting mailings to the same list – not the same people, but people from the same list (e.g. the list may have 50,000 people on it, and we're mailing a small portion of that list each time).

Prior to utilizing the schedule above and doing the first 5,000 person prospecting mailing, I would expect the organization to do a smaller test mailing of 1,000 – 2,000 letters to make sure that the list is good and the letter works with the list. Direct mail is a funny business. You may have a letter that works great with one list and terribly with another. Alternately, you may have two lists that look relatively the same on their face, but one is profitable and the other is not.

The only way to be sure that you've got a great letter and a great list and that they work well together is to test them by sending a test mailing to a portion of the list. If the response rate from the test mailing is 1% and the average gift is $50, you can then extrapolate that out and assume that if you mail another portion of the same list with the same letter, the averages will be the same. Thus, after the test mailing, you will be able to tell whether or not mailing the rest of the list will be profitable, break-even, or disastrous.

If the test mailing doesn't work well, make changes to your letter and do another test mailing, or change lists and do a test mailing to that list. Don't ever send the same letter to the same list after a disastrous test mailing and assume that the results of the second mailing will be anything other than equally bad.

How to Use Direct Mail Prospecting at Your Organization

Now, let's take a look at the steps you'll take to use direct mail prospecting at your non-profit organization. After that, we'll look at effectively using direct mail consultants as well as tips or maximizing your return from direct mail prospecting.

Find a Promising List

One of the most important aspects of successful direct mail prospecting is finding a promising list. As noted above, it is imperative to test each list to make sure it will work for your organization with the mailing you are sending out.

Where can you find good lists? Your non-profit has two main options for finding lists:

List Brokers

List brokers are companies that are in the business of renting out lists. Companies like this usually maintain thousands of lists for every possible demographic, ranging from subscribers to *National Geographic* to "Rich Republican Donors," and everything in between. Their lists can be sliced and diced anyway you want. So, for example, if you are an environmental organization in Baltimore, you may decide to rent a list of all Sierra Club members in Maryland over age 25.

When you rent a list from a list broker, you get to use it one time – meaning for one mailing only. Some organizations that rent their lists through list brokers require you to send a copy of the letter you will be sending out for approval beforehand, to make sure you aren't sending anything that will negatively impact the list and make it less valuable / lucrative in the future.

Don't try to game the list brokers – if you rent a list for one mailing and your letter gets approved by the list owner, but then you send a different letter, or you mail the list more than once, not only are you being unethical and possibly breaking the law (and certainly breaching your contract with the broker), but the broker will know, because they usually seed the list with a couple of addresses that they control, so that they will see what and when you send the list members.

List Sharing

While the majority of all direct mail prospecting is done to lists rented from list brokers, another way to obtain a list to mail is to do a list share. This is where another organization that supports your cause allows you to mail *their* housefile list, or (more likely) trades lists with you... allowing you to mail their list and in return they mail your list for their own fundraising purposes.

List sharing can work well if you find a good fit, but just because you get the list for free or in barter doesn't mean you shouldn't still test it... sending out direct mail is expensive (printing, materials, postage) and you don't want to waste money, so even if the organization you are sharing with seems like an amazing fit, you should still test a small portion of the list to ensure that a larger mailing will ultimately be in your best interest.

Consider Hiring a Copywriter

Writing prospecting letters is much, much more difficult than writing housefile letters. With housefile letters, your organization is a known quantity to the recipients. You don't need to both introduce your organization as well as try to convince the reader to make a donation. Instead, you are simply asking a person who already supports you financially to do so again. With prospecting, on the other hand, your one letter has to do it all.

If you're new to direct mail prospecting, I want to make a suggestion: consider hiring an experienced non-profit copywriter / direct mail consultant. Direct mail prospecting really is a bit of a science that has been honed over the past 40-50 years since the real launch of the direct marketing industry.

Good copywriters aren't cheap, but they're not overly expensive either. Consider hiring one as a consultant to help you write your first couple of prospecting letters. After working through the process with him or her, you'll be in a much better position to be able to write effective direct mail prospecting letters in house.
Of course, if you decide to write the letter in house the first time, it can be done, but be doubly sure to test, test, test before doing a larger mailing.

Write a Compelling Letter

When writing a prospecting letter, remember that the recipients haven't given money to you before – in fact, depending on the size and profile of your organization, they may not have even heard of your non-profit. Thus, you'll need to do some things different in a prospecting letter than you so with a housefile mailing. Here are the various components to a successful prospecting letter (these components need not be in this order):

- What is your organization? What do you do?
- How is your organization changing the world for the better?
- Why should we trust you? Show you are real and trustworthy.
- How much money do you need?
- Why are you raising this money? What will you do with it?

In general, all of the rules and suggestions we discussed in the section above on writing effective fundraising copy still apply, but with the added caveat that you are writing for a different audience, one you do not have a relationship with yet. Thus, your letter has the added goal of introducing your non-profit and quickly (very quickly) building a baseline relationship with your reader.

Test Your Letter to a Portion of the List

Once the letter is done and edited, it's time to test the letter / list combination. I suggest you test the mailing by sending it to between 500-1,500 people. For most organizations 1,000 pieces seems about right.

Then, carefully track response. You want to track:

1. Response rate – how many people send back in a donation?
2. Average gift – what size donation are people sending back in?
3. Bounce rate – how many letters are returned as undeliverable?

If lots of letters are bounced, or returned as undeliverable, you'll want to have a conversation with your list broker to (a) get a partial refund for the letters that were returned and (b) decide if maybe this particular list is just too old and out of date to use. Note that you will always get *some* bounces, and because of this, most list brokers give you some small amount of extra names with your list at no cost. That being said, you should not be getting 5% of your letters bouncing back.

Make a Decision Based on the Results of the Mailing

A month after the mailing hits mailboxes, you will have gotten the vast majority of the donations that will come in. If people haven't given a month after they get the letter, it is highly unlikely that they will do so at all. Now, it is time to make a decision as to whether or not it makes sense to mail to the rest of the list based on the test mailing.

Assuming the list doesn't get too many bounces, the only real metric to look at to make your decision is, *what is the cost for me to acquire a new donor for our housefile?*

The equation you want to use is:

$$Cost\ of\ New\ Donor = \frac{Cost\ of\ Mailing - (Total\ \#\ of\ Gifts \times Average\ Gift)}{Total\ Number\ of\ Gifts}$$

So, for example, let's say it cost you $1,000 to send out 2,000 letters. You received 25 gifts, with an average gift size of $60. Thus, your equation is:

$$Cost\ of\ New\ Donor = \frac{\$1,000 - (25 \times \$60)}{25}$$

The cost to acquire a new donor through this mailing was -$20. Negative, meaning you actually made $20 for each new donor you acquired. That's an outstanding result, and clearly you should mail out to the rest of the list.

On the other hand, if the same mailing cost $1,500 to send out, and your average gift was only $35, the equation would look much different:

$$Cost\ of\ New\ Donor = \frac{\$1,500 - (25 \times \$35)}{25}$$

Now, the cost to acquire a new donor through this mailing is $25... meaning that the mailing lost money, and cost you $25 per new donor that you added to your housefile. Not as great a deal, right?

The question becomes: what is a new donor worth to you? If the mailing makes money, you have a winner... your organization is basically being paid to add new donors to its housefile list by using this list and this letter... so keep going. If the cost of a new donor is $0, meaning that you are breaking even, it's likely that you should keep going as well – you are adding new donors without cost, except for the staff time to run the program. Again, a winner.

But... what if you are losing money on each donor you are adding? Then, it's really a value question. First ask yourself, is there some way I can make this letter better, to increase our response? If so, do it and test. If not, think about whether or not you should try another list.

What is the lifetime value of one of your direct mail donors? Lifetime value (LTV) is the measurement of how much money the average direct mail donor to your non-profit will give over the course of their relationship with your organization. Specifically, for those donors you acquired through prospecting, how much money will the average such donor give over the course of their relationship with you?

Once you know that number, it becomes a values game... how much return on your investment do you need to make it so that a letter makes sense for your non-profit? If a certain letter / list combination is costing you $1 for every new donor you add, but your average direct mail donor LTV is $500, is the $1 worth it? Would $5 be worth it? $25?

The answers to these questions will vary for every non-profit and every development budget.

Add New Donors to Your Housefile Donor List

Finally, once you have made your decision and either mailed the entire list or decided to stop the campaign, take the donors that you did generate and add them to your housefile list, so that they can be mailed again and again. Remember – with direct mail prospecting, the money is in the follow-up.

Using Direct Mail Consultants

As I mentioned above, fundraising direct mail, and particularly prospecting mail, is a science that has been perfected over the past 40 or 50 years by professional practitioners. Today, there are hundreds of qualified (and some not-so-qualified) non-profit direct mail shops, consultants and copywriters in the United States, Canada and many in other countries as well.

If you're going to be using lots of prospecting mail then I recommend you use a qualified direct mail shop. Depending on the scope of your contract with them, these firms will write your letters, cull your housefile, choose which prospect lists to mail to, work with the print shop to print, stuff, stamp, and mail letters, and help you analyze the returns, all for a reasonable price.

In order to work successfully with a direct mail consultant, I suggest the following:

Check references. Interview potential consultants in-depth, and then check at least 3-4 references. There is no licensing in this industry, so the rule is, "buyer beware."

Remember that everything is negotiable. Be sure to negotiate your fees before you sign the contract.

Trust but verify. Your consultant may be a professional, but he or she isn't infallible. Check and double check the lists, the letter, and the returns.

You have to be comfortable with the letters. Have someone on your staff review each and every letter before it goes out. Don't approve any mailings where you are not comfortable with the language or theme of the letter.

Watch your return on investment. If your letters are consistently losing money or not performing the way they should be, change course, change the text, change the lists, or change consultants.

Tips for Successful Direct Mail Prospecting

Let's take a look at a few other tips for successfully using direct mail prospecting:

It doesn't make economic sense to do direct mail prospecting if you don't have a strong housefile mailing system in place. If you're only mailing your housefile once per year, the LTV of a direct mail donor to your non-profit is going to be far lower than if you are mailing to your housefile 3 or 4 times per year. Get your housefile program in place, and then worry about prospecting.

Numbers and metrics matter. You may think a letter is good. You may think it is bad. You may scoff at a list. You may think another list is a goldmine. It doesn't matter. What matters is testing and metrics. If the numbers say a list is good, then it is. If the numbers say a letter is working, then it is. Track your results and trust your numbers.

How to Write Amazing Annual Appeal Letters for Your Organization

Of all of the different types of fundraising mail that are utilized by non-profit organizations, perhaps the most ubiquitous is the annual appeal letter. In many cases, annual appeal letters are used by non-profits that don't send out any other direct mail at all, even to their housefile. Because annual appeal letters are so common, and yet in many ways "different" from other types of direct mail, this section focuses specifically on how to write amazing annual appeal letters.

What is an Annual Appeal Letter?

An organization's annual appeal letter is a yearly letter that gets sent out to the housefile asking for general operating funds for the non-profit. It usually gets sent to every donor in your donor file (or at least, every donor that has been active over the past several years) and normally gets sent out around the same time each year (the time of year differs by non-profit, but once you pick a time of year, you normally stick with it).

While not every non-profit organization utilizes annual appeal letters, it has been my experience that most do. The reason for this is that it gives the charity a good reason for contacting donors for general operating funds as opposed to asking for designated dollars, and it is a great opportunity to cast a wide net through an easily scalable medium (direct mail).

Why is an Annual Appeal Letter Different from Other Types of Direct Mail?

In some ways, an annual appeal letter isn't all that different from other types of direct mail. When writing an annual appeal letter, you'll still want to follow all of the rules that we discussed earlier in the book and use all of the design and copywriting techniques we mentioned. This is, after all, still a piece of direct mail.

There are many ways, however, in which an annual appeal letter differs from other types of fundraising mail. For many organizations, the annual appeal may be the only time that the non-profit specifically asks for non-designated general operating funds. The annual appeal letter also normally serves as a sort of summary of the year that was and grand vision for the future of the organization.

Because most organizations that use annual appeals send them out at the same time each year, donors come to look forward to the letter and many make additional donations simply because this is the annual appeal (even if the organization sends out other fundraising mail throughout the year).

Running a Coordinated Annual Appeal

The best and most successful annual appeal letters are sent out as part of a coordinated, system-wide annual appeal for the organization. This means that the non-profit not only sends out the annual appeal through direct mail, but also posts about it on its website, makes it a board priority, sends out appeal e-mails, and makes calls to higher and mid-level donors to seek support for the annual appeal campaign.

Effective annual appeals start with an idea, or theme, for the appeal that is then carried through each of the tactics that will be used to raise money for the annual campaign.

The 5 Rules of Successful Annual Appeal Mailings

As you plan your annual appeal mailing, keep the following rules in mind:

#1 – Consistent Mailings Produce Better Results

If your annual appeal letter is the only time that your donors hear from you via snail mail, then your mailing will not raise its full potential. Consistency produces better results.

When your appeal is the only real live letter your donors get from you, they are more likely to feel "sold" by your organization. On the other hand, if you are regularly communicating with your donors via snail mail (even if it's only by sending them two mailed newsletters per year) your supporters will feel like the annual appeal is a natural part of the ongoing conversation they are having with your non-profit.

#2 – Preach to the Choir

Remember that your annual appeal letter is going out to your housefile, and only to your housefile. This means that when you're writing your letter, you're "preaching to the choir." Thus, don't belabor your explanation about what the organization does or the mechanics of your work. Talk about your mission, of course, but don't treat your readers like they are prospects who have never heard of your non-profit before.

#3 – Summarize Your Work

As noted above, your annual appeal letter serves, in part, as a summary of the work that your non-profit is proud to have carried out over the course of the past year. Summarize your work in emotional and compelling terms, tie it to your mission, and remind your donors that they played an integral part in your success over the past several years through their generous donations to your organization.

#4 – Spell Out Your Need

In addition to summarizing your work and mission, your annual appeal letter serves as a tool for laying out a *bold* and exciting mission for the future of your organization. Use the letter to tell your donors what you hope to accomplish going forward. Tell them why you need them to get involved. Then invite them to do so.

#5 – Be Creative, but Not Cute

My rule for annual appeal letters is always to be creative, but not cute. Your annual appeal mailing isn't the time to try out that velvet printing paper you've always wanted to use or to test out a new premium to include with the letter.

That being said, you can and should be creative with your letter. Remember, these are donors who in many cases have been with you for a long time. They've gotten tons of letters from you. Even if they are in fact expecting and looking forward to receiving your annual appeal, try to spice things up a little by being creative, emotional, and visionary.

Don't Forget the Ask!

Perhaps the most important part of your annual appeal letter is the *appeal*... the ask. Don't forget to include a concrete ask in your letter.

Example of a Successful Annual Appeal Letter

Beginning on the next page, you will find an example of an annual appeal mailing that worked extremely well for the organization that mailed it. I wrote the letter, which was part of a coordinated annual appeal campaign at the non-profit several years ago. Note that this letter is both a summary of the work completed as well as a vision for the work ahead, and includes a concrete and compelling ask.

The name of the non-profit (and identifying characteristics) has been changed to protect confidentiality.

London Children's Clinic
Oxford Street • W1b 3Be

Dear (First Name),

<u>I'm nervous, and excited...</u>

Last year, the London Children's Clinic set an ambitious goal: to do *whatever it takes* to be able to offer our services to every single child in London who is in need of urgent medical care. Last month, we took a major step to make that goal a reality...

We leased new space on Oxford Street which will significantly increase our capacity. Now, it's too late to turn back!

For the past 18 years, the Children's Clinic has been located in Wembley. It's been a great home, but it's a small facility. As we've increased the number of children we see every month, we've added staff... and equipment... and family resources... and now <u>we are out of room</u>!

Thanks to your support, we've grown dramatically over the years. During our first year in existence, we saw fewer than 100 children. This year, the Clinic is on track to see over 8,000 child patients and their caregivers. But we can't stop there...

Each year, over 20,000 children are unable to afford ongoing medical care in the city.

Today, the London Children's Clinic sees less than half of these children. Within the next five years, our goal is to see every single child in need and offer them the life-saving services that the Clinic provides.

Last month, we signed a lease for a new office that will <u>triple the amount of space we can use to provide free healthcare to suffering children</u>. We've cancelled the lease at our old location, and we're hiring new staff members who will be ready to treat children and counsel families the minute we move early next year.

We are pushing ahead to make sure that **every child in the city who is unable to afford adequate medical care will be served at the London Children's Clinic.**
There's no turning back now... how could there be? We know that ailing <u>children who are not seen at the Children's Clinic</u>:

- Often receive only emergency medical care, and receive no follow up treatments, well-visits, or testing

- Receive sub-standard care outside of the supervision of a general practice pediatrician

- Do not receive the medications and life-saving therapeutic treatments that so many of them require

<u>At the Clinic, every child receives</u>:

- A complete physical exam by a board certified pediatrician

- Prescription and non-prescription medications and outpatient therapies at no cost to them or their families

- Referrals for specialist and mental health services, as well as other services the family might need, such as nutritionists and physical therapy.

- The ongoing support of a caring family practitioner to guide the family through ongoing medical treatments

Because you have been so generous, we have been able to *dramatically* increase the number of children we see every year. It is your support, year in and year out, which has enabled us to save so many children from the devastating effects of disease and illness – and which has emboldened us to set this goal and take these steps to see every child who needs our help.

The truth is that signing this new lease on larger office space is the biggest leap we've ever taken – and it will require significant financial support to maintain a larger facility and provide our services to a growing number of children. In short...

...We need your help!

Last year, the Clinic raised over $1,900,000 to fund our mission. This year, we will need to raise over $2.1 million – It's a lofty goal, but I know we can do it. In fact, we are well on our way. **But we can't do it without your help.**

Will you contribute $50, $100, or more to help us serve the children of London?

Your contribution is needed today, more than ever, and will enable the Children's Clinic to move into our new office, and bring our expert doctors and medical services to more of London's most vulnerable children.

Thank you for helping us save lives.

With gratitude,

Louise Pontarelli, MD
Medical Director

P.S. We've taken a big step – we're moving into new office space and we've hired new staff. Our goal is to be able to help every child in the city who cannot afford adequate medical care. But we need your help! Will you contribute $50, $100 or more today to help us increase our services and stop the suffering?

P.P.S. Please be generous. The London Children's Clinic is a private, non-profit organization that relies on the financial support of our friends and donors to be able to provide our services to children in need.

Even More Tips for Supercharging Your Direct Mail Fundraising Strategies

We've covered most of the basic and advanced topics your organization will need in order to run successful direct mail fundraising campaigns, including copywriting, design, prospecting, and annual appeals. In this section, we're going to wrap things up by talking about 10 strategies you can use to really supercharge your direct mail fundraising efforts. These strategies are a combination of ideas that simply didn't fit in other areas of this chapter as well as expanded tactics that were only lightly touched on earlier in this course.

Strategy #1: Directly Show the Impact a Donation Will Make on the World

In general, philanthropically minded people are continually haunted by one question: "How can I make a difference in the world?" As a non-profit engaged in direct mail fundraising, you need to send them a letter that screams, "You can make a huge difference in the world by donating to US!"

If they do anything, your fundraising letters should directly show your donors and prospects the impact that making a donation to your organization – today – will make. Do this by telling donors what an impact your organization is already making, what their money has been used for in the past, telling compelling stories of the people you are helping, and laying out a huge and compelling vision for the future.

Strategy #2: Focus on Both Immediate Gifts and Lifetime Donor Value

When you send out a direct mail fundraising letter, you want an immediate gift. You want donors to take out the enclosed reply card, fill it out, and place it (and a check!) in the pre-addressed reply envelope you supply. Easy-peasey.

But an immediate gift is not the only (or even the biggest) thing you want from a donor. What you really want is to build a lifelong relationship with a new and committed supporter of your organization. Rather than a one-time $50 gift, you'd prefer $25 (or $50, or $100) per month each and every month for the next three years. You'd prefer someone who gives $1,000 per year to your annual appeal over someone who gives $2,000 this year and is never heard from again. In short, while immediate gifts are nice, what you are really looking for is lifetime donor value.

The moral here is that you don't want to do anything in your initial direct mail letter that will encourage your prospects to give now, but hurt your potential relationship with them such that it will reduce the amount they give in the future. Thus, make a concrete ask, but not a hard sell. Ask for money now... but don't (as one organization I recently talked with did) tell people that if they just give now, you won't bother them again all year. You're not bothering them... they are your partner in making the world a better place!

Strategy #3: Measure ROI, not Cost

Which mailing would you rather send out at your organization?
Mailing A costs $1,000 to send to 5,000 donors, and returns gross donations in the amount of $8,000. *Mailing B* costs $5,000 to send to 5,000 donors, and returns gross donations in the amount of $37,000. Which is a better mailing?

It may seem obvious that Mailing B, which netted $32,000 for the organization, is the preferred mailing because it netted far more than Mailing A, which only resulted in net profits of $7,000 for the organization. Yet every day, I see non-profits that send the cheapest possible mailings to save money on the front end, thinking they are making the best decision for their organization.

Expensive does not always equal good and cheap doesn't always equal bad. Remember that the measurement you should care about is *not* the cost to send out a mailing, but what the overall *return on investment (ROI)* is for the letter/package.

Strategy #4: Time Your Mail Drops Prudently

Be very, very careful in when your direct mail letters "drop." Take a good long look at the calendar to make sure that your letters aren't going to be received right in the middle of a direct mail crush or near a holiday when people aren't in the mood to open mail.

For example, if you're sending out a Christmas mailing, would you rather it drops on December 21st or December 24th?   Many organizations would say the latter, but I would rather have my letter drop on the 21st, while people still have some bandwidth available for things other than egg-nog and Christmas carols.

Similarly, if you are mailing to an area with a large Jewish population, have you taken a look at the Jewish holiday calendar? You don't necessarily want your mailing to hit mailboxes on Yom Kippur or Passover, when people are occupied with other things.

Elections are another tricky mail time… in many countries including the US, political campaigns heavily rely on direct mailers to get out their message.   This means that during the week before Election Day, people are going to be inundated with direct mail from multiple (in some cases dozens) of candidates.   Do you really want your fundraising letter to have to fight for attention with dozens or hundreds of other "urgent" letters? Be sure to time your mail drops prudently!

Strategy #5: Direct Mail Is a "Program," Not a "Tactic"

Stop thinking of direct mail as a one-time tactic or as a series of independent events (mail drop 1, mail drop 2, prospecting letter 1, etc.). The best direct mail efforts are *programs*, not one-time tactics. Start thinking of your direct mail as one big interconnected program. Direct mail has a cumulative effect. As you continue to mail your housefile, your donors will get used to giving to you through the mail. As you continue to send out prospecting letters, more and more people will hear about your message.

Develop a complete direct mail program and calendar for your organization and stick with it… your results will multiply over the years.

Strategy #6: Ask for a Second Gift Sooner than You Think

Experts say that for most things, it takes doing something at least 5 times before it becomes a regular habit. I have found that for direct mail prospecting it takes at least 2 gifts before giving to your organization becomes a regular occurrence for a donor.

Sadly, many of the new leads you receive from your prospecting mailings will drop off of the radar screen after they make that first gift. The best thing you can do to keep them giving – and to get them to become a regular giver – is to make a second ask by mail sooner than you may otherwise think.

First, send a thank you note immediately after getting that first gift. This reinforces the importance of this new donor to your organization. Then, within 8-12 weeks of that first gift, send a second direct mail letter (this time, it's a housefile letter!) to ask for another gift. Even if the person doesn't give this second time, the mere fact that they received both a thank you letter and a second ask so soon after first contact encourages a long-term relationship. And for those that do give the second time around, you are well on your way to a great long-term donor relationship!

Strategy #7: Constantly Build Your List

With direct mail fundraising, you need to constantly build your list through prospecting because people will constantly be falling off of your housefile list. People die, move, change interests, lose their job, etc. Thus, people will constantly be falling off your list, often through no fault of your organization.

The only way to keep your direct mail fundraising program growing and moving forward is to keep testing and mailing new prospecting letters. Sadly, many non-profits don't do this. They send out one prospecting mailing, add 50 or 100 new donors, then move back to doing only housefile mailings. Those 100 new donors will dwindle over time, and in five years, of the original 100 new donors gained from the prospecting mailing, only 8 are still giving.

Now contrast that to an organization that continually prospects and adds 50 or 100 new donors three times per year, every year. Even though some (or most) fall off over time, they consistently profit, and their list consistently grows.

Strategy #8: Always Write to an Individual

You can't build a relationship with a corporation, a partnership, or a foundation. The only way to truly build lasting relationships is person to person. Thus, you should never, ever write a direct mail fundraising letter that begins:

> *Dear Friend of the Council,* or
> *Dear Supporter,* or
> *Dear Leadership Committee Member,*

These impersonal greetings show the recipient that this isn't a personal letter, but is instead a pitch. People don't like pitches... they like to know that *you* know who they are... they like proof that the good feelings they have for your organization are mutual. Always write your solicitation letters to an individual, even if you are asking for corporate or foundation money.

Strategy #9: Always Write from an Individual

Similarly, never write a letter signed by your organization. Always have one or two real, identifiable people from your staff or board (or some other supporter) sign your letter. Write the letter as if it comes from that person. Use I, you, me, we, and other words that show that this is a person-to-person letter and not a solicitation from a friendly but faceless entity.

Strategy #10: Diversify

When sending out housefile mailings, you should send out more than one housefile fundraising letter per year. The more housefile letters you send out, the more diverse they should be. Test new and creative ways to reach your list – people get tired of reading the same 12 point Times New Roman double-spaced three page letter on your organizational letterhead every other month. Be creative.

The same goes for your prospecting mail. Don't be afraid to test your creative letter ideas to see what works and what doesn't. That being said, always <u>test</u> before you invest in larger mailings.

Chapter 11:
Supercharging Your Non-Profit's
Online Fundraising

Online fundraising matters to your non-profit. No matter how small you are, or what an amazing direct mail operation you run, or how big you are, or how you're "grant-oriented," raising money online matters for you – and it will matter for you tomorrow even more than it does today.

Within the next decade, nearly every person in the first world will be online. Just as you have the ability to reach anyone you want via postal mail, you will (and pretty much now do) have the ability to reach anyone by e-mail or social network. Each year, people are spending more and more time online, taking market share not just from the postal service, but also from television, radio, and even real-life interaction. More people are spending more time online, year after year. If your non-profit wants to reach them, you'll have to do the same.

There's an old adage in advertising that says, "Go where the people are." That's as true in fundraising communications as it is in the ad world. You need to be prepared to use the internet *passively* (making it easy for people who are looking for you to find you online, get the information they want, and connect with you) as well as *actively* (going out and finding new prospects, cultivating them, and getting them to give). Other non-profits are out there doing both, very effectively. Are you?

What We Mean by Online Fundraising

Lest you think that when I say "online fundraising," I am only talking about that big "Donate Now!" button on your website, let's define what we mean when we're talking about raising money online.

First, online fundraising is, well… *online*. It's not just your website. It's everything you do over the internet. It's your website, sure, but it's also your e-mail communications, your social media presence, your crowdfunding campaigns, and even things like the profile you set up on Guidestar. It's all of the places you're available online.

Second, just as offline fundraising isn't solely about making asks, online fundraising isn't solely confined to those times when you are asking people for their credit card information. *Everything you do to communicate with donors or potential donors online is "online fundraising."*

Most non-profits don't think this way. They think of online fundraising as asks only. Don't make that mistake. See your online efforts holistically: You find new donors online. You cultivate them. You ask them for money. You steward them. It's all fundraising, and it's all online.

The Five Key Principles of Online Fundraising

As you explore more of the strategies and tactics available to you when fundraising online, keep in mind the following five key principles that underlie everything you do to raise money on the internet:

#1 – It's Fundraising... Relationships Matter

Online fundraising is still fundraising – and like every single type of fundraising, relationships matter. Far too many non-profits think that they can hop online and hit "publish" on their website, and – voila! – the money will start rolling in. That's the exception, not the rule.

The rule is that in fundraising, relationships matter. And in online fundraising... relationships still matter. During this section, we'll talk about different ways to build strong relationships with your online prospects, donors, and friends.

#2 – You Need an Online Fundraising Plan

Just as every type of fundraising requires relationship building, every type of fundraising – include online – requires a plan. Not a 40 page plan, but at least a thumbnail sketch of your activities, deadlines, goals, and who is responsible for what. Don't fly by the seat of your pants just because you're online. Figure out what you want to do beforehand... then implement.

#3 – Coordinate Your Online and Offline Fundraising Activities

It's not a good practice to build artificial boxes around your online and offline fundraising efforts. Instead, you should be coordinating your offline and online efforts to make sure they are complimenting each other – not competing with each other.

Draw up a master communications plan for your organization that details when people will get snail mail, when they'll get event invitations, when they'll get e-mails, when you'll launch that new fundraising campaign on your website. Coordinate your online and offline fundraising, don't compete.

#4 – Online Fundraising Isn't Magic

Above, we (hopefully) debunked the myth that you could simply "get online" and the money would roll in (it takes work, and relationship building). But, equally important to acknowledge is that raising lots of money online isn't magic. It's not something that only online whizzes can accomplish – it is knowable, understandable, and doable for every non-profit.

I can't guarantee that you'll raise a million dollars online, but I can guarantee that you can learn online fundraising best practices and apply what you have learned to your own web activities.

#5 – Not Every Communication Should be an Ask

Not every communication you have with a donor should be an ask… this is true in offline fundraising, and even *more* true in online fundraising, where people are already wary of spam and can easily delete what you send them, take your website off of their bookmarked-pages list, and unfriend you on Facebook.

Build relationships with your online prospects and donors by sending them e-newsletters, posting relevant links to your social networks, keeping interesting pictures of your work on your website, soliciting their input through e-mail polls, etc. Vary your communications to deepen your donor relationships.

How Online Fundraising Differs from Offline Fundraising

You already know that online fundraising differs from offline fundraising in many ways, but here are three important differences you may not have thought about, which will greatly impact your ability to raise money online:

Attention Span

People's attention spans online are short. *Very short.* I would say that for the average person, their attention span online is shorter than almost every other fundraising method... perhaps save for telemarketing. People like to be entertained and enlightened on the web and this means that they are willing to click links or the "back button" on their browser (or delete your e-mail) if it doesn't garner their attention.

Ability to Spread Your Message

Nowhere else can your non-profit's message spread as quickly as it can online. People forward e-mails and links, post things to Twitter, Facebook, LinkedIn, et al, and create personal fundraising pages for the causes they like. In short, people share online in a way that has never happened offline. This means your message needs to be "shareable" and worthy of sharing. More on both of those later in this book.

Ease of Measurement

Finally, just about everything you do online can be measured. Sending out an e-mail appeal? You can see how many people opened your e-mail (try that with snail mail!). Posting a link on a social network? You can track how many people click it and in many cases how long they spent looking at the page you send them to. Everything is trackable and measureable.

This means your non-profit can do split testing (sometimes called A/B testing) to see what e-mail headlines get opened more... and what works best on your website, etc. The most successful non-profits measure everything they can online to make the best decisions possible about their online fundraising campaigns.

You understand that online fundraising is important and encompasses everything you do to communicate online. You know that online fundraising is still *fundraising* and thus requires the building of strong relationships... and you understand that your online and offline fundraising activities must be coordinated, and not created in competition with each other. Now... what are the advanced concepts your non-profit needs to understand in order to maximize your online fundraising strategy?

The Online World is a Permission Economy. Attention Matters.

Well over a decade ago, Seth Godin wrote a groundbreaking book called *Permission Marketing*. In it, he posited that the dot-com revolution had moved the marketplace from an "interruption economy" to a "permission economy."

In an interruption economy, businesses pay money to interrupt people who are doing something they find enjoyable or necessary and use the interruption deliver an advertising message. Thus, TV shows and radio programs have commercials, magazines and newspapers have ads, and roads have billboards.

In a permission economy, people can easily tune out interruption. They can change to one of the other 200 channels when your ad comes on. They can switch to satellite radio. They can click out of your pop-up ad or delete your e-mail at the press of a button. What really matters in a permission economy is *permission* – people who give you their permission to communicate with them and thus are likely to give you their attention.

The online world is a permission economy. The best way to communicate with your friends and donors online is to get their permission to do so... and then to hold on to that permission by not abusing and losing it.

What does permission look like online? When someone signs-up for your e-mail newsletter, they are giving you their permission to communicate with them by e-mail. Don't abuse it by sending an e-ask every week. Instead, send a monthly newsletter and run one big e-mail ask campaign each year.

When someone follows you on Twitter, they are giving you permission to post updates that will show up on their Twitter feed. Don't abuse it by sending 250 public tweets a day, two-thirds of which ask for money. Instead, post some relevant links, re-tweets, and thoughts every day. Drive people to your website gently.

Now, you may be saying, hey.... I don't need permission. I send out tons of direct mail to rented lists, so why can't I send out tons of e-mail to people I don't know? I'll tell you why... because online, people are hypersensitive to SPAM. If they get an unsolicited glossy self-mailer from you offline, they know that at least you paid to have it designed, printed, and mailed. When you send SPAM online, they know that it didn't cost you anything... and that they're probably one of a million people who got that e-mail from you.

In short... online, people don't give their *attention* to your organization until after they have given you their *permission*.   Later in this book, we'll talk about specific strategies for gaining that permission (it's easier than you think).

The Most Efficient Accelerator in Online Fundraising is Social Proof.

For most people, when they are online, they have their guard up to an extent that they don't offline. Think about it... when was the last time you passed by a fast-food restaurant when you were hungry and didn't go in because you were worried that the restaurant was just a front to steal your credit card number? I'll wager that thought never crosses your mind.

Yet, when was the last time you saw an ad or a product online and wondered whether or not it was safe to use your credit card to buy it, or whether the e-mail you got was "real?" I'll bet that's happened to you at least once and more likely dozens of times since you've been on the internet.

When people are asked to give their e-mail address, their personal information, or their credit card number online, they worry. Alarms go off. They want to make sure that they can trust you.

In the offline world, it's much easier to build this type of trust. People can see your office building. They can shake the hand of your Executive Director and Board Chair. They can attend your events. They can know that you are "real."

Online, it's harder. There are a number of things you can do to build trust: you can have a professionally designed website and nice looking online materials. You can avoid having typos in your posts and poorly-produced videos on your site. You can post pictures of your staff, and host your payment pages on a secure server (you know, one of those sites that start with https:// instead of just http://). And, you can accelerate that trust, and those relationships online, by offering social proof.

What is social proof? It's confirmation that you are trustworthy because so many other people have dealt with you and found you to be so. It is the "herd mentality" in action... where people trust you because others do and take action because others are. There are any number of ways you can offer social proof to your online prospects and donors that will encourage them to trust you:

- Include written and video testimonials from donors on your site and social networks

- Post testimonials from well-known, well-respected people who support your cause

- Be active on social networks. Having a decent number of "friends and followers" online shows that you are real and that other people trust you

- Ask your supporters to tell their friends about you – nothing says "trustworthy" more than being told about your organization by someone a person trusts and knows in real life or online

- Post a physical address and phone number for your organization on your website so that people can contact you offline if they so desire

- Share pictures and testimonials from those your organization has helped

Be Human. People Give to Humans, Not Machines.

When organizations first get serious about their online activities, there is often a temptation to be very anti-septic about their activities. They post only the necessary details about their non-profit. Their tweets and updates come out of the blue from an account with an organization logo and name... not from a person. They never show the personal side of their organization.

Imagine trying to raise money offline that way! Imagine telling prospects, you can call the office and ask for the organization (not a specific person) and someone who shall remain nameless will respond to you. No way! You want them to call your Development Director or the major gifts officer with whom they are building a relationship. You want them to put a face to your organization, to know that you are real people with a real passion for your mission.

If you wouldn't present your organization so devoid of personality offline, don't do it online either. All fundraising – including online fundraising – is about building relationships. People build relationships with humans, not machines.

So... post "staff member of the month" articles in your e-newsletter. Have your Executive Director tweet under her real name, sharing all the positive things that are going on at your non-profit. When writing about planned giving, don't tell people to e-mail info@yourorganization.org to get more information, tell then to call Sara, or Joe, or Katelyn. Be human, and show your personal side.

Of course, when doing this, be smart about it. Your Executive Director *should* be tweeting about your non-profit's new coat drive, but should *not* be tweeting about the upcoming presidential election. Similarly, keep your donor relationships mission-centered, because your mission matters and you want that mission to be front and center.

It's Easy to Go Crazy Online. Don't. Use Your Resources Wisely.

As you think about starting or expanding your web presence, it's easy to go crazy – to think you have to spend tens (or hundreds) of thousands of dollars on your website, the time to be on Facebook for three hours per day, and the bandwidth to obsess constantly about your site content and e-mails.

You don't. Your time, energy and money are limited resources. One of the best things about the internet is that it has allowed non-profits to communicate with the outside world effectively and relatively cheaply. Use that to your advantage!

You may need to spend some money to set-up or upgrade your website. You want it to look good, so you may want a professional's touch. That being said, very few organizations need to spend outsized sums on setting up a good looking and functional website. Similarly, you don't need to spend hours per day online. In fact, it is my belief that you should be able to effectively communicate on social media using my "1+15" strategy. This strategy says that you should be able to spend 1 full day setting up your social media sites – choosing which sites you will be on, setting up your profiles, and getting connected with some of your supporters. Then, you should be able to maintain and grow your presence on all of your selected sites in just 15 minutes per day, per social media outlet.

Thus, if you decide that you need to be on Twitter and Facebook, but not any other social sites right now, then you would need to invest just 30 minutes per day (15 minutes for each of the two sites) to build a presence on those sites, after your initial set-up is complete. This is an easy, and eminently doable investment for your non-profit organization.

Don't fall victim to the idea that you can't do great fundraising online without spending gobs of money and time on it. Finish this course, understand what you need to do, then make some decisions and upgrade your online presence (and start raising more money online too!)

How to Raise Money through Your Organization's Website

Now that you know the fundamentals of online fundraising, let's turn our attention to your organization's website. In this section, we will go over the fundamentals of your website: what you'll need, tools for setting it up (if it isn't already) and the purpose of your website – where it fits in to your online fundraising strategy. Then, we'll look at a strategy for supercharging your website revenue.

The True Fundraising Purpose of Your Website

Your website probably has lots of purposes. You may sign up volunteers through your website, advertise your client services or schedule appointments, offer information to the press and public, or post public resources on your website. You may even offer brochures or white papers through your site. Of course, your website has a fundraising purpose as well – you use it (or should be using it) to raise money as an integral part of your development strategy.

Your non-profit's website serves as the *central hub* of all of your organization's online fundraising efforts. Everything you do online, including e-mail marketing and social networking, should be focused on driving people back to your organization's website. When you're working on Facebook... drive people back to your website. When you're sending out an e-mail newsletter... include lots of links that drive people back to your website.

Why? Why do you think it is important to drive people back to your website? What do you want them to do there that they can't do almost any place else?

Do you think it is so they can click on your big green "DONATE NOW" button to make a gift to your organization? That would be great, but no, that's not the primary reason to drive them back to your website.

Do you think it is so they can read all of the great information you have there, or see all of the pictures you have posted from your latest mission trip or fundraising event? Nope... that's important too, but it isn't the main reason to send them back to your site.

The first and foremost reason you want people to visit your organization's website... the reason you spend the majority of your efforts online trying to drive them back to your place on the web, is so you can *collect their e-mail address*.

Think about it... with any luck, thousands of people will be viewing your website and looking at your social media pages each month, week, or day. For most of those people, you will never, ever know who they are... you won't have any way to get back in touch with them, either. Even if they like you on Facebook or follow you on Twitter, they'll only read your stuff if some serendipity happens – if they're online when your message comes across their feed, and happen to be in the mood to read what you are writing. In other words... for most of those people, you don't have any control in communicating with them.

With e-mail, on the other hand, you're in the driver's seat. Most people check their e-mail more than once per week, and most people at least scan each and every e-mail they get (at the very least, they look at who each e-mail is from and what the subject line is, then decide if they want to read further). When you have someone's e-mail address, and their permission to e-mail them, *you* get to control the pace of the communication and you know that you have at least a fighting chance of getting through the clutter and getting people to read what you send.

Remember what we said earlier in this chapter: we're in a permission economy. The best type of marketing that you can do is *permission marketing*, which means sending messages about your organization to people who have given you their permission to do so.

So – the goal of your online activities is to drive people back to your website and the purpose of your website is to get people to give you (a) their e-mail address and (b) their permission to communicate with them.

The 5 Things You Will Need to Have an Effective Web Presence

In order to offer information, collect e-mails, and raise money online, you need to have at least a minimally effective web presence. Here are the 5 things you need to have in place in order to do so:

1. Professional Look

I am not a big believer in the idea that your website has to be flashy and over-the-top. I have seen hundreds of non-profits that raise a good amount of money online with basic, functional websites. There's one thing, though, that is shared by almost every website that raises decent money online: it has to look professional.

People won't give to you through your website unless they feel like they can trust you. They won't feel like they can trust you unless your site looks professional. Remember, I'm not talking about using a $100,000 per site web designer. I am talking about a basic level of professionalism that shows you place importance and pride in your website.

The most important part of a professional look is professionally designed web graphics. Unless you're a design pro, this is one area where I highly recommend bringing in outside help. For far less than $1,000 you can have professional web designers create a great looking banner for the top of your site and secondary graphics to place throughout your site. You can commission really great designs through 99Designs (99Designs.com), which uses a competition format where designers compete and you award the project fee to the design you like best, or through KillerCovers (KillerCovers.com) which, despite its name, designs more than just book covers. I have used both services in the past with complete satisfaction.

The second most important thing in making sure your site looks professional is editing – making sure you use correct grammar, spelling, and punctuation. Nothing looks worse than an organization encouraging readers to "Donate noW to our orgnziation."

Finally, be sure that all the information on your website is up-to-date. If you're still showing information for *last* year's gala fundraising event, it's hard for potential sponsors to take you seriously about *this* year's event.

2. Ease of Editing

Which brings us to another key requirement for an effective web presence... your website has to be easy for you to edit in-house. Sure, if you're a major national organization, you can afford to have an IT consultant update your site each week. But for most non-profits, you'll need to be able to perform basic web edits in house. This means adding new articles and links, changing dates on the calendar, etc.

Don't get frightened, though! Currently available web tools make it extremely easy to build an easily editable website, without anyone on your team learning advanced coding or HTML. If you're building a website from scratch, check out Wordpress, an amazing, free and easy to use backend system that can do almost anything. (Note that you'll want Wordpress.org, which is the backend system you install on your own site, instead of Wordpress.com, which is a less-editable blog you can host on *their* site).

If your website is already set up, and it is not easily editable by your staff, talk with your web designer (or any web design company) about migrating your site over to an easy to use backend like Wordpress or Expression Engine, so that your team can make regular changes to your site.

3. Regular Updates

Why is it important that your site be easily editable by your team? Because it is important that your site get updated regularly!

No one wants to visit (or trust) a website that is bogged down with last month's (or... yikes... last year's) content. They want to know that your website is fresh and updated regularly before they fork over their hard earned dollars on it. Thus, it is important that your site is updated regularly with news items, event information, staff profiles, asks, etc.

What qualifies as "regularly" will differ for every organization, but at a minimum, some new content should appear on your website at least monthly. If you followed my advice and found an easily editable backend to build your website on, these updates should take no more than 2-3 hours for your organization to make. Thus, at a minimum, you should be investing 2-3 hours of staff time into updating your website per month, if not per week.

4. E-mail List

If you're going to be collecting e-mail addresses on your website, you'll need an easy way to allow people to give you their e-mail address (using an online form), and also an easy and secure way to store those addresses and send mass e-mails to your list. There are two great, and very affordable, solutions I recommend that you check out:

My top recommendation goes to AWeber. While fewer non-profits use them than Constant Contact, they offer, I think, a very powerful suite of tools that requires only minimal learning in order to be completely customizable.

My second-highest recommendation goes to the aforementioned Constant Contact, which is slightly easier to use but offers far less customization on e-mail templates and web forms to collect e-mail addresses.

5. Way to Process Donations

Finally, you will need a way to process donations that people make to you through your website. This means that you'll need a way for people to safely and securely enter their credit card information to process donations on your site.

If you already have a merchant account (a credit card processing account) through your bank for processing credit cards *offline*, talk with them to see if they have a solution for processing donations *online*, or use a service like Authorize.net which acts as an online "card swipe machine" for your offline merchant account.

If you don't already have a merchant account, there's probably no need to get one unless you are processing massive amounts of credit card donations. Instead, use a service like PayPal Web Payments, or Google Checkout, or a credit card processing service geared for non-profits, like Network for Good or CauseVox (which allows you to set up a separate, off-site donation page).

Now that we've gotten the basics out of the way, let's get into the good stuff... how can your organization raise exceptional money through your website? What are the tactics you can use – starting tomorrow – to turn your website into an essential part of your fundraising strategy?

The Money Is In the List – How to Get the E-mail!

As noted above, the money is in the list... the e-mail list. The main fundraising purpose of your website should be to get people to give you their e-mail address and permission to use it. How do you get your visitors to give you their e-mail addresses?

The best way is to copy what we do on The Fundraising Authority – by starting an e-newsletter for your non-profit and inviting people to sign-up for it. Tell your visitors you will be sending out a newsletter highlighting the issues you are working on and the people you are helping. Make it clear that the newsletter will only come out once per quarter or once per month, and that you won't sell, rent, or trade their e-mail address with any other person or organization.

You can also offer a special report or whitepaper in return for the e-mail address, either with or without a newsletter. Some organizations have also found success with offering free invitations to events in return for an e-mail address. Whatever you do or offer, make sure to ask for an e-mail address from your visitors.

My suggestion to you is that you ask for an e-mail address on every page of your site by placing an e-mail sign-up box on the top right hand corner of every page. Most e-mail list companies, including AWeber and Constant Contact, offer simple, copy and paste code for placing an e-mail sign-up box on your site. When someone fills out the box and clicks "Sign Up" they will automatically be added to your list.

You can also experiment with "pop-ups" and "pop-unders", those somewhat annoying boxes that pop up to ask people to sign-up for your e-mail list. The general consensus on those boxes is that they are effective in increasing your sign-up rate, but that some visitors will be very turned off by them. Most non-profits avoid using them, but your mileage may vary.

Many people have asked me what a good sign-up rate would be... I would say that if you are converting over 1% of your sites visitors into newsletter subscribers, you are on the right track, over 3% means you're doing really well, and over 5% means you are knocking it out of the ballpark.

Secondary Fundraising Purposes

Ok, we know that we have a primary fundraising purpose for our website: to get visitors to give us their e-mail addresses so that we can proactively communicate with them. We also know that we have a second, but somewhat less important, primary fundraising purpose for our website: to get visitors to click the "donate now" button to make an immediate gift to our non-profit.

Now, let's talk about the secondary fundraising purposes of your website – all of the things your website can do to support your fundraising operations, if the site is properly designed:

Information

One big thing your site can do to support fundraising is to offer compelling back-up information and resources to your prospects and donors. Many times, prospects will check out your organization's website *before making a gift*, to get a basic understanding of what you do, have their questions answered, and make sure that you are an organization they can trust. Likewise, many current donors will visit your site often to stay informed and make sure that they have made a wise investment.

Thus, you need to make sure that your website provides compelling content in an easy-to-understand format. You should include all of the basics about your organization: your mission and case statement, a listing of your staff and board, links to your public financial information and annual report, contact information, etc. You should also include compelling fundraising content: stories and testimonials from those you have helped, testimonials from donors on why they are glad to be part of your organization, videos, pictures, and stories that describe the good that you are currently doing in the world and what your goals are for the future.

Credibility and Social Proof

Earlier in this chapter, we talked a little about social proof. Social proof is a group of testimonials, social media followers, donor stories, etc. that "prove" that your organization is trustworthy and worthwhile because of the positive experiences that others have had with your non-profit.

Your website is a great place to offer social proof to prospects and donors. Include testimonials and references. Show pictures of happy donors, your offices (to show you are a real organization!) and your board and staff. Include links to press stories about your organization. In short, your website is a fantastic place to showcase any and all information that will add credibility to your organization.

<u>Two-Way Communication</u>

Finally, your website can be a good place to provide non-intimidating two-way communication opportunities to your donors and prospects. Include an e-mail contact form (and be sure to answer those e-mails that come in promptly and professionally). You can also include phone numbers, "chat with the staff" options, or even an "ask the Executive Director a question" page. All of these options make it easy for those with questions or concerns to receive an answer quickly and from the right person on your team.

Making it Easy to Give on Your Website

Have you ever visited a non-profit webpage and thought, "gee, I'd really like to make a donation... I just can't figure out how?" I know I have... and it is very frustrating... so frustrating, in fact, that most prospective donors will click away if they can't find an easy way to give on your site.

You need money. Donors want to give. Make it easy for them to do so:

<u>The Ubiquitous "Donate Now" Button</u>

Most non-profits have a "Donate Now" button on every page of their website... if you are one of the few that doesn't, you should. The ubiquitous Donate Now button ensures that no prospect ever has to leave the page in order to make a donation. The button is linked to your payment processor and allows donors to simply click and make a gift.

Your Donate Now button should be large enough to be easy to find, yet not so big that it is garish or takes over the whole page or navigation bar. The color, look, and feel of the button should fit in with the overall color, look, and feel of your site.

Giving Levels on Your Website

Another great way to make it easy to give on your website is to offer a number of different giving levels, just as you would in a direct mail campaign.

Many non-profits have their Donate Now buttons prominently displayed, but when people click on the link in order to donate, they are simply asked to enter the amount they want to give. Instead, offer your donors choices by placing "radio buttons" on your donation page that people can click to make varying levels of donations (e.g. $25 / $100 / $250 / $500 / $1,000 --- or whatever levels seem appropriate for your organization and your website).

Even better, tie the giving levels to concrete items or services your organization needs or offers. For example, if you are an affordable housing agency, you could say:

$25 – Covers move-in costs for one family
$100 – Provides one family with a utilities stipend for one month
$500 – Provides one family of 6 with a house for one month
$1,000 – Provides one family of 4 with a house for six months

Showing people that their donation will make a real, positive difference for a person, family, or the world at large will encourage them to not only make a donation, but to give more than they otherwise would.

Getting Traffic to Your Website

You've got your website up and running. It looks good, and is chock full of information about your organization. You're updating it regularly, offering a prominent "Donate Now!" button, and encouraging people who visit your site to sign-up for your e-mail newsletter. Now: how do you get people to visit your site to take advantage of all of those wonderful features? Here are four great ways to get traffic to your website:

#1 - Driving People to Your Website

The most basic thing your organization can and should be doing is driving people (donors, volunteers, prospects... anyone you can think of or come across) to your website. You can do this by making sure your website URL (your web address) is displayed prominently on anything you print or hand-out, by constantly encouraging your friends and supporters to "go online for more information," and by mentioning your website in press releases, interviews, during events, etc.

Take every opportunity you can to drive people to your website, and offer value there that will convince them to keep coming back.

#2 - Getting Links to Your Website

Another great way to drive traffic to your website is by getting other websites in your niche and your geographical area to link to your website. This will encourage visitors to *those* websites to click on the links to visit *your* website, and also offer additional SEO benefits (more on that below).

There are a number of effective ways you can get other sites to link to yours. The most effective (and also the most time consuming) is to personally call or e-mail the creators of other websites that have audiences that would likely be interested in what your website has to offer and to ask them to link to you. For example, if you run development for a small private high school, you might ask local news sites in your area as well as education blogs and websites run by your school's alumni to link to your site.

Another good way to get links to your site is to "guest post," which means that you write an article that appears on another website, along with a link to *your* site. For example, if you are doing development for a local hospital, someone at your hospital might write an article on "The Top 5 Ways to Avoid Getting Sick this Summer," which a local news site or blog agrees to post along with a link to your hospital's website. Reach out to local websites that might be interested in a guest post from you, and suggest some topics to whet their appetites.

A final way to get quality links to your site is by posting "link bait," extremely strong content and articles on your site that are so important or compelling that other sites link to them simply because they know that their readers will benefit from the information you are offering. Great link bait includes whitepapers, tip-sheets, research papers, and even photo galleries that are particularly captivating.

#3 - Search Engine Optimization (SEO)

Search engine optimization (SEO) is a tactic for making your website appealing to search engines like Google and Bing in such a way that your site appears at the top of the results for search queries that matter to your potential donors.

For example, if you are a homeless shelter in Cleveland, you want to appear in the first three results for searches like "homeless in Cleveland," "how to help the homeless," etc. Appearing at the top of the results for search queries is important for driving traffic because the vast majority of people who search for something on a search engine will click on one of the top three links that are shown in the search engine results pages (SERPs).

While the nitty-gritty of SEO is beyond the scope of this chapter (whole books are constantly being written and re-written on the changing tastes of the search engines) you should know that there are two basic ingredients that you need to focus on in order to get your website to appear in the top three results for appropriate search queries:

The first is *on page content*. When someone searches for "helping the homeless," the search engines want to show pages about "helping the homeless." Obvious, right? Thus, if you want to rank well for "helping the homeless," you will need to write an article (a complete webpage) about that topic, which includes the phrase "helping the homeless" several times.

The second factor in strong SEO is *inbound links.* The search engines want to know that not only is your article about the topic people are looking for, but also that other people have found your website useful. The metric they use to determine this is whether or not other websites have linked to you, presumably because they found your information worthwhile. Thus, the more links you get to your site using the tactics mentioned in #2 above, the higher your page will rank in the search engines, and the more people will visit your site.

#4 – Social Media Traffic

Later in this chapter, we will be talking in depth about using social networks like Facebook, Twitter, and Google+ to drive fundraising for your non-profit. One of the primary ways to use social networks is to drive traffic to your online hub, which is your organization's website. This is done by constantly including links to various pages on your site in the information you send out over social networks. Doing so can provide a significant boost to your traffic numbers. More information on how to do this is in the section on social media below.

How to Raise More Money through E-Mail

In the previous section, we focused on raising money through your organization's website – but we still spent a lot of time talking about e-mail, because, as we mentioned above, getting permission to stay in touch with prospects through e-mail should be the single biggest focus of your organization's online fundraising activities.

In this section, we're going to move from the website side of the equation over to the e-mail side. We're going to discuss how to find even more e-mail addresses for potential supporters *offline*, as well as the mechanics of raising money through e-mail. Then, we'll talk about what your e-mail communications should look like, and what the purposes of your various e-mails should be.

Remember: e-mail is an incredibly important mechanism for your fundraising operation because it is one of the few online ways you can actively reach out to your supporters, and be sure that a significant portion of those that you reach out to will see your message. Your e-mails are important for fundraising both because you can raise money right through e-mail (more on that in a minute), and also because your e-mail communications will reinforce your other messages to donors and are an inexpensive method for keeping your donors up to date.

Ways to Build Your E-Mail List Offline

Note that throughout this section, I will refer to your e-mail list as your "newsletter list." While you don't have to have an e-mail newsletter in order to collect e-mail addresses, I have found it to be the easiest and most effective way. Basically, you have three options when asking people to give you their permission to e-mail them. You can (a) ask them to sign-up to get fundraising letters, (b) ask them to sign-up to receive periodic updates, or (c) ask them to sign-up for your newsletter. In my experience, (c) is the most appealing option to your website's visitors.

As noted above, the largest share of your e-mail newsletter subscribers will likely come from your website, including all of the "sign-up boxes" you scatter across your site asking people to get on your newsletter list. That being said, let's take a look at a couple of other ways you can add e-mail addresses to your list:

Donor E-Mail Addresses

Every time you send out a donor solicitation with a reply card, donor reply envelope, or a donor information sheet, be sure to include a spot that asks for an e-mail address. You'll want to do everything you can to make sure that as many of your donors as possible are signed up for your e-mail newsletter list.

Of course, just because someone puts their e-mail address on your donor reply card, it doesn't mean that they are giving you permission to e-mail them every month – they may think you only need it "for your records" or for a tax receipt for their donation. Thus, you have to make a note on your reply cards / envelopes that allows you to add the donor to your newsletter list. There are several ways you can do this. You can include a checkbox that says something like "Please send me your monthly e-newsletter," or, my favorite, which is simply to include a note that all donors will receive a free subscription to the organization's monthly e-mail newsletter as a thank you for their generous gift.

Newsletter Sign-Up Sheets

You'll also want to capture e-mail addresses (and permission to use them) at all of your organization's events (both fundraising events *and* non-fundraising events). You can do this by making sure to ask for an e-mail address (and permission to use it, as noted above) whenever you register attendees, and also by placing e-newsletter sign-up sheets around your events that ask guests to write down their name and e-mail address in order to sign-up for the newsletter.

Forwarded Newsletters

A third way to gain additional newsletter subscribers, though it isn't really an "offline" method, per se, is to make sure that there is an easy way to sign-up for your newsletter from within your newsletters and other e-mails themselves. You may be thinking, "if I am only sending out my newsletter to people who subscribed for it, why would I need to include a "Subscribe to this Newsletter for Free" link in each newsletter? The answer, of course, is forwards.

If your e-mail content is compelling enough, your subscribers may, from time to time, forward you newsletter on to friends, family, or colleagues who might be interested in what you have to say... when they do, if you have a "Subscribe" button or link in your newsletter, some portion of the recipients of these forwards will sign-up to receive further updates. Make it easy for them to do so! Every little bit helps...

A Word about Spam and Rented Lists

Often, organizations will add people to their e-mail newsletter lists that they think would enjoy receiving the newsletter. These include friends of the organization, volunteers, local reporters and philanthropists, friends of the staff, etc. The thinking is that these are people who wouldn't mind receiving the information or would probably find it valuable… so why not add them?

Don't make this mistake. Over the past decade and a half, as e-mail newsletters and communications have become ubiquitous, people have become hyper-sensitive to SPAM. Most people wage a constant battle to keep spam e-mails out of their inboxes, cluttering up what has become a valuable personal space. If you add people to your list willy-nilly, without receiving their permission to do so, you *will* make people mad. They *will* complain, or even worse, *not complain*, and instead secretly seethe that you are sending spam, and thus be turned off from your organization forever.

Likewise, I always advise against using rented e-mail lists. There are many list brokers out there who will sell you "opt-in" e-mail lists that you can send a mailing to, claiming that the people on the lists have agreed to receive e-mail newsletters from organizations like yours. While this may or may not be true, I can guarantee you that renting these lists are a waste of money for two reasons:

First, many of the people on the list, even if they initially agreed to receive e-mails, will see your mailing as spam.

Second, the people on these lists are *not* good prospects for your organization. Think about it – even if they *did* agree to receive e-mails from non-profits, how many organizations have bought this list and sent them e-mails? A dozen? A hundred? Do you really think the recipients are making donations to all (or most… or any…) of the non-profits that are e-mailing them?

Don't spam, and don't use rented e-mail lists.

How Do I Raise Money Through E-Mail?

So... how exactly do you raise money through e-mail? There are basically two different ways you can collect donations through your e-mails:

The first is by including a link that leads directly to the payment page... the page where people enter their credit card information. The payment processor you choose to process credit card donations can provide you with a link that you can use in your e-mails that will send people directly to this page. The benefit of using this method is that it takes less clicks to get the donation, so you won't lose people by asking them to click through two pages.

If you use this method, just be sure that the link you provide them says something like:

"Donate Now!"

(where the words are linked to the payment page) and not something like:

"To Donate Now, Click Here: http://www.PaymentSite.com/NN23376/payment/creditcard?89732"

People don't trust clicking on long URL's like that, and it will cut down on your response rate.

The second method for collecting donations through your e-mails is to send people to a special page on your website that talks more about why you need the money, and which also has a "Donate Now!" link that sends people to the payment page.

The downside of this method is that donors have to click through two pages to make a donation (first clicking from the e-mail to your website, then clicking from your website to the payment processing page), and some will inevitably drop off before making that second click. The benefit of using this method is that your webpage can provide more detail about the ask, including an up-to-the-minute fundraising thermometer, pictures, video, and other things your e-mail can't provide.

My suggestion is that when you're making simple asks, such as for general donations, you send people directly to the payment processing page, and when you're making more complicated asks with giving levels or tied to a campaign or an event, you send people first to a page on your site that talks more about the ask and levels, and then sends people to make a donation.

As with all types of development communications, e-mail fundraising is part science, part art form. In this section, we'll take a look at what types of communication you should send out to your e-mail list, how frequently you should contact them, and how to make your e-mail fundraising letters deliver strong results.

Types of E-Mail Communications

Just as your "snail mail" communications with prospects and donors should not be all fundraising letters, so your e-mail communications with prospects and donors should not be all asks. If they are, people will soon tune you out.

Similarly, if your e-newsletter subscribers only hear from you once or twice per year, they will either forget that they signed up for your newsletter and think you are sending spam, or they will not feel a strong enough connection with your organization to encourage them to make a gift when you do send an ask.

Thus, the best practice for e-mail communications for your non-profit is to send out a mix of e-mail communications to your list, including a blend of the following:

Regularly Scheduled Newsletters

Your e-newsletters form the basis of your e-mail communications strategy. These newsletters should include a nice mix of content including information on the work you are doing, events you are holding, staff and client profiles, etc. Each newsletter should include 1-2 pictures, and anywhere from 3-7 articles of varying lengths.

No more than 1 of these articles should be about fundraising campaigns or events, or else you run the risk of having your newsletters be perceived as fundraising letters. They're not. Instead, think of them as an inexpensive way to stay in touch with your friends, donors, and volunteers as well as to prime the pump for future asks.

I have found that newsletters work best when they are delivered at regular intervals, so that your prospects and donors know when to expect them. You should send out an e-newsletter at least quarterly, and no more than monthly.

Special E-Blasts

From time to time, you may have special announcements you want to make or opportunities you want to mention to your newsletter list. Do this through the use of one-time "E-Blasts," which are basically short newsletters that you send out to your list on an infrequent basis. I would recommend not sending more than 2 or 3 of these per year, or else they will start to lose some of the attention recipients give them as something "special."

Event Invitations and Announcements

Have a seminar coming up? Holding a walk-a-thon, fundraising event, roundtable, open house, tour, or other in-person event? Use your newsletter list to publicize the event by sending out event invitations or announcements.

I would generally suggest that you limit stand-alone event announcements/invitations to no more than 2 or 3 times per year, to avoid overkill. Thus, use them only for your biggest events. For other events, simply include a listing in your regularly scheduled e-newsletters.

Volunteer Opportunities

Many non-profits have found great success with sending out quarterly or yearly e-mails listing volunteer opportunities available with their organization. Sending out such e-mails will also bolster fundraising by allowing prospects multiple ways to get more connected and feel like part of your team.

Fundraising E-Mails

Last, but certainly not least, are fundraising e-mails. One of the main goals for your e-mail communication program is to raise money for your organization, so you will need to include a mix of fundraising e-mails as part of your strategy. Remember, people don't give unless they are asked.

Types of Fundraising E-Mails

There are several types of fundraising e-mails you can send out to your e-mail list. These include:

Connected Appeals

Connected appeals are e-mail fundraising letters that are sent out in conjunction with a larger offline fundraising campaign. For example, you may send out an e-mail ask as part of your annual appeal, which also includes phone calls and snail mail letters. Likewise, you may be running a capital or endowment campaign utilizing multiple online and offline asking strategies, and decide to include an e-mail ask as part of that appeal.

In general, connected appeals work best when they are well coordinated with the other parts of the appeal, so that the e-mail's content, message, look and feel all match up with the other online and offline portions of that fundraising effort.

Non-Connected (E-Only Appeals)

Non-connected appeals (also called e-only appeals) are appeals that are not being run as part of a larger online & offline appeal, and instead are a stand-alone appeal being run through e-mail, or in conjunction with a supporting webpage. For these appeals, you will generally want to send more than one e-mail to pitch the effort, and many organizations send out as many as 4 or 5 separate e-mails over the course of 1-4 weeks while running non-connected appeals.

Online Fundraising Campaigns

Very similar in nature to non-connected appeals, online fundraising campaigns are online fundraising efforts that combine a number of different strategies into an all-encompassing fundraising effort – using things like your website, social media networks, crowd-funding sites, and even publicity through online blogs and news sites to drive donors to make donations to your online fundraising campaign.

Events

Your organization can and should use e-mail to directly sell tickets and small sponsorships to your fundraising events.

Should You Include a Donate Now Button on Every E-Mail?

Yes. My experience has shown that every e-mail you send out should include a "Donate Now" link that leads to your payment processing page, including your non-fundraising e-mails. You don't want the donate button to take over the page or be the first thing people see (otherwise they will think they are getting bombarded with fundraising e-mails), but you do want to make sure that if someone is moved by one of your e-mails and wants to give, they can find a quick way to do so by clicking a button or a link.

This means that each of your fundraising newsletters and e-blasts should include a Donate Now button or link on the navigation bar, in the sidebar, or under the content that allows people to give. It also means that your staff should include a way for people to make a donation as part of their e-mail signatures that are automatically added to every e-mail they send out. This can be something as simple as including the staff member's contact information, and then, at the bottom, including a link to your payment processing page that says:

"Save Lives. Make a Donation to Hope for Children Today."

...or whatever is appropriate for your organization. You would be surprised how many donations come in this way. It won't fund your whole organization, but you will add new donors and revenue that you otherwise never would have found for your non-profit.

How Frequently Should You Contact Your E-Mail List? What Should the Mix Be?

The reason that I included a list of all the different types of e-mail communications and fundraising e-mails you can send out in the sections above is because it is imperative that you include a wide-ranging mix as part of your e-mail strategy.

If the only thing your subscribers ever receive from you is the same old thing: a newsletter with a header, three articles, and a picture... they will tune you out. Likewise, if the only type of fundraising e-mail your subscribers ever see is a four paragraph fundraising letter, they will quickly tune them out after the second or third one they see.

To keep people's attention online, you need to mix things up and include lots of different types of communications... maybe sending out a regular newsletter, some free event invitations, a special announcement blast, running an online fundraising campaign, etc... keeping things different makes your e-mails interesting for your subscribers.

My recommendation is that you stay in touch with your e-mail newsletter list at least monthly, if possible, and e-mail them no more than twice per month, on average. If you can't e-mail them at least quarterly, then running an e-mail list is likely a waste of time, as anything less than that will not create the relationship or connection that you will need to turn your subscribers into donors.

Furthermore, I suggest that you maintain, at the very minimum, at least a 3-1 ratio in your e-mails, meaning that you send out at least 3 non-fundraising e-mail communications for every fundraising e-ask that you send out. This ensures that your subscribers feel they are getting real value from your content, and not just getting bombarded by fundraising asks.

Staying in touch via e-mail does *not* need to take up days and days of staff time. With a little practice and experience, you can easily stay in touch with your donors via e-mail on a monthly basis and not use up more than 4-6 hours of staff time per month to do it.

Writing E-Mail Fundraising Letters that Produce Results

Ok, we know that not every e-communication should be an ask, and that we need to stay in touch with our subscribers regularly with a good mix of content styles and asks. What do good, high-producing e-mail fundraising letters look like? What are the best practices to get the best results? While your e-mail fundraising letters will vary depending on whether they are part of a coordinated campaign, selling tickets for an event, etc., there are some basic rules of thumb that will allow you to see maximum results with your e-mail fundraising efforts:

Similarities to Offline Direct Mail

In many ways, e-mail fundraising letters are similar to offline fundraising letters. Just as with offline letters, e-mail fundraising letters must be compelling and emotional. Remember, for your readers – your organization and your mission matters! Tell people stories that tug on the heart strings, that make them cry. In fundraising letters, people don't want to hear a list of boring statistics and facts. Sure, one or two surprising or super-compelling facts might make all the difference. But a list of twelve percentages with footnotes supporting them? Not compelling when sent as part of as fundraising letter.

Instead, tell stories, use charts, make people cry. Think: if I had 30 seconds to tell someone about my non-profit, and the success of our group depended on that one person writing a check on the spot... what would I say? Then write that pitch as your first draft.

The second key similarity with offline fundraising mail is: write your e-mail in such a way that your compelling content gets read. People are busy. Even if they aren't really busy, most people think they are. Very few people think they have the time to read through your fundraising e-mail. Most people will skim your e-mail to see if it is worth reading. Where do they look to make their decisions? The e-mail subject and first sentence, the pictures, the headlines and bolded or underlined words, and the P.S. That's it... just 20-30 second of skimming.

How do you capitalize on this tendency? First, give them lots to skim. Use section headlines, a great subject and opening sentence and P.S., pictures, and bolded/underlined words. Then, make sure that all of this "skim-able" content works together to tell the entire story of your letter. Ask yourself: if someone only skimmed my letter, using the items listed above, would they know what I am saying? Would they "get" the whole story?

Differences from Offline Direct Mail

The primary difference between offline fundraising letters and e-mail fundraising letters is length. For many organizations, long (or super-long) snail-mail fundraising letters work. Some organizations send 3, 4, or even 5 page fundraising letters and know that their constituencies appreciate the length because they make money with these letters.

The rule online is less, less, less. I have never seen an e-mail fundraising letter that was the equivalent of a 4 page offline letter get read. When writing online fundraising e-mails, keep it relatively short – I would suggest trying to keep your e-mail asks to 400 words or less. Anything more than that, and people simply won't want to read it. If necessary, you can include links to your website to explain additional information, but for the actual e-mail, keep it short and to the point.

The Ask

Remember – as we said earlier, people don't give unless they are asked. If you are sending out an e-mail fundraising letter, be sure it includes a clear, concise, and understandable ask. Tell people that you need money. Tell them how much you need and why you need it. Then make an ask, by asking the reader to click on a button or link to donate now. Make the button or link big and bold, and don't be shy about asking – your mission matters, and you need money to carry out the good work that your organization does!

How to Raise More Money through Social Media

Facebook. Twitter. LinkedIn. Google+. How can your non-profit harness the power of these and other social networks, and their billions (yes, billions) or members, to help you raise money? In this section we're talking all about raising money through social networks.

First, we'll define social networks, talk about how to get started on these sites, and discuss what social networks you should be on. Then, we'll look at the keys to successfully using social networks for fundraising at your non-profit, how to build a following on social networks, how to effectively communicate through this medium, and how to run fundraising campaigns through social media. Let's get started…

What Do We Mean by "Social Networks" and "Social Media?"

A "social network" is an online site or platform that exists to connect people online. These sites usually connect people through shared interests, activities, or real-life (offline) relationships. Generally, social networking sites allow people to set up a profile, connect that profile to other users, and then share information, links, pictures, etc. between themselves and their connections.

The most popular social networks in the world are Facebook, Twitter, Google+ and LinkedIn. There are dozens of other social networks as well. Some are very popular and widespread in certain areas (for example, Orkut is big in Brazil and Mixi is popular in Asia). New networks pop-up often (for example, Pinterest has recently gotten lots of traction in Western nations).

"Social media" is an umbrella term that encompasses all of these social networking sites.

Should My Non-Profit Really Care About Social Media?

The short answer is: *Yes. Your organization should care about social media.*

Fifteen years ago, non-profits were asking the same thing about websites… "Do we really need one?" "Isn't this just a flash in the pan?" "Our thing is direct mail. People never get tired of getting letters."

Can you imagine an organization in 2013 asking whether or not they needed a website? Over the course of just 10-15 years, websites (and e-mail) have allowed non-profits to reach more prospects, volunteers, and donors than ever before, and to do it quickly and cost-effectively.

The reason that websites became so important is because, starting in the late 1990's and accelerating at the turn of the millennium, people around the world started to spend so much time online. As the old saying goes, if you want to catch fish, you have to go where the fish are.

The same thing is true for social networks today. Over 1 billion people around the world are now using social networks. In the developed world, the vast majority of your target audience is likely to be active on social media sites. Social networks provide a quick, cheap, and easy way for people to stay in touch with each other, share what they like, and keep abreast of each other's lives. Similarly, social networks provide a quick, cheap, and easy way for *your non-profit* to stay in touch with your donors, prospects, and friends.

Your organization can and should be active on social media.

Important Disclaimer: You Don't Own Your Social Media Profiles and Followers

This is very, very important to understand: unlike your website, you don't really own your social media profiles and followers. Social networking sites may act like you do, but you don't. You don't own your Facebook profile, Facebook does. The same goes for Twitter and every other social network out there.

If a social networking company thinks (rightly or wrongly) that you have violated their terms of service, they can disable your account at any time. You can lose any information you keep on their servers, including your content and your followers' list. The sites can change the rules at any time, delete accounts at any time, or decide they don't want non-profits on their site.

Some of this sounds outlandish and yes, it probably is unlikely that your profile will be disabled or deleted from a social networking site, but it is important to understand that is can happen. There are many, many instances where companies, individuals, and organizations have had their social profiles and pages disabled or deleted for various reasons, including times when the sites themselves (and not the people or organizations) were clearly in the wrong.

This being said, you should still be active on social media. Why? Because the opportunity is there -- the people are there – and *you* have to be there. Of course, you should try to do everything you can to make sure your time isn't wasted on each site. You can do this by making sure you follow each network's terms of service, and most importantly, you can do this by <u>constantly driving people from the social network back to your site</u>.

This is something most non-profits (and many for-profit companies) don't understand. One of the primary purposes of your social media activity is to drive people back to your site using the links that you post. You want people to come to your site and bookmark it, know where it is, and sign up for your e-mail newsletter. Then, you will truly "own" that contact, and nothing a social network does can disable that relationship. Remember: actively drive people from your social networks back to your site by regularly posting interesting links back to your website's content.

What Social Networks Should Our Organization Be Active On?

One of the first questions non-profits generally ask me when talking about getting online is: what social networks should we be on? The answer I give comes down to two guidelines:

<u>Go Where Your Prospects Are</u>

Find out where your prospects hang out online. If you're in the English-speaking world, they will likely be on Twitter and Facebook, at a minimum. In many first-world nations, business people can also be found on LinkedIn. Some communities, including photographers, "geeks" (I say that with a positive connotation, meaning someone who is interested in technology and online activities), and non-profit staffers can be found in large numbers on Google+. In non-English speaking countries, your prospects and donors may be found on other sites.

Take some time to talk with your board, staff, donors and friends to find out what sites they are active on online. Then go where the fish are...

Go Where Your Resources Allow

If you're a one person development shop, you don't have time to be on 20 different social media sites. But even though you're busy, you *do* have time to be on two or three. No matter what you find out in your research phase, don't bite off more than you can chew. In order to be successful with fundraising on social networks, you need to be *active* on the sites where you choose to establish a presence (more on this later) so take your time and don't get on more sites than you can handle.

How Do We Get Started With Social Networks?

Social media sites generally go to great lengths to make sure that their sites are easy to get started on... For most sites, you simply go to the site and click the "Sign Up" button. Then, you fill out your profile. Filling the profile out is important, because this is the image most people on the site will have of your non-profit... so make sure it is professional, personal, and uses appropriate photos.

Once your profile is complete, use the tools available on the site to "connect" with the people you already know on the site – your board members, staff, donors, volunteers, etc. This will provide a base of 10-100 followers / connections for your organization's profile, and you can grow from there.

Then, it's off to the races – start posting good content, and you're on your way.

Now that you understand what social networks are, how you can get started with them and what sites you should be on, let's take a look at how you can raise more money through social networking...

The Four Goals of Your Social Networking Activity

Your ultimate objective in using social networks for your non-profit is to raise money. Here are the four main goals you should keep in mind for your social media activity that will allow you to raise more money and find new prospects on the site:

#1 – Drive People Back to Your Site

Remember what we said above: your most important activity on social networking sites should be to drive people back to your website. While you want to connect with as many people as possible on each social media site, you want to be sure to direct them back to your own site as often as possible.

I have seen far too many non-profits that have pushed their Facebook profiles so hard that when their donors think about finding information about the non-profit online, they immediately go to Facebook. This is a big mistake on the part of the non-profit. When people think about your online presence, they should think WEBSITE first. Your website should be such a wealth of information, photos, videos, whitepapers, etc. that they don't think of going to social sites first.

Sure, you want to connect with people on social sites and get them to share the information you are providing, but it is ALL for the purpose of driving people back to your organization's website.

#2 – Connect with New Prospects

The second main activity you want to conduct on social networking sites is connecting with new prospects. The best way to do this is to get your current supporters and followers on the site to hit the "share" button – that is, you want to post such interesting, entertaining or compelling items on your social media sites that people want to share it with their own followers and friends on the site. This will help you grow your presence on the site and will encourage new prospects to follow you.

As noted above, the best way to get people to share what you are posting is to post extremely compelling content. Another great way is to simply *ask* your supporters to share some of your content with their own circles and networks online. Many times, people will happily do so. You don't want to do this with every post, but from time to time, consider sending out a message to some of your supporters like this:

"I just tweeted out an important message about our event this weekend. Would you consider retweeting it to your friends? This is our most important event of the year! Thanks in advance for your help!"

I have found that one of the best ways to get people sharing what you are posting is to launch a "Social Media Leadership Team" or "Social Networking Committee" for your non-profit. The idea is to gather a group of your supporters who are very active on social networks, and get them to commit to share or repost a couple of your items per month. Treat this group like any other committee, with occasional meetings, lots of appreciation and recognition, etc.

#3 – Stay in Touch with Current Donors

The third main goal of your social networking activity is to stay in touch with current donors. Social sites are a great way to unobtrusively stay "front of mind" with your donors. By sharing content on these sites on a regular basis, your donors will have a constant reminder of your good work and their commitment to be part of your team.

Be sure to remind your donors about your social networking profiles on a regular basis and spend time building connections on each site with your team of donors and volunteers.

#4 – Maintain an Active Conversation On-Site

The fourth and final primary goal of your social networking activity is to maintain an active conversation on each social media site where you are engaged. This means allowing people to send you messages on the site, and responding in a timely manner. It also means asking interesting questions, seeking advice, and listening to what people have to say on those sites.

Why? Because it shows you are a real, caring organization, it will help you reach new people (people are drawn to conversations and questions, and people like to share content like this) and it will provide a valuable way to "keep your ear to the ground" and see what people are saying / thinking about your non-profit.

How Much Time Does Our Organization Need to Spend on Social Networks?

The number one reason why many non-profits are not using social media is because they don't understand what social networks are or how to use them. Hopefully, we're clearing up that confusion in this chapter.

The second main reason why many organizations aren't using social media is because they worry that it will take too much time. I want to dispel that myth right now: social networks do *not* have to take a ton of time.

Yes, social networks *can* take a lot of time... in fact, if you let them, they can take up your entire day. But that's if you let yourself get sucked in to playing games, goofing around, blindly following links, etc. Don't let that happen and don't let your staff tell you that they need to spend three hours a day on Facebook. They don't.

I would suggest to you that, in order to meet the minimum requirements of being "active" on a site, you need to spend 15 minutes per day, per social network. Thus, if your non-profit is active on two social networks, you would need to spend 30 minutes per day on social media. If you are active on five social networks, you would need to spend an hour and 15 minutes per day on the sites.

What should you do during those 15 minutes per day, per site? Until you get comfortable enough with the site to vary your schedule, I would suggest using the following 15 minute routine:

- Checking to see if anyone mentioned your organization, as well as seeing if any of the people you are following posted anything that you might want to repost: 5 minutes

- Seeing who your new followers are, following them back (if appropriate) and looking for new prospects to follow: 5 minutes

- Posting an interesting thought, link to another site, or a link back to your organization's website: 5 minutes

Yes, you can spend 2 or 3 times as long per activity, per site, but you don't have to if you don't want to – you can do each of these items "well enough" (but not perfect) in just 5 minutes per item, or 15 minutes per site.

The Five Keys to Successful Social Network Fundraising

Now that we've talked about the goals for your activity on social networking sites, let's take a look at the five keys to making sure that your activity successfully connects you with current and new donors, and ultimately helps generate new gifts for your organization:

#1 – Be Active

You have to maintain an active presence on each site you are targeting, or else you won't be successful. This means, at the very minimum, that you visit each site at least three times per week and post or tweet or link to a new item. Ideally, you will be on each of the social networks you are targeting once per day, every day, Monday through Friday.

#2 – Be Personal

The best way to connect with people on social networking sites is to be personal, not "corporate." Have the person who handles the social networks for your non-profit post his or her picture, tell their name, and post in the first person. If you post and interact as an anonymous corporate-like entity, you will find people will engage with you far less online.

#3 – Have a Goal (Don't Just "Connect for the Sake of Connecting")

Far too many self-appointed social media "gurus" will tell you that you should be active on social networks just to "have a presence." "Connect for the sake of connection," they will tell you. "Listen, learn, be there."

Hogwash.

You're too busy to be doing work (and it *is* work, when done right) for the sake of "connecting." Have a goal for your social networking time. Do you want to raise money? Find new volunteers? Build buzz for your organization? All of these are respectable goals. Go into your social networking work with a goal in the back of your mind and then work towards completing that goal successfully.

#4 – Link to Your Site Often

I know I have said it a number of times, but I am going to say it again, because it is so important – link to your own site often. Send out stories and articles from your own website often. Get people to follow you back to your website, sign-up for your e-newsletter, and donate to your organization. One out of every three things you post should be a link back to some compelling content on your own site.

#5 – Become an Authority

One great way to help you connect with new people is to be seen as an authority in your non-profit's area of expertise. If you run a soup kitchen and notice that there is an ongoing conversation about homelessness, jump in. Point people back to that paper your organization released on the causes of homelessness, and offer to answer any questions people may have.

Be seen as an authority by joining the conversation on the social networks you are targeting, and more people will follow you and connect with you and with your organization.

How to Raise Money through Social Networks

Remember, people only give when they are asked… this is as true on social networks as anywhere else. In order to raise money on social media, you have to make asks. These asks should only happen occasionally. Just as with e-mail, you'll want to maintain a good ratio between the non-ask information you send out and the asks you make. If you're active every day on a site, you wouldn't want to send out an ask more than once per month, and once every 6-8 weeks would be preferable.

For the purposes of timing, you can consider multiple asks for the same campaign as one "ask." This means that if you're running a fundraising campaign on Twitter, you can send out 10 tweets about it over the course of a week. You don't need to wait 6-8 weeks after the first tweet to send out a follow-up. If, however, you send out tweets about your annual campaign and then want to send out some tweets asking for donations to your annual event, you *should* wait 4, 6, or 8 weeks before sending out this next "round" of asks.

Where the Transaction Happens

It's important to note that the actual financial transaction doesn't happen on the social networking site – it happens on your own website. This means, in most cases, that your Donate Now button and payment processing page will *not* be on the social media site – instead, you will put an ask on your social media page, and/or send it out to your followers, and send people back to your own website to make the donation. In other words…

On Social Networks, You Fundraise Through Links

You send out an ask by sending out a link to a page on your website that tells more about the ask, and that includes a link or button people can click on to donate. So, you might send out a tweet that says something like:

"Help us save 20,000 acres from deforestation. Join the campaign for 20,000 today: http://www.LINKTOYOURPAGE.com"

Your asks on social media can be part of an larger fundraising effort, such as when you are running an annual campaign and you send out asks for it over Twitter and Facebook, in addition to through e-mail, direct mail and phone calls, or your asks on social sites can be for a social-only campaign.

Either way, because space and attention on social networks is hyper-limited, I suggest that you ALWAYS set up a page on your website that explains your ask in further detail, provides contact information, reiterates the ask, and provides a Donate Now button to allow people to make their donation immediately. Then, direct all of your social media links about that ask to the special ask page you have set up for the campaign on your non-profit's website.

How to Raise More Money through Crowd-Funding

Let's turn our attention to one of the real frontiers in online fundraising, something that has become very popular recently, and looks to be taking its place among the other high-impact online fundraising strategies. The name of this new kid on the block is *crowd-funding*

What is Crowd-Funding?

If you have never heard of crowd-funding before, I want you to stop what you are doing, open a web browser and visit Indiegogo.com - Go ahead, click over and when you get there, click on "Browse Campaigns." Take 15 minutes and look around. I'll be waiting right here when you're done.

Did you do it? Great. What you just browsed were examples of crowd-funding campaigns, some geared at raising money for non-profits, some not.

So... what is crowd-funding? Simply put, crowd-funding is the process by which certain websites offer the chance for businesses, designers, non-profits, political campaigns and others to post a request for money, along with a description of what the money is needed for and what the donors will get in return for their donation, and then raise money from any number of people in increments from $1 to $10,000 and beyond.

Sound crazy or unreal? It's not. Here are some very real examples of projects that have been successfully crowd-funded over the past few years:

The Pebble Watch

For-Profit Example – received over $10,000,000 (that's 10 MILLION DOLLARS) in funding from 68,000+ funders to launch a new iPhone and Android connected watch.

The Marc Doty Fundraiser

Non-Profit Example – raised over $84,000 to pay medical bills for an individual diagnosed with cancer.

One for My Baby Fundraiser

Arts Example – raised over $67,000 from 345 people to launch a new show in New York City.

Let's Give Karen the Bus Monitor a Vacation

Non-Profit Example – raised a whopping $600,000+ to send a bedraggled and abused bus monitor on the vacation of a lifetime. (Seriously). Raised so much, in fact, that she decided to retire with the money.

Think about the amounts that were raised in those crowd-funding campaigns, and you'll get a good feel for the amounts of money that organizations and individuals are raising through crowd-funding.

How Does Crowd Funding Work for Non-Profits?

The process of crowd-funding is deceptively simple for non-profit organizations:

- First, the non-profit picks a project that they would like to fund through crowd-funding.

- Then, the organization chooses a crowd-funding website that meets their needs.

- Third, the charity writes a compelling page about the project, posts a video, photos, or both, and lists both how much they would like to raise as well as the perks or donor benefits that people will receive in return for donating at various levels.

- Finally, the non-profit launches the crowd-funding campaign, promotes it as best as possible, and waits for the results.

Please note that your non-profit should check with a qualified legal advisor before beginning your crowd-funding effort to ensure that you are complying with any state-level fundraising registration rules or other requirements.

Funding Types

It is important to note that there are two main funding types for crowd-funding campaigns. The first is "defined funding," under which you set a fundraising goal and only receive the money if you reach the amount of your goal in pledges. The second type is "flexible funding," in which you receive any amount pledged, even if your total pledges don't reach your overall goal.

Different crowd funding websites offer different funding types, and some even offer more than one type and allow your organization to choose which you would like to use.

What are the Major Crowd-Funding Websites?

Given the recent popularity of crowd-funding, there are now several hundred crowd-funding sites that have popped up to cater to the needs of both for-profit and non-profit fundraisers. Most don't have enough traffic to make them worth your while. Here are the crowd-funding sites with the most traffic and which deserve your consideration for your next crowd-funding campaign:

Kickstarter – the largest and best-known crowd-fundraising site. Has a strong emphasis on business / for-profit / product design projects, but does host a significant number of non-profit fine arts, indie music, and publishing projects.

Indiegogo – A well-known crowd-funding site focused, in large part, on the arts. Hosts many non-profit arts projects, particularly in the theatre, music, and visual arts niches.

Fundly – Non-profit-only crowd-funding site that allows charities to raise money easily, including letting your supporters set up their own fundraising pages on your behalf.

CauseVox – Another crowd-funding site focused on non-profits.

Fundraise.com – Charity-focused crowd-funding site that allows organizations to set-up and publicize flexible funding campaigns.

Before deciding on a crowd-funding platform for your next fundraising project, check out each of the five major crowd-funding sites linked above and look at their variable fee-structures, marketing opportunities, and project restrictions to see which is right for you.

Is Crowd-Funding Right for Your Non-Profit?

Honestly, I believe that there are very few non-profit organizations that couldn't benefit from crowd-funding. So the answer is yes, it is highly likely that your organization should take a shot at running a crowd-funding campaign this year. My advice to you is to pick a mid-level project you need help funding, and use it to give crowd-funding a shot this year.

If you're contemplating running a crowd-funding campaign, you should know that running a successful campaign is both an art and a science. In the next section, we're going to take a look at how you can make sure your crowd-fundraising efforts are successful.

The Components of Your Campaign

One of the most important things you can do to ensure the success of your crowd-funding campaign is develop a project page that is emotionally compelling and draws people in to donate. In order to do that, you'll need to optimize each of the five main components of your project listing:

The Project

First, you'll need to choose a project that you want to fund through crowd-sourcing. If this is your first crowd campaign, I would suggest starting with a mid-level project, something in the $5,000-$10,000 range.

As you'll see later in this chapter, a portion of the money you raise through this campaign will come through your own current donors, so think through how much you think you will be able to raise for the campaign through your own list. Ideally, you should know that your e-mail and online lists will donate at least 25% of your funding goal. Thus, if your goal is $10,000 you should be reasonably certain that your own donor base will be willing to donate at least $2,500 through the crowd-funding campaign.

If you are a very small non-profit, you may need to start with a smaller campaign in the $2,000-$5,000 range. If you're a very large non-profit, you may be able to start higher, in the $25,000+ range. But be careful... even though there have been lots of successful crowd-funding campaigns for non-profits over the past couple of years, only a small percentage of them have raised in excess of $25,000.

The project you choose should be concrete and easy to understand for your potential donors. Remember: many people will be on the site browsing and they won't want to spend 45 minutes trying to figure out what your project is all about. The project you choose should be easily explained and should be able to be broken down into giving levels that make sense based on what the project entails.

The Funding Goal

As mentioned above, the funding goal should make sense based on the project size and the size of your non-profit. If you really want to raise funding for a larger project, but you don't think you have the donor base to pull it off, you can always raise just a portion of the total fundraising goal for the project through crowd-funding.

For example, let's say you need to raise $100,000 to open a new health clinic, but you realize that your donor base online probably couldn't support that size goal. That's ok – instead, launch a $20,000 crowd-funding campaign to pay for building renovations… make that your project, and leave the remainder of the overall $100,000 project costs for your other offline fundraising activities.

Your ultimate goal should be to raise 100% or more of your funding goal for the project – meaning that you don't want to launch a $50,000 project and only raise $17,000. Instead, launch a $15,000 project, and that $17,000 will look amazing – you'll have exceeded your goal, which will build your organization's credibility on the crowd-funding site you are using, making future projects that much more doable.

The Video

A video is perhaps the most important part of your crowd-funding campaign's project page. Every super-successful project on sites like Kickstarter and Indiegogo features a well-produced video.

Now, when I say well-produced, I'm not saying it has to be professionally done, but it should be done with as high-quality a video camera as you can find, shot using a tripod (shaky videos are bad, bad, bad), and using good audio input. You should be able to find someone on your staff, board, one of your volunteers, etc. who is good enough with online video to be considered a hobbyist or "semi-pro" for the purposes of your video.

The content of your video is also important – it should be compelling and it should use stories that appeal to viewers' emotions. You should include video or pictures of the work you are doing and the work that you want to fund, and feature at least one person from your organization talking on camera directly to the viewers of the video (this is important, because it shows you are real and makes a strong connection with browsers on these sites).

There is no "perfect way" to do a video for a crowd-funding site, but you should make sure that your video is easy to understand, that at some point you talk directly to the viewers, and that you clearly describe what the project is and why you need the money.

The Text Content

In addition to the video, the text content on your project page explains what the project is all about. The rules here are similar to direct mail – most people will simply skim the page, with only a few reading each and every section. So... write for both skimmers and readers, by using short paragraphs with lots of bolded headings throughout.

In the text content section, explain the project and why it is important. Explain how much money you need, and why you need the money. Talk about the perks you are offering, and who is involved with the project. Then – make an ask. In both the video and the text content section, you should be making a real and defined ask, something like, "Will you help us by donating to this project today?"

The Perks

Crowd-funding sites allow you to offer different giving levels to your donors, with donors at each level receiving different perks or benefits... things like t-shirts, tickets to your show, producer credits on your film, buttons, gift cards, etc. Obviously, you want to make sure the perks are valuable to your audience, but also make sure that it doesn't cost you more to send out the perks than you raise through the crowd-funding campaign.

I suggest that you use lots of perk levels – at least 4, preferably 5-7, maybe 8 or 9 if you really have lots to offer. Offer a perk at the $1 level – something like, "a heartfelt thank you" for everyone who donates. Then offer several perk levels in the $10-$50 range, more in the $100-$250 range, and some higher-level perks as well.

Take a spin around the crowd-funding sites to see the types of perks that work well – there's no real right answer… it depends on what your project is all about. Generally, the perks that work best are benefits that are tied to your mission somehow, and that show your great appreciation for the donations you receive.

Where the Money Comes from: Internal vs. External "Crowds"

It is important to note that the money you raise from a crowd-funding campaign will come from a mix of sources: some will come from your current donors and their friends and colleagues (I call this your "internal" crowd), and others will come from friends-of-friends-of donors and people who are just on the crowd-funding site (I call these folks your "external" crowd).

Much of the early money raised during your campaign will be from your current donors – you will need those who are already close to you to "seed" the campaign by getting them to donate early on – this will show others that your organization is serious and make them take note of the project.

Then, you will ask your friends and supporters to e-mail out the campaign to *their* friends and colleagues. This will generate a new round of donations from folks who may not have made a donation to your organization were it not for this campaign.

Finally, if you've gotten some traction and have a well-designed campaign in place, you will get donations from people who are just browsing the site or from people who are distantly connected to your supporters and who see the campaign because of re-shares, etc.

Building a Campaign Committee

One thing that your non-profit absolutely has to do to generate momentum for the project, but which most organizations who try crowd-funding *don't* do, is build a crowd-funding campaign committee.

Gather your most ardent supporters who are also the most active online – those with huge Facebook followings, or who are on Twitter all of the time, or who are connected to lots of other folks either online or offline – and get them to join a committee to lead your crowd-funding campaign.

The goal of the crowd-funding campaign committee is simple – they are responsible for building the initial buzz for your project. This means that they make a donation to the campaign, no matter how small, and e-mail, tweet, and post about your project over and over again, encouraging their friends (both offline and online) to get involved, make a donation, and send out the project page to other folks they know.

The campaign committee is a key step in building a baseline layer of buzz for your project. You should hold a meeting with your committee, keep them updated by e-mail, and generally treat them with the same appreciation and give them the same level of responsibility that you would offer an event host committee.

Marketing Your Campaign

Once your committee is in place, and your campaign is launched, your organization will need to do some marketing to keep the dollars coming in. I recommend that you do several rounds of marketing for your crowd-funding campaign, depending on long it is running. For example, if you're running a 90 day campaign, you'll want to figure out a way to be constantly marketing it over the course of those three months. Some of the ways you can market the campaign include:

E-mail Blasts – Send out e-mail blasts mentioning the campaign to your entire list.

Social Networks – Mention your campaign regularly on Twitter, Facebook, etc.

Your Website – Put a link to the campaign front and center on your organization's homepage.

<u>PR</u> – Try to get the local newspaper, news radio station, or other media outlets to run a story about your crowd-funding campaign.

<u>Offline Buzz</u> – Mention your campaign at offline events, in your snail mail letters, etc.

You'll also want to stay on top of your campaign committee and other supporters and remind them to keep e-mailing out about the campaign as often as they feel comfortable.

Where Does Online Fundraising Fit In?

In the past few sections, we have delved into the most important topics in online fundraising, including how to raise money through your website, through e-mail, on social networks and through crowd-funding. Before we move on to monthly giving, I want to spend some time looking at where online fundraising fits in as part of your overall development program.

Online Fundraising as a Stand Alone Model

The first place where online fundraising will fit in your development strategy is as a stand-alone model. If you structure your activities properly (in accordance with everything you are learning in this book) your organization will be able to run online-only fundraising campaigns during the course of the year. The primary tactics you will use to do so include:

- Running online fundraising campaigns on your website
- Sending out e-mail fundraising letters
- Launching crowd-funding efforts

By building a website where you capture e-mail addresses, communicating with your online donors and prospects regularly, and maintaining a presence on appropriate social networks, your organization will be able to hold profitable stand-alone online fundraising campaigns that add significantly to your revenue year in, year out.

Online Fundraising to Complement Other Activities

The second place where online fundraising will fit in to your overall development strategy is as a complement to your other, offline fundraising activities. We'll go into more detail about this topic below, but the general gist is that you can use online strategies to boost revenue for your offline campaigns in areas like events, annual appeals, and direct mail solicitations.

Building an Organization Where Online Fundraising Works

It is important to note that while online fundraising provides a tremendous opportunity for your non-profit to grow fundraising revenue, it won't do so unless you commit to it and build an organization where online fundraising "works."

Inevitably, every year I talk to organizations that tell me that they tried the whole online fundraising thing, and it didn't work for them. I ask them what happened, and they'll tell me that they put up a Donate Now link on their website and nobody used it, or they sent out an e-mail fundraising letter and no one responded.

Sure enough, when I delve deeper, I find out that nobody ever visits their one-page website because they never update or promote it, or that they only have 45 names on their e-mail list because they don't make collecting e-mail addresses a priority for their organization.

Online fundraising is work... and like all fundraising, 90% of the work comes *before* the ask, as you find new prospects, communicate with them, and build relationships.

If you want to be able to successfully use online fundraising, you need to build a development culture where that is possible. You need to maintain an active website. You need to be present on social media. You need to collect e-mail addresses. You need to have an online communications plan for staying in touch with your online donors and prospects. In short, you need to do the work, before you can benefit from making the asks.

The Goal: An Integrated Strategy

The ultimate goal for your non-profit is to maintain an integrated strategy for your online fundraising. You need to keep your online efforts as part of the mix as you develop your fundraising strategy for the year. As you launch other, offline fundraising efforts, your staff should be thinking, "how can we use our online presence to boost return from this campaign / letter / event / appeal?"

Online fundraising doesn't solve all of your problems and won't transform your fundraising overnight, but when added as a key and properly-resourced component of your overall development strategy, it will provide a major boost to your fundraising efforts.

How to Boost Your Offline Activities through Online Fundraising

Did you know that you can add online components to your offline fundraising activities, and in doing so, raise more money than would be possible with an offline-only strategy? Here's how...

The Two Goals for Adding an Online Component: Reach and Revenue

Your organization has two main goals when adding an online component to your offline fundraising activities:

Reach

Adding an online component is a phenomenal way to add more reach to your fundraising campaign or activities. This means that by utilizing online strategies, your organization will be able to include new audiences and networks in a fundraising campaign, or amplify your message to a certain group of donors who are more susceptible to online appeals than offline efforts.

For example, if you are running a capital campaign, adding an online component may enable to you to communicate with a key network of donors that you don't yet have offline connections with. Similarly, if your young professionals network is hyper-connected online, adding an online component to your sales efforts for your next fundraising event will allow you to communicate with that group better than simply sending out paper invitations will.

Revenue

The second mail goal for adding an online component to an offline campaign is, obviously, increasing the amount of revenue you raise through that campaign. Online components can help you generate additional revenue both because of the increased reach and visibility of your campaign, as noted above, but also because it allows your campaign to "be everywhere" for your donors – they will hear about it through your direct mail, through events they are invited to, through a phone call from the development staff, and through e-mail, your website, and more.

More communication with your donors through more mediums means more revenue for your organization.

Three Keys for Successfully Adding an Online Component

I have found that there are three keys for *successfully* adding an online component to your offline fundraising campaigns:

1. Don't Make Online an Afterthought

So many organizations say they are going to add an online component to their next fundraising campaign, and then simply copy and paste the text from their snail mail letters into an e-mail program and send it out to their donor list... meaning many of the recipients will receive the same letter twice, once online and once offline. This is *not* a good method for generating online revenue though your campaign.

Don't make your online component an afterthought – it is easy for your donors to see when you do, and it turns a valid opportunity for you to communicate more with your prospects into a pathetic attempt to harass them with the same message over and over again.

Instead, as you develop your fundraising plan for a particular campaign, appeal, or event, put the online component on equal footing with the offline tactics. Take the time and energy to write the online portion into your plan, and implement it with the same care you use for offline activities. (Here's a hint: if your organization requires three levels of approvals before you send an event invitation to the printer, but your intern sends out an e-mail invitation to the same event without anyone else looking at it, you are *not* giving equal weight to your online activities).

2. Use Online's Unique Ability for Conversation and Community

There are lots of things that your organization can do better offline than online. Because you can meet, shake hands with, and dine with your donors offline, you can build a stronger personal bond with them offline than on, at least for most donors and prospects.

That being said, there are also lots of things your organization can do better online than offline. Primary among them are holding real, ongoing two-way conversations with a large group of people who are interested in your work, and building a strong community around your non-profit without spending lots of money to do so.

Use online communication's unique abilities for conversation and community when designing your online fundraising efforts. Don't just ask for money – hold a conversation with your donors and prospects, build relationship and community over time, then move to the ask. When you do, your return will be much greater than when your online efforts are one-sided.

3. Encourage Your Supporters to Spread Your Online Efforts

One of the biggest benefits of online fundraising is the ease with which those who support you can spread the word about your campaign or event to their own network of friends and colleagues. But, it won't happen unless you ask. Be sure that for each online component that you add, you have a plan for getting people to e-mail / tweet / post / talk about your efforts with their own networks.

Adding Online Components in All Four Areas

In this book, we have talked about four primary areas of online fundraising. Each can be used to add an online component to offline fundraising campaigns:

Your website can easily be turned into an online hub for your offline fundraising campaigns, allowing you to post additional information, seek comment, and keep your donors updated on the campaign's progress. Likewise, your site's homepage is prime real estate, and including a feature about the campaign on the homepage will help you generate new prospects for the effort.

Your e-mail list can be used to drive people back to the campaign's page on your website, to remind people about an upcoming event, or as the online equivalent of offline direct mail.

Social networking sites can build buzz about your offline fundraising efforts, make it easy for your supporters to spread the word, and help you find new prospects and donors, and

Crowd-funding sites can help you raise a portion of your overall offline fundraising goal by engaging donors in a fun and relatively new way to raise money online.

In short, online fundraising can and should be an excellent complement to your offline fundraising campaigns.

Chapter 12:
Supercharging Your
Monthly Giving Program

Does your non-profit have a monthly giving program?

When I say "monthly giving," some non-profits may be thinking of year-long pledges, where the organization sends out letters and envelopes each month to collect a portion of the pledge from its donors. Other organizations may be thinking of monthly direct mail campaigns or e-mail efforts that ask for small one time gifts over and over again. These are *not* monthly giving programs, at least not in the context of this book.

A monthly giving program involves preauthorized or recurring gifts. These are gifts that the donor has authorized you to deduct directly from their bank account or charge to their credit card every month on a recurring basis. In monthly giving, the donor makes a pledge to give a certain amount to your organization each month, and then provides you with a credit card or bank account number, or some other means to directly deduct the money from their account.

Monthly giving programs are very popular with non-profits in Europe, and have been gaining popularity with organizations in the US and elsewhere, and for good reason, they work. Let's take a look at some of the many benefits of monthly giving programs…

Why Monthly Giving Matters

Launching a monthly giving program can be a powerful strategy for non-profits both large and small. Studies over the past decade have shown that monthly givers give more money and stay with a non-profit longer than non-monthly givers. Here are some of the reasons why monthly giving is so important for every non-profit:

Monthly Donors Give More

Once a donor signs up for a monthly giving program, they stay more loyal to the non-profit and tend to give more than they otherwise would. This isn't because of any "slimy" or ethically grey development practice... it's because monthly donors, if cultivated right, build stronger relationships with the non-profits they support, and because that relationship won't be stopped just because the donor forgets to put a check in the mail. Stopping a monthly giving relationship takes a proactive step from the donor, one they are unlikely to take unless they really mean to stop their support for a particular non-profit.

Monthly Giving Programs Build Strong Relationships

One of the most amazing things about monthly giving is that once a donor signs up for a monthly giving program, you can stop asking them for money, because the person is giving you money each and every month. Instead of making regular asks, you can focus 100% on stewarding your donors. Imagine, donors that get tons of attention from your non-profit, and none of it is an ask!

Ok... the truth is that you'll want to send your monthly donors *one* ask per year, an opportunity to upgrade / increase their monthly gift. But other than that, all of your communications are based on cultivation and stewardship. You can build amazing and strong relationships with your monthly donors, confident in the knowledge that the money is coming in every month.

Monthly Giving Programs Provide a Stable Foundation for Your Non-Profit

Good monthly giving programs build a nice monthly income that your organization can rely on, month in and month out. Instead of waiting around for donor checks to arrive or worrying about whether or not this donor or that donor will make a gift this quarter, you know that you are starting every month with a nice-sized deposit in the bank. Monthly giving is one of the very few strategies you can use in the non-profit fundraising world to provide your organization with *predictable* income.

I've seen non-profits with strong monthly giving programs starting each month with $2,500 -$25,000 in income, and some large regional and national organizations bring in $100,000 or more per month from monthly giving. What a way to start each month!

Monthly Giving Programs Lower Fundraising Costs

While there can be some expense in launching a really good monthly giving program (including doing mailings and preparing materials), overall the larger your monthly giving program becomes, the lower your fundraising costs will be. As donors sign-up for monthly giving, you can stop sending them direct mail solicitations and stop worrying about scheduling asks and follow-up calls. And... because monthly givers are more loyal to your organization, you can spend less money trying to find new donors to fill in for all of the donors who lapse each year.

The Importance of Board and Staff Buy-In

Now that you know why monthly giving programs are so valuable for non-profits, you'll need to share that information with your board and staff. Why? Because moving to a monthly giving program requires a *shift* in thinking at your organization. You see, once you start a monthly giving program, you're going to start looking at donors for their lifetime donor value, instead of just their one time giving potential.

Looks look at an example. Let's say that right now, your organization is sending out its annual appeal letter. You have two prospects, Mrs. Jones and Mrs. Smith. Mrs. Jones is an attorney and sends in a check for $250. Mrs. Smith is a school teacher and sends in a check for $30. You certainly appreciate both gifts, but which donor is going to get more of your time and attention? For most non-profits, the answer is simple... Mrs. Jones, because she has a higher "capacity."

Next year, you start a monthly giving program. As part of your annual appeal, Mrs. Jones once again sends in her $250 check. Mrs. Smith, on the other hand, signs-up for your monthly giving program, and authorizes you to charge her credit card $30 every month to support your work. *Now* who gets more of your time and attention? Now who is your bigger donor? Can you see how monthly giving can shift your organization's perception of donor commitment and lifetime donor value?

I'm not suggesting that once you start a monthly giving program you should abandon your events, direct mail or annual appeal programs. You may certainly find that over time some of those lessen in importance, but you'll probably always have donors who prefer to give through events, in-person meetings or direct mail rather than through monthly giving. But that being said, monthly giving does require a subtle shift in strategy and perception at your organization. Because of this, it is important that both your board and staff understand and commit to monthly giving. The best way to get your board and staff "on board" is to explain the facts. Tell them what you already know... that monthly giving programs work and are extremely beneficial for non-profits big and small. Share the information in this book with them, and get them to commit to launching a monthly giving program at your organization. You'll want to get your team on board before launching, so that you have the support you need for the adventure ahead.

How to Prime Your Organization for Monthly Giving Success

As you make plans to launch monthly giving at your non-profit, there are several things you can do to prime both yourself and your organization for success:

#1 – Understand that this is a Process

Launching a monthly giving program is a process… it takes time. If your non-profit has 2,000 donors in its database, it is highly unlikely that you will launch your program and in 6 months have 1,000 donors giving on a recurring monthly basis. On the other hand, there's no reason that at the end of the year (and with some good, sustained effort) you can't have 100-200 donors signed up for the program.

Monthly giving programs start slowly, and build on themselves. Because donor retention is so much better for monthly giving than for other donor programs, Once you get started, your numbers will grow steadily. As more and more donors sign-up for the program and most stick around, you will see a steady increase in your monthly revenue. Before launching your program, commit to at least two years of solid effort to get it off the ground before deciding that it isn't working for your non-profit.

#2 – Be Willing to Think Differently

As mentioned above, monthly giving programs allow your non-profit to think in terms of long term donor value. Be willing to embrace this thinking… be willing to think differently about fundraising and about what it means to be a "key" donor.

For example, you may previously have spent $5,000 at your organization holding a small "thank you" event each year for your major donors… those that give $5,000 or more per year to your non-profit. Once you launch your monthly giving program, you may need to change your definition of just which donors qualify for expenditures like this. Remember, if a donor gives you $50 per month for 10 years, that means the donor has given you $6,000 on a predictable basis, without you having to chase them down twice a year to write checks. That's a valuable donor in anyone's book.

#3 – Have Good Financial Controls in Place

We'll talk at length about setting up your processing and other monthly systems later in this chapter. It's important to note, though, that if you're planning to launch a monthly giving program, you'll need to have good financial controls in place at your organization.

It's easy to assign a trusted volunteer the task of running a deposit full of checks down to the local bank. It's harder to entrust a volunteer with credit card numbers for your monthly donors… in fact, you probably shouldn't. You'll need to set up secure systems for handling donor information and safely disposing of confidential account info to avoid having an embarrassing harmful data breach / theft at your organization.

#4 – Know that You Can Do This!

The fourth and final thing you need to do to prime yourself for monthly giving success is understand that you can do this… you can make this jump and make it work at your non-profit. Whether you are a new organization that is just starting out and wants to focus on finding monthly givers, or an established non-profit that wants to turn your legion of loyal supporters into predictable recurring donors, it can be done. Thousands of organizations large, small and otherwise have done it, and you can to. I'm looking forward to helping you along the way!

Launching Your Monthly Giving Program – Be Intentional

In this section, we're going to talk about how to actually launch a monthly giving program at your non-profit. This includes not only what infrastructure you will need in place in order to successfully run a monthly giving program and the steps you need to take to launch, but also how to brand your program and build some momentum behind your monthly giving launch.

Before we start, I want to point out one thing. In order to be successful with monthly giving, you have to be *intentional*. Far too many non-profits come to me and say they tried monthly giving and it didn't work out, but when I inquire further it turns out that all they did was slap a line on their donor envelopes that says, "check here to make this a recurring monthly gift." That's not launching a program, that's just an after-thought.

All of the non-profits I have seen that were super-successful with their monthly giving programs launched in a well-planned and intentional manner. This means that they thought through the program, put the infrastructure in place, and then launched through a step-by-step process. It also means that they gave the program time to catch on... instead of calling it quits after one or two months, these organizations committed to running a monthly giving program for at least one or two *years* to give the program time to grow.

If you want to be successful with monthly giving, my best advice is to have a plan and be intentional about launching your program. In this chapter, we'll walk you through everything you need to do to start your program on the right foot. Let's get started...

Monthly Giving Infrastructure: What You Need to Launch

In order to run a really great monthly giving program launch, you'll need three primary pieces of infrastructure in place:

<u>Monthly Giving Case for Support</u>

The first thing you'll need is a case for support tailored specifically to your monthly giving program.

Remember, a non-profit's case for support (sometimes called "case statement"):

- Is donor-oriented / donor-facing (written for donors)
- Clearly illustrates your organization's mission and vision for the future
- Tells donors why you need funding and what outcomes you are seeking from their investment

- Offers strong reasons why prospects should make gifts to your organization.

Simply put, your case for support is a document that tells donors who your organization is, what it has accomplished in the past, outlines your vision for the future, tells the donor why your organization's vision matters and why the donor should care, and gives the donor a chance to get involved by making an investment in your non-profit. Case statements cast a bold vision for a better future, and invite donors to get caught up in that vision.

When you launch a monthly giving program, you need to create a short case for support tailored specifically to this program. In addition to casting a vision for the future of the organization, this case statement needs to explain (a) why monthly giving is so important to your non-profit, (b) what impact a monthly gift / recurring gift could have for your organization and what impact it will have for the people you serve, and (c) the benefits of the monthly giving program for your donor.

For example, you might say that (a) monthly giving is important for your organization because it will allow your non-profit to build a base of support to grow and serve a new group of people or geographical area. You case for support can note that (b) a monthly gift of $25 per month will allow you to feed 1 hungry child for the month, and a gift of $36 per month will allow you to provide primary medical care to one family per month. Finally, you can show (c) that a recurring gift will reduce the number of letters the donor gets from your organization, saving you money and saving them time, and that a recurring gift of at least $10 per month will enable them to join your "Superstar Supporters" club (more on monthly giving clubs later in this chapter).

Creating a short case for support for your monthly giving program shouldn't take long, and will allow you to write stronger monthly giving materials and appeal letters.

Recurring Billing Processor

The second important item you will need to have in place prior to launching your monthly giving program is a processor to run your monthly credit card bills.

Remember – with monthly giving, your donors are authorizing your non-profit to bill their credit card each month for a set pledge. There are two ways you could go about processing these cards. One would be to store the credit card numbers in a file at your organization and run the numbers every month on the anniversary date of the pledge. This is time consuming, can lead to forgotten transactions, and requires you to store sensitive information in paper files at your facility.

The second and much better option is to use a credit card processor that will provide you with software or an online portal where you can store the credit card information securely, and which will automatically bill the credit cards each month at the right time and for the right amount, and all you have to do is print out the thank you notes at the appropriate time. Many of these processing programs will even integrate with your accounting software to make record-keeping a snap.

There are a number of different options when it comes to recurring credit card processors, and we will refrain from endorsing any single option in this book, because different processors and methods may work better or worse for any one organization.

One option is to use your current donor database to process recurring transactions. Several non-profit donor databases that have the ability to process credit cards right in the program also can handle monthly giving. If you are interested in this option, check with your database provider to see whether this is included with your software and what the additional costs and fees are to process recurring payments.

Another option is stand-alone software. Many companies that offer payment processing to non-profits also offer software or online portals that allow organizations to process recurring payments. If you are interested in this option, check with your payment processor to see whether they offer this service and what the additional costs and fees are. Also see if the software will integrate with your donor database to allow you to easily track recurring payments with your donor files.

An alternative to credit processing is EFT, or "electronic funds transfer." Perhaps your monthly utility payment or gym membership is processed as an automatic bank debit. The beauty of EFT is that there are no credit card expiration dates. Once it's in place, EFT tends to be seamless....but setting it up can be more complicated. Check with your organization's bank to determine if EFT would work for you.

No matter which option you choose, be sure to check out the fees that each payment processor charges for monthly / recurring giving, as the differences can be substantial.

Your Donor File

The final key piece of infrastructure you will need to launch a strong monthly giving program is your donor file. We'll talk more about this later in the book, but remember that we'll be targeting your regular donors with asks for monthly giving. In order to make these asks, you'll need to know who your regular and annual givers are... thus, we'll be using your file of current donors to make our asks.

Branding Your Monthly Giving Program

The next step in preparing for your launch is to create a brand for your monthly giving program. Sure, you could always just ask people to make a monthly gift without creating a brand around it, but many non-profits have found that creating a strong and identifiable brand for their monthly giving members helps to build the relationship and increases the feeling of being part of something special among monthly donors.

Remember that your monthly donors really *are* something special. They trust you and support your work so much that they are willing to give you their credit card numbers and tell you to charge them monthly to help you carry out your mission. They will likely be your most loyal and longest-supporting donors. Shouldn't that be celebrated?

The first step in creating a brand for your program is to give it a name. The name should reinforce your mission and make it clear that this is a special group of people – one that other donors should want to join. For example, Habitat for Humanity calls its monthly donors the "HopeBuilders" and Food for the Poor calls its program "Angels of the Poor." Be creative, but keep it mission focused with a slight air of exclusivity.

Next, consider creating an inexpensive logo and tagline for your monthly giving program. Treat this program like you would any fundraising campaign – give your program a public persona and make it easily recognizable as a distinct and important program for your most committed donors.

How to Set Ask Amounts and Benefit Levels

One of the primary goals for your monthly giving program is to take occasional and annual givers and get them to upgrade to a monthly recurring gift. These are people who already know a little about your organization and have supported it with a financial gift. Thus, you will now need to convince them that signing up for a monthly gift is an even better way to move your mission forward. The first way to do this is through the case for support we talked about above. The second way is to set smart ask amounts for your monthly giving appeals.

As with all fundraising appeals, you will be setting gift levels for your monthly giving program. Set these levels based on your mission and how much it costs to fund your work. Make them bite-sized and easy to understand. For example, if you are a private inner city school that allows children living in poverty to attend for free, you could set your giving levels as follows:

$15 per month – Provides 3 free breakfasts for students each month

$22 per month – Subsidizes 1 hour of instruction for students each month

$40 per month – Provides art supplies for 8 students each month

Or, if you are fundraising for an animal shelter, you could say:

$8 per month – Provides immunizations for one animal per month

$25 per month – Sponsors food for one animal each month

$50 per month – Allows us to offer animal education program to one school each month

The key with setting giving levels is to make sure that your donors understand what each level sponsors or allows you to provide, and that the ask amounts are realistic based on your donors' giving capacities (e.g. if your average donor gives $125 per year, don't set a monthly giving level at $60 per month… you are unlikely to get it).

A second consideration when setting your giving levels and planning your monthly giving program is what benefits you are going to offer to your monthly donors. My advice is to think of your monthly giving program as you would a "giving club." Offer donors at different levels certain benefits that encourage them to give and that easily build a stronger relationship with the donor. Obviously, you should also make sure that any benefits you offer don't cost more than 10-15% of the total amount given by the donor to receive those benefits, otherwise you will be giving away a substantial portion of your recurring revenue.

Most organizations with large monthly giving programs offer some basic benefits for *everyone* who signs up to be a monthly donor. These benefits are usually things that are free or almost free, such as a monthly *Partners* e-mail newsletter, a refrigerator magnet with the giving program's logo, etc.

As donors go up the giving ladder, you can offer increasing benefits. For example, you could say that monthly donors who pledge $25 or more per month with be receive an exclusive lapel pin from the organization to show their support, and those who pledge $40 or more per month will be invited to an annual recognition event with a prominent guest speaker.

For more examples of giving levels, just turn on your local public television or radio station during pledge week to see all of the levels they offer for monthly givers. Unlike those stations, though, I recommend that you limit your benefits program to just 2-4 levels (I have found that 3 seems to be the best, but others suggest 2 or 4 levels can work well) so as not to overwhelm your donors and prospects.

How to Target Your Monthly Giving Asks

When launching your monthly giving program, you are going to be targeting a certain subset of your current donors to ask them to become monthly givers. I do not recommend approaching new donors and asking them to become monthly givers. In my mind, that is like asking someone to marry you before you ask them out for a first date. It's way too much commitment with far too little relationship built.

Most good monthly donors start off by making one time gifts to the organization. This allows them to "kick the tires" a little and get to know the organization. As you cultivate these donors and build a relationship with them, they become better and better targets for a monthly giving ask.

So… who should you be asking to commit to monthly gifts as part of your monthly giving program launch? Current donors. Your goal is to get these supporters to give more each year, pledged on a monthly basis. Your best prospects are those who give every year or, even better… multiple times each year. That being said, you should probably target your initial mailing at everyone who has given to your organization at least twice over the past three years.

The 7 Steps to Launching a Monthly Giving Program at Your Non-Profit

Ok, now that you have the infrastructure in place and know who you are targeting with your monthly giving program launch, here are the 7 steps you should use to make your launch a success:

1. Create a Monthly Giving Launch Letter / Appeal

The first step of your monthly giving launch is to create a strong monthly giving appeal letter. You'll be sending out a traditional snail-mail / direct mail letter to your current donors to ask them to sign-up for your monthly giving program. This is where all of the preparation work we talked about above comes into play – you'll use your case for support, program branding, giving levels and donor benefits to craft a compelling letter that moves donors to action.

2. Develop a Web Page for Monthly Giving

The second step of your launch is to develop a web page that explains your monthly giving case for support, includes a call to action, and allows people to click on a link to sign-up for recurring giving.

You want to design and publish this webpage *after* you write your monthly giving appeal letter but *before* you put it in the mail. This is because you want the web page to match the look, feel, tone, and language of your letter, but you also want people who receive the letter and want to find more information on your website to have somewhere to go to get that information.

3. Drop Your Monthly Giving Launch Letter

Once your web page is up and functional (be sure to test those payment buttons!) you're ready to drop your appeal letter in the mail. Remember the basic rule of thumb for program launch letters such as this one: they are much more effective in the Spring and Fall than they are in the Summer or near the Christmas / Hanukah / New Year's holiday season.

4. Send Out a Monthly Giving Launch E-Mail

Several days after your letter goes into the mail, send out an e-mail solicitation to your entire e-mail list asking them to sign-up for the monthly giving program and giving them links to click on to sign-up right away. As with your monthly giving web page, your e-mail appeal should match the language and look of the direct mail letter which you sent out... this way, your donors will be getting a consistent message and ask across all mediums.

5. Follow Up with Phone Calls

Ok, this is where it gets tricky and a little controversial. In my experience, organizations that follow-up their direct mail and e-mail solicitations with phone calls asking donors to become monthly givers are far more successful than those organizations that don't use phone calls as part of the mix. These calls can be done in house or through a reputable telemarketing firm. Not every consultant would agree with me about adding phone calls to the mix, so your mileage may vary.

I know not every non-profit has the manpower or financial resources to call through their donor file as a follow-up to the direct mail and e-mail campaigns. That's ok. If you can't make the calls, skip this step, and do all of the others. You will still be successful.

That being said, if you have limited resources and are willing to give phone calls a shot, have your top development folks call through your top donors... maybe the top 5-10% of your annual givers... to ask them to join the monthly giving program.

The call script can be as simple as, "Hi Mary, I just wanted to make sure you got my letter about our new *Champions for the City* monthly giving program. Did you get the letter? Great! This new program will allow us to offer hot meals and clean beds to 50% more of our city's homeless this year. Would you be willing to sign-up with a monthly pledge?"

6. Welcome New Monthly Donors

Remember – your monthly giving program is important not only because of the financial benefits it provides your organization, but also because it allows your non-profit to build stronger relationships with your donors. Get this new relationship off to the right start by sending your new monthly givers a welcome letter highlighting how important they are and reminding them of the benefits they receive as part of their membership in the program.

7. Add Monthly Giving as an Option

Finally, after you complete the launch of your monthly giving program, add monthly giving as an option to all of your fundraising materials. Add an option on your online giving forms for monthly giving, include monthly giving language on your donor envelopes, and include information about monthly giving in your e-mail and snail mail newsletters.

Keep it Up! How to Build Momentum Behind Your Program

Following the 7 steps above will allow you to launch your monthly giving program the right way and poise it for sustained growth. Remember that monthly giving programs grow through sustained effort. Thus, each year that you focus on the program, you should see more and more growth and expansion.

As you grow your program, remember the following:

Be Willing to Test and Measure

As with all programs and appeals, as you try things out, measure the return and make decisions based on what you learn. For example, you may find that your e-mail list responds better to certain monthly giving levels and certain asks, or that your phone program works well for low-dollar donors but not for higher-level ones. Your monthly giving program should be a long-lived, ongoing effort. Test and measure!

Make an Appeal Each Year!

Once you complete your monthly giving program launch, your program goes into "ongoing" mode, meaning that at any time, people can sign-up through your website or donor envelopes, etc. just by clicking yes and giving you their monthly pledge.

That doesn't mean that you should only do one monthly giving appeal to your list. Far from it! I recommend doing one "all hands on deck" monthly giving appeal (snail mail + e-mail + phone) each year to help you grow and expand your monthly giving program.

Ask for Upgrades

Remember to ask for upgrades from your monthly givers! One of the best ways to do this is during your annual monthly giving program appeal. Send out one set of e-mails and letters to those on your list who *aren't* monthly donors to ask them to sign-up, and send out another set of e-mail and letters to those who *already* give monthly to ask them to upgrade. Many will!

How to Create an Effective Monthly Giving Appeal

In this section, we'll be covering the nuts and bolts of writing your monthly giving appeal. We'll be talking about the differences between direct mail appeals and email appeals, and we'll be covering why you need the right mindset when you begin drafting your organization's campaign.

I can hear you now. "Mindset? What is he talking about?"

Before we get started, I want you to tell yourself that you're proud, proud, **proud** to be a fundraiser. You're about to ask for a serious commitment of your donors, and you can't go into this being afraid to ask. So, I want you to ask with the assumption that you're going to get lots of yes's. And remember: you're not asking -- **you're offering an opportunity** -- *a rare and precious invitation* -- to change the world.

Your "Secret" Weapon: Know your donors

Gaining a solid understanding of who your donors are will help you write monthly giving appeal letters that speak to them, in their language. You've got to understand them from a demographic perspective -- and that goes beyond a mere understanding of their giving patterns. Where do they live? What is their income level? Education level? Where do they shop? You've got to know why they give to your organization.

In the classic book, "Relationship Fundraising," author Ken Burnett prefaces every chapter with a "Donor Profile," an in-depth story about one particular individual and how and why they give. Each profile describes, in-depth, a particular donor's day-to-day life, his/her likes and dislikes, the kind of car that he/she drives, even his/her upbringing.

Remember that the *"who is so much more important than the what."* Before you spend hours crafting a monthly giving appeal – spend some time giving some thought to the person who will be reading it!

While a natural disaster may bring out nearly everyone's humanitarianism, you will strengthen your monthly giving appeal by spending some time really getting to know your donors. Do what Ken Burnett does and truly envision that person. What they do for a living, what they wear, where they live, how many children they have, where they worship – give that person a name!

Here's an example: Years ago I worked with a small nonprofit organization with a dual mission: they provided inner city middle school children with the tools they needed to reach beyond their public school education and go on to scholarships at private schools or the city's best magnet schools, and eventually college. The programming was taught by talented high school and college students, which, in turn, drew talented teachers into urban education where they were most needed. A definite win-win.

After reviewing a sampling of our most loyal donors, when I envisioned this agency's "ideal donor," I arrived at "Lisa," a 47-year-old woman with a master's degree in political science. Lisa didn't grow up in the area and moved here with her husband for his career. She considers herself politically progressive and an environmentalist and believes in the importance of giving back. Lisa and her husband enjoy a relatively affluent lifestyle and live in the suburbs of Philadelphia. Their eldest son is in his junior year at Berkeley and their daughter is in her junior year at the local public high school. She drives a Honda Civic hybrid and shops at Whole Foods. Lisa volunteers for three organizations and serves on two boards.

A Package, Not a Letter

When you choose to appeal to monthly donors via direct mail, it's important to remember that now is not the time to cut corners. In the book *Monthly Giving: The Sleeping Giant*, renowned copywriter Jerry Huntsinger says that your letter must be *"totally and highly personalized, right down to direct addressing and a first class commemorative postage stamp. No short cuts. No worry about postage costs. No compromises and, for goodness sakes, no windows and no postage boxes."*

But don't despair if you believe that your budget can't handle high postage, design and printing costs. Remember my mantra: *everything is figure-out-able!* No money for a logo? No problem. Can't afford expensive paper? That's ok too! I've personally developed monthly giving packages that were created and printed completely in-house.

Step-by-Step: Your Monthly Giving Ask

Here's how to create a compelling monthly giving ask for your donors:

Show your appreciation

Always begin your direct mail monthly giving appeal with appreciation. After all, you're targeting those donors who have already demonstrated their appreciation for your work and mission. Shower the donors you love with love and come right out and tell them that you couldn't have accomplished what you have without them!

Is there a special story your donors have responded to in the past? You might say something like "Remember _____? Thanks to you _____."

Issue your invitation

Now you'll be issuing your donors a very special invitation. You might lead off with something like: *"We're writing to you, as one of our most committed supporters, to ask you..."* Stress the exclusivity of your offer -- **and their past support.**

Extol the benefits of monthly giving

Here is where you'll point out the benefits of monthly giving to the donor. Stress the ease of monthly giving. If you have a monthly giving program in place that you're looking to grow, you might choose to insert a donor testimonial here.

One monthly giving program that I launched was started by a handful of donations from board members. One of the board members contributed a quote attesting to the fact that she'd been able to increase her own yearly gift to the organization by a third through monthly giving.

Your case...and how your donor makes it possible

This is where you reinforce the impact that your donor's gifts have already made -- and stress what could be possible.

Return now to your case for monthly giving support. Remember that the best cases demonstrate your organization's <u>impact vividly</u> and with <u>emotion</u>. The stronger your case, the stronger your ask.

<u>The ask</u>

Now is when you'll again circle back to the purpose of your letter. Use phrases such as:

With your gift of just $5 a month we can _____

Your gift of just $10 a month means that _____

<u>Thank Again</u>

You can never be too effusive with your gratitude.

<u>Don't forget your PS</u>

Never neglect your PS! It's your opportunity to reinforce the benefits of monthly giving.

Your letter should be warm and personal and your main point (aside from making your case!) should be to convey to your donors how special they are.

Email and Your Monthly Giving Campaign

Are most of your donors already giving to you online? You'll want to use the same channel through which you acquired your donors to upgrade them to monthly giving. Email is an inexpensive way to grow your monthly giving program.

The key to success lies in developing a comprehensive campaign (one email does not a campaign make!) and having a dedicated monthly giving landing page that's succinct, focused and seamless.

It Has to Be Seamless!

One of the first things I do when I'm working with non-profits on online giving is to have the executive director make an online gift to their own organization. It's invariably a humbling experience. Test, test and test again. What kind of "thank you" or "welcome" message do you receive once you've made a gift? Is the process easy and straightforward? What kind of error message do you receive if you enter your card's expiration date incorrectly?

Your email monthly giving campaign will follow much of the same processes as your direct mail approach, with a couple of notable exceptions. Your email messages will be tighter and you will follow a traditional campaign model of 3-5 sequenced emails.

Taking It Multi-Channel

If your organization is using a direct mail campaign this year, you're already halfway there in developing your online campaign. Your message series quite simply tells your organization's story. Remember: our focus is on your outcomes and what your donor is accomplishing through their gift.

It can be easy to fall back on numbers. Don't. Reflect on the emotional stories that best reflects your agency's work. At this point, you don't need to worry about writing your subject line as much as getting a very clear picture in your head of the stories and opportunities that will make an impact on your donor.

Chapter 13:
How to Launch Planned Giving at Your Non-Profit

Planned giving... for many non-profits, particularly small and mid-sized organizations, it's something we say we want to get around to, but never do. Sure, if someone leaves us a gift in their will, we'll take it, but for many of us, we never quite get around to launching a planned giving campaign at our charity, even though we talk about it at board meetings and put it on annual "to-do" lists.

The reason so many non-profits keep putting off planned giving is because it *seems* like it's complicated. When we think of planned giving, so often we think of lawyers, accountants, legal documents, research... all of the things that sound time consuming and expensive. The truth is, though, that setting up your first planned giving effort can be relatively smooth and painless. In this article, we're going to look at how small and mid-sized non-profits can go about setting up their first planned giving effort.

Defining Planned Giving

For the purposes of this section, "planned giving" is the act of making a commitment to give a charitable organization a major gift, over time or at death, as part of the donor's overall financial and estate planning.

Planned giving vehicles can get quite exotic. Planned gifts can range from the relatively simple bequest made in a will, to gifts like charitable gift annuities and charitable remainder trusts that provide major gifts to a non-profit while at the same time returning income to the donor.

While you will eventually want to explore all of the options available to you, my recommendation if you are just starting out is to stick with launching a campaign to generate bequests – that is, supporters who agree to leave a portion of their estate to your non-profit. Then, once you have your planned giving campaign gaining momentum, you can investigate all of the other forms of planned giving available to your charity.

Why Planned Giving Matters

Before we go into the six steps you'll need to take to launch your campaign, I wanted to talk briefly about why planned giving matters, particularly for small and mid-sized organizations. Simply put, every non-profit should be focused (in part) on finding benefactors to leave them planned gifts because there is no better way to plan for the future growth and strength of your organization.

Planned gifts can be game-changing for your organization. Even relatively smaller planned gifts can be used to sustain certain programs or facilities, add capacity, establish endowments, or launch major new initiatives. Plus, to my mind, planned gifts are an excellent return for relatively little cost or upfront investment. You can ask for planned gifts on a regular basis without it costing much money or time, and yet reap amazing windfalls for your organization. So if you haven't yet launched planned giving, now is the time to start!

Step 1: Research

The first step in launching a planned giving effort for the first time is to do some amount of research. You'll want to make sure you understand (at a basic level) how planned giving works, and what basic wills look like. If you're going to be focused on bequests, you won't need to do much more research than that. Of course, if you're going to be using more complicated instruments like charitable remainder trusts, you'll need to spend more time doing research. In either case, spending an hour or two with an attorney focused on estate law would also be worth your time, just to make sure you're headed in the right direction.

Step 2: Write

Once you've gotten a basic understanding of planned gifts, you'll want to write up a short (1-2 pages would be fine) document explaining why people should remember your organization in their will, and briefly explaining just how easy it is to do so.

You should also provide a contact person at your organization who will handle calls relating to planned gifts.

Step 3: Publish

Next, I always suggest non-profits publish the information they developed in Step 2 in several places to make sure prospects and donors can find it easily. First, create a planned giving page on your website. Second, create a quick and easy planned giving brochure that you can hand out to prospective donors. Such a donor could be a more expensive full-color tri-fold brochure or something as cheap and simple as a flyer run off on your in-house copy machine.

Step 4: Launch

You've done your research, written compelling copy, and published the information to make sure your donors can find it. Now, you're ready to launch your first ever planned giving campaign.

First, go to your board. (Preferably, the board chair should launch this type of campaign at a board meeting, by seeking 100% board participation). Ask your board members to take the lead by remembering your non-profit in their will.

Next, go to your key donors and supporters, and ask *them* to make a planned gift to your organization. This should be treated like any other fundraising ask – and for significant donors, should be done on the phone or in person.

Finally, depending on how often you make direct mail asks of your donor file, consider sending a mailing to your entire donor base asking them to consider remembering your organization in their wills.

Step 5: Recognize

One great way to encourage participation in your planned giving efforts is to recognize your planned giving donors in a Legacy Club or other donor group comprised of everyone who has told you that they have written your non-profit into their will.

As you approach new planned giving prospects, showing them a list of people who have made planned gifts to your organization will help them feel as if they are making a wise investment. Likewise, a Legacy Club will allow you to stay in constant contact with your planned givers to ensure that they don't fall off of your radar and move their support to another organization.

Step 6: Include

Finally, be sure to include a small note on planned giving in almost everything your non-profit does. Planned giving information should be on your website, included in your newsletters, mentioned on your reply devices ("Check here to receive information on how to support our organization through a planned gift"). The more you remind your donors that you are seeking planned gifts, the more likely they will be to make them.

Chapter 14:
Writing a Successful Fundraising Plan for Your Non-Profit

In this section, we're going to take an in depth look at how to write a fundraising plan that works for your organization. Note that throughout this section, we will use the terms "fundraising plan" and "development plan" interchangeably.

Why You Need a <u>Written</u> Fundraising Plan

It is my belief that every single non-profit, no matter how small or large, needs a *written* fundraising plan.

If you're just starting your non-profit, only have two board members (your close friends) and $1,000 in the bank, you need a written fundraising plan. It may not be long and complicated, but it needs to be well thought out.

If you're running a major worldwide organization, have millions of dollars in the bank, serve hundreds of thousands of people, and have affiliates on every continent, you still need a written fundraising plan. Don't think that just because you're big it means you've got it covered and don't have to write it down. You need a fundraising plan.

The same goes for every organization in between: every non-profit needs a written fundraising plan. Here's why…

1. **Provides organization** – a detailed fundraising plan creates organization and order in the chaotic world of non-profit development.

2. **Defines responsibilities** – a fundraising plan determines who does what, and adds accountability to your fundraising efforts.

3. **Sets deadlines** – a good fundraising plan tells you when you need the money. Deadlines help motivate your team to perform.

4. **Provides a credible fundraising tool** – when an investor purchases a business, he or she wants to see the financials that prove the company can be a success. Often, it's no different for major donors to your organization. Your fundraising plan shows why you need the money and lets your donors know you are serious about your mission.

5. **Measures progress** – a detailed fundraising plan lets you measure your fundraising progress, thus allowing you to make needed adjustments before it is too late.

Creating a Fundraising Plan: The Process

Writing a great fundraising plan takes time. My suggestion would be that you dedicate at least 1-2 months to the process, particularly if this is your organization's first written development plan. There are several key steps to writing a great plan:

Research

First, you'll need to gather information and do some research. How has your non-profit traditionally raised money? What is the state of your donor file? How many donors do you have, and at what levels? What tactics have worked for your organization in the past? What tactics have failed, or at least failed to perform as you had hoped? How many prospects do you have? Where can you find more prospects?

Meetings and Consensus Building

The next step is to hold a series of meetings (one on one or in small groups) with your staff, your board members, and with some key donors, supporters, and advisors to your non-profit. During these meetings, you'll want to see what these key stakeholders think about your organization's fundraising efforts. Talk to them about what programs and mission-related items they'd like to see your non-profit engaged in, and try to build some consensus on the direction for your fundraising efforts for the coming year.

Writing the Plan

Once your research and stakeholder meetings are complete, it's time to sit down and write the plan. I have found that it is usually best to have <u>just one person</u> writing the plan. Many organizations and consultants would argue with me on this point and suggest a team effort, with each team member taking responsibility for a different portion of the plan. I have found this method to lead to disjointed fundraising plans where the constituent parts don't add up to a strong whole.

I do think you should get a team together to discuss and revise the plan, but I advise having one extremely competent person sit down to write the first draft in its entirety. Depending on the size and complexity of your organization, this person may need 1-3 weeks to actually write the plan. I would then bring the whole team in once the plan is written, for the purposes of refining and strengthening it.

Building Support

Once the plan has been completed, reviewed, edited and strengthened, it's ready for prime time. You should now "shop the plan around" to your staff, your board and some of your key donors to get their support for the plan. I also suggest going through the formal step of having the board of directors vote to approve the plan. This puts the board on the record as supporting the initiatives contained in the plan, and makes it easier when it comes time for your staff to seek the board's help with fundraising.

The Key Parts of Your Fundraising Plan

Every organization, consultant, and fundraiser has a different formula and structure for writing fundraising plans. Here's a secret I learned early in my development career: it's generally not the structure of the fundraising plan that matters... it's the content, and even more so, the fact that you sat down and wrote a plan in the first place. So don't agonize over structure. Just start putting pen to paper!

Here is how I like to organize my fundraising plans:

<u>Cover Page</u>

<u>Background</u> – Briefly explains what is currently going on at your non-profit that will influence the plan.

<u>Goals and Objectives</u> – What your organization hopes to achieve with this plan. Include numbers (fundraising targets)!

<u>Assumptions</u> – The assumptions you are making in formulating the plan.

<u>Fundraising Infrastructure</u> – What infrastructure do you currently have in place for fundraising, and what infrastructure do you anticipate needing over the coming years? Infrastructure includes things like your staff, your donor database, your marketing materials, your case for support, your website, etc.

<u>Donor Prospect Plan</u> – Where will we find new prospects?

<u>Donor Communications and Cultivation</u> – How are you planning to communicate with your donors? What will your cultivation paths look like? What are your donor and prospect communication calendars?

<u>Fundraising Tactics</u> – What tactics will we use to raise money, and how will we use them? Each tactic should get its own subsection. Common tactics include:

- Direct Mail
- Events
- Online Fundraising
- Grants and Government Support
- Annual Giving Programs
- Planned Giving
- Endowments
- Capital Campaigns
- Affinity Groups and Fundraising Networks

Fundraising Needs and Goals – A numbers-driven summary of what your organization needs to raise (budget) and how you are going to raise it (tactics) with monetary goals for each tactic.

Action Step Timeline – Finally, I like to include a list of action steps in each section that lists what needs to be done by which deadline in order for the plan to succeed, as well as include a consolidated timeline at the end of the plan with each action step listed chronologically.

Remember, your fundraising plan *will* change. It is important to write down your plan, but it is also important to be willing to change course when events dictate. Review your plan often, and make changes as necessary.

The Two Most Important Parts of a Successful Fundraising Plan

The two most important parts of your plan are firm DEADLINES and set RESPONSIBILITIES. If you want your fundraising plan to succeed, you absolutely need to include actual, details deadlines and responsibilities as part of your written draft.

Many non-profits write nebulous fundraising plans that set general strategy but don't spell out what it will take to reach the organization's fundraising goals. This is a mistake. Your fundraising plan should include not only general strategy but also the key action steps that your organization will need to take to carry out that strategy this year. For each action step, there should be a deadline (telling you when the action needs to be completed) and a responsible person (showing who will be responsible for meeting the deadline).

Fundraising plans without firm deadlines and responsibilities aren't very helpful for your organization. Be detailed. I like to say that an organization should be just a little worried about implementing their fundraising plan. They shouldn't be scared or write a plan that is clearly not achievable, but the plan should be ambitious enough and clear enough on deadlines that everyone thinks, "gee, we've got a lot to do. I've got a lot to do. We better get started."

Supercharging Your Fundraising Plan

The best way to supercharge your fundraising plan, as you write it, is to think big about it. Now, I'm not suggesting you go crazy… we've all seen fundraising plans that bear no relation to reality (e.g. you raised $100,000 last year at your major event, and now your plan says you are going to raise $2,000,000 this year. How exactly are you going to do *that*?)

What I *am* suggesting, though, is that you think bigger about your plan this year than you ever have before. I see far too many organizations that set the same goal for their major event each year ("we'll raise $15,000 again this year, just like last year!") when they really could come up with a strategy for raising <u>more</u> this year. The same goes for direct mail, major gifts, endowments, etc.

Don't write "just another" fundraising plan. <u>Think big</u>.

Chapter 15:
How to Implement the
Rapid Growth Fundraising System ™
at Your Non-Profit

Rapid Growth Fundraising™ is a proprietary fundraising strategy that I developed over a decade of working with organizations that want to raise more money quickly and efficiently. The goal of this system is to double or triple an organization's revenue in a short period of time – months or years – while maintaining high quality standards for donor interaction. This chapter shows you exactly how we do it. Over the course of this section, I will refer to "Rapid Growth Fundraising," "The Rapid Growth Fundraising System," and "Rapidly Growing Your Fundraising" interchangeably.

Prerequisites for Rapidly Growing Your Fundraising

If you truly want to rapidly grow fundraising at your organization, you'll need to make sure you have the following two prerequisites in place before you begin:

#1 - A Big Vision. Donors don't invest in small visions. You can't rapidly grow your fundraising if your goal is to increase services by 1% or to help 10 more people next year. You need a big vision, one that is worthy of your non-profit. Doubling the number of people you serve, helping every single person that has a certain problem, and eradicating a disease are all examples of BIG visions.

#2 - A Willingness to Do the Work. It's easy to maintain the status quo with your fundraising. It's hard to DOUBLE your fundraising... even harder to triple it in just a year or two. Rapidly growing your fundraising will take the commitment of your board, staff and volunteers, a willingness to follow the plan, and most importantly, a willingness to do the work.

The Four Pillars of the Rapid Growth Fundraising System

There are four key components of the rapid growth fundraising system that allow it to work quickly and efficiently. These "pillars" must be put in place by your non-profit if you want to double or triple your fundraising revenue over the next 1-2 years.

Pillar #1: Order

Disorganized development programs can't and don't dramatically increase fundraising year over year. Sure, you can raise a little more each year, but not double or triple your revenue. This is <u>particularly</u> true if you want to dramatically increase your fundraising revenue in <u>a short amount of time</u>.

Rapid Growth Fundraising requires ORDER. That means it that you need to have your fundraising program well organized and planned, whether you're a one person shop or a major university with 400 fundraisers on staff. You have to get a good handle on what is going on in your fundraising shop.

The first thing you need to do to have order is get the craziness and disorganization of most non-profits remedied, and remedied quickly. Here's the strategy I use to get development offices in order when they feel disorganized:

Get organized, and have all of your fundraisers get organized.

Have everyone take an hour to go back to their desks and sort through what they are working on. This does NOT mean that they should try to get anything done. On the contrary, the only thing they should be doing is sorting papers and keeping a list of the 5, 10, or 50 projects they are currently engaged in.

Then, hold a thirty minute meeting (or just sit down by yourself, if you're a solo fundraiser).

Get your team together, and tell them to bring the lists they created in step #1. Each member of your development staff should take a turn explaining, as briefly as possible, what they are working on. There should be no discussion. Just a list. The goal of this meeting is for the Executive Director or Development Director to get a handle on every single thing that is going on in the organization. At the end of the meeting, allow 5 minutes for people to ask questions and get answers. Keep this meeting to 30 minutes or less.

Have the lead fundraising staff member develop a master project list for the fundraising operation.

Use the 80/20 principle here – what 20% of the work is going to result in 80% of the benefit to the charity? The end goal is for the development director to come up with a priorities list for the organization that includes all of the important tasks that must be done. For each task, the director should list what person or persons are responsible for the project, and what the deadline is for completion. Project priorities are no good without deadlines, and won't get done unless everyone knows who is responsible.

Then, publish this to do list for your team.

Tell them to throw away all of their post it notes and mini-lists. This list is it. These are the projects you are all working on, and the deadlines that need to be met. Hold a 30 minute meeting with your team each week (or with yourself, for solo fundraising shops) to review the list and see where you are hitting deadlines and where you are late. Bring order to your fundraising organization

It doesn't take weeks to get a handle on your projects. Don't put this off. The system outlined above could be done in one day – TOMMORROW, for instance!

Once you have the craziness in check, you need to make sure you have a bold fundraising plan laid out for the coming year. This is connected to the project to do list we just talked about, but more forward looking.

If you're going to rapidly grow fundraising – where? How? Who will do the work? What are the deadlines? What strategies will you use? You need a fundraising plan, and it needs to be written and concrete.

Pillar #2: Story

The second pillar of the Rapid Growth Fundraising System is story... the story your non-profit is telling. Make no mistake about it, your non-profit IS telling a story. The only way to get donors rapidly engaged with your non-profit is to get them *caught up* in the story of your organization. As we mentioned earlier, that story, that vision, needs to be a BIG vision if you want to get people excited about it.

Remember, we human beings, we like to think in terms of stories. There's something about them that speaks to the innermost part of our being. We like to get caught up stories... and not just any stories, but **big stories**. We like to get caught up in stories and adventures bigger than ourselves, to join together for a common goal and a common good.

These stories have heroes, who fight clearly on the side of the good and right and just, and villains (who may be people, but could be organizations, diseases, or bad situations) that are squarely on the side of wrong.

<u>We all want to be part of a story</u>.

Your non-profit has a story like that... I know it does. You need to refine it, bring it out, tell it to the world. This should be as part of your case statement... but if refining your case statement would take three months and lots of board approvals, then at the very least, you should modify your fundraising communications RIGHT NOW to tell a better story.

As you are fundraising, ask: what comes next in the story? What is the plan that will lead your heroes to final victory over the bad guys? And... this is key... what resources will you need? How much money will you need to raise?

That's what you need to talk about when you make your ask. The stage has been set. The story told. All that remains is for others (your prospects) to join your cause, to stand on the side of right and good. And all that requires from them is a simple "yes."

Every non-profit, no matter how small or large, can think bigger about their story.

Pillar #3: Movement

The third pillar of Rapid Growth Fundraising is movement – you can have your shop in order, you can have a plan, you can develop your story, but if your non-profit is stagnant, if your fundraising doesn't have any movement, you'll never be able to rapidly grow your fundraising. Movement is key to your fundraising efforts. There are two primary types of movement that you need at your organization: Internal Movement and Donor Movement. Let's look at each...

Internal Movement

How much is your fundraising team getting done? It probably seems like a lot, and maybe it is, but are you really moving the ball forward? Not all movement is created equal. For example, you could spend 3 hours sending out thank you letters, or you could spend 3 hours holding meetings and making three $25,000 asks to qualified prospects. Thank you letters are important, but which of these tasks really moves the organization forward more? You see, when I say movement, I don't mean activity. I mean really MOVING the ball forward.

For movement, it is important to remember the Pareto (80/20) Principle: 20% of your activity will generate 80% of your results. For rapid growth fundraising, some things will have to be left undone. I know this is scary... but you can't do it all, so focus on what really matters. Make sure you are focusing on and completing the 20% of your work that is really game changing. The rest can be handled by support staff, interns, volunteers, or left undone.

Donor Movement

The second type of movement you need at your organization is DONOR MOVEMENT. Donors should constantly be moving down your fundraising funnel. If they are not, your development operation will STAGNATE.

This is a big problem at many organizations. They find new prospects and talk to them, and then.... NOTHING. Or someone makes a gift and is added to the donor database, and then... NOTHING. This is NOT the way to rapidly grow fundraising.

You need to constantly be pushing to get people moving through the four stages of the donor pipeline that we talked about earlier in the book:

- Prospecting
- Cultivation
- Asking
- Stewardship

Be sure to track prospects through this process. Make sure they are moving through it. See where your bottlenecks are. Keep your staff focused on donor movement!

Remember, moving donors through the fundraising funnel doesn't need to take forever! In rapid growth fundraising we try to move people from new prospect to Ask in 4-6 months, tops. How quickly you can make an ask depends on the person, of course, and you should always cultivate before you ask, but fundraising doesn't need to take forever.

Pillar #4: Leverage

The fourth and final pillar of the Rapid Growth Fundraising Formula is leverage.

If you are trying to TRULY grow your fundraising RAPIDLY, it is nearly impossible to do so with your current prospect universe – the people you currently know. Otherwise, you would already be raising everything you need in order to thrive!

In order to have a donor universe that is large enough for your new expanded fundraising profile, you need to LEVERAGE your current connections to bring in new donors. You do this by building FUNDRAISING NETWORKS.

A fundraising network is a group of people who have committed to raise money on behalf of an organization or charity. It is a formal committee, loose group of support, board of directors, or other coalition that is systematically opening up its rolodex on your behalf, introducing you to new prospects who may be interested in giving to your organization.

Some common examples are finance committees, development committees, or young professionals fundraising groups. Many organizations have multiple... or even dozens of... fundraising networks working for them, all of which combine to form one gigantic network that raises a lot of money on behalf of a charity.

Fundraising networks are important because they allow you to multiply your fundraising efforts. Instead of asking just one person for just one donation, by building a fundraising network you can ask that one person to fundraise on your behalf, thus turning one ask into several, or even into hundreds, depending on the skill of your network members.

One of the biggest problems faced by non-profits is their ability (or inability) to constantly feed their fundraising funnel with new prospects. How many times have you said to yourself, "Gee, I wish we had more folks to approach for a donation!" or "Wow, I wish we had more prospects for this event..." Building good fundraising networks will allow your organization to have a never-ending supply of leads.

The Two-Ask Process

Good rapid fundraising relies on getting good referrals. I like to think of all donor relationships in terms of "two asks." The first ask is for money, the second ask is for your donors to make referrals and open up their fundraising network to you. This process builds on itself into a constantly growing network of donors... one donor refers another, who refers another, and so on...

Use the leverage of referrals to fill your pipeline with new donors!

Why Keeping Your donor Pipeline Full is So Important

The donor funnel is a true funnel – wide on one end (PROSPECTING) narrow on the other (STEWARDING). People weed themselves out as you approach and cultivate them. It is important to keep feeding new prospects into the funnel so that as people weed themselves out, you'll have enough people moving through that you can make the asks you need to fund your mission.
Many organizations have trouble feeding their pipeline. If you have trouble feeding your pipeline with new prospects, you will find it impossible to reach your fundraising goals.

Upgrading and Reactivating Donors

Crucial to the success of Rapid Growth Fundraising is upgrading current donors (so that they give more this year than last year) and reactivating lapsed donors (who used to give, but no longer do). Current and lapsed donors are the *low hanging fruit* of your fundraising program.

Remember… the people most likely to give to your non-profit are people who have given in the past. Likewise, the people most likely to give a $1,000 gift this year are people who have given $250, $500, or $750 in previous years.

If you're seeking to rapidly grow fundraising, you have to put lots of focus on the low hanging fruit. This includes UPGRADING CURRENT DONORS by getting them to give more this year than they did last year and REACTIVATING LAPSED DONORS to get them to start giving again.

How to Upgrade Your Current Donors

In order to get your current donors to upgrade, you have to ASK. It's that simple. Most nonprofits never actually go out and ask their donors to give more this year than last year. The best upgrade asks are made in person or over the phone, but for lower level donors you can also ask through the mail.

I have a 5 step strategy for asking donors to upgrade:

Step 1: Acknowledge the Most Recent Gift or Current Pledge - the first step in asking a donor to upgrade is to recognize your donor for their most recent gift or the current pledge they are paying off. Thank them for their support and investment in your organization and let them know the crucial role they play as part of your team.

Step 2: Show the Positive Outcomes from the Most Recent Gift or Current Pledge - explain to your donor all of the great things you have been able to do with their money – all of the people that are being helped, all the good that is being done in the world as a result of their gift. Alternately, if you are asking the donor to upgrade a pledge, show them all of the wonderful things that your WILL be able to do as they pay off their commitment.

Step 3: Explain Why You Need More Money - The next step is to explain why your organization is seeking more money. Have things changed? Has your vision gotten bigger? Are you extremely close to your goal, and asking current donors for more support to end your campaign? Are you launching a new project or trying to serve more clients? You're going to be asking this donor, who has already given you money, for a larger gift. Explain to him or her why you need more.

Step 4: Ask Your Donor to Upgrade – This is where you make your ask. Your ask should be concrete (for a specific amount) and an actual question. Don't make a statement like "we could really use more support," and don't ask for a wishy-washy amount (asking for "as much more as you can give" is not an effective way to upgrade). Instead, ask something like, "Would you be able to increase your pledge from $25,000 to $50,000 over the next five years?"

Step 5: Be Quiet - As with all asks, the final step is to be quiet. Once you make the ask, stop talking. Let your donor think. Then let them talk first. It may seem awkward, or like too long a pause, but it's not. Sit tight. You'll receive far more yes's if you stay quiet after the ask than if you keep on talking.

Make a plan for upgrading your donors *this year*! Your current donors truly are the low hanging fruit for your non-profit.

How to Reactivate Lapsed Donors

Lapsed donors are important because (a) they have already shown an affinity for your organization and (b) they have already demonstrated their willingness to write a check for charity. If you want to bring them back into the fold, you need to reach out to your lapsed donors to find out why they stopped giving and to encourage them to start giving again.

As with all things, the best way to do this is with a personal visit or call for large or mid-level lapsed donors, but you can use snail mail letters or e-mails for lower-level lapsed donors, if you like.
The best way to reactivate a lapsed donor is to be direct. Tell them:

- We appreciate all of the support you have given us in the past
- We miss you
- We're doing great work, and have a huge vision for the future

Then... make an ask – either for a gift, or ask them to come to a non-ask event or other cultivation event that will help ease their way back into the non-profit. Remember, lapsed donors don't come back unless you ask!

Bringing it All Together – A Step by Step Plan for Using the Rapid Growth Fundraising System ™ at Your Non-Profit

Let's say you want to implement this strategy this year to raise dramatically more money at your organization. You're chomping at the bit. Your board is supportive, your staff is ready. What steps should you take – starting today – to implement Rapid Growth Fundraising?

Preparation

First you need to prepare using the 4 pillars of the system:

Order – get your development office in order. See what programs and strategies you are currently using. What projects are on the horizon? Get everyone on the same page with deadlines and responsibilities. Then create a plan for the coming year using the tactics we talked about in the first two webinars.

Story – Frame your non-profit's story in the most compelling way possible. How is your organization changing the world or making your city a better place? What is your BIG vision for the future? Figure it out and write it down.

Movement – Remember, there are two kinds of movement. The first is internal movement... have your team commit to focusing only on what truly matters in moving the ball forward. Focus on the 20% of your work that results in 80% of your results. Delegate the rest to volunteers and interns, or drop those items this year.

Then, focus on donor movement. Draw up a prospect map to show the universe of prospects you can go after. Develop a plan for reaching out to them. Schedule non-ask events and other methods for bringing new donors into your pipeline. Have a plan in place for cultivating those donors such that you can make asks within 4-6 months of first meeting them. Then steward your donors to leverage their relationships.

Leverage – Ask your donors for referrals. Set up fundraising networks. Make a plan for getting your donors to open up their rolodexes to you.

Then it's time to take action:

Action

Upgrade Current Donors – Divide your donors into high-level, mid-level and low-level donors. Figure out how many donors your team can visit, how many you can call, and how many you have to send letters to. Then go out there and ask for renewals and upgrades from every single donor you have.

Reactivate Lapsed Donors – Set up meetings and make calls to people who haven't given in 1 year, 2 years, 3 years. Tell them you miss them. Ask them make a gift and get involved again.

Find New Prospects – Use the strategies we talked about in the first webinar. Most importantly, set up fundraising networks to get your donors in the habit of bringing new donors into your orbit.

Cultivate Current Prospects – Hold small group meetings, lunches, send out special e-updates. Have a plan for cultivating all of the new prospects in your pipeline.

Make Asks in Short Order – Don't wait around. Remember, an ask needs to be concrete (for a specific amount) and a question. Once you ask, wait silently for an answer.

Steward Your Donors into Providing Referrals – Take good care of those who make a gift to your organization, and prepare them for that second ask – to open up their networks to you and help you find new donors.

Appendix A: Sample Case for Support

Amber   **is hurt…**
                 is afraid…
                 is alone…

Together, we can change her world.

Every month, over 150 cases of child physical abuse are reported in the City of Montreal. For these children, the nightmare is far from over.

After suffering physically and emotionally scarring abuse - often for years, and more often than not at the hands of someone they know – these children must undergo extensive medical tests, hours of interviews by different investigators, multiple court appearances and a sense of shame and guilt after being abused and victimized. They are put into a system that is confusing for them… one that wasn't designed for a child's emotional or physical needs, and where they feel afraid and alone.

With Your Help, It Doesn't Have to Be this Way

Today, over one-third of children victimized by physical abuse in Montreal are taken to the Montreal Children's Home. Here, in a child-friendly facility that is built around their needs, they are seen by an expert staff trained to work with child victims. Here, they avoid multiple interviews by different investigators, and are seen by one specially trained interviewer, who gives the child an opportunity to tell their story and get the truth out into the open.

At the Home, every child and his or her family is assigned a Victim Advocate who walks them through the process, gives the family referrals for medical treatment and counseling, and accompanies the child to court when he or she needs to testify. In fact, because other family members may also be witnesses in the case, our Victim Advocates are often the only friendly face a child will see in the courtroom when they are facing their abuser – an experience many abuse survivors say is the most harrowing experience of their lives.

Your support enables the Home to provide these services, and many more, at absolutely no charge to victims or families, and has emboldened us to set an ambitious goal: having the resources within the next five years to see every single child in Montreal who is victimized by Physical abuse.

The Shocking Statistics on Child Physical Abuse…

- 1 in 4 girls in North America will be physically abused before the age of 18
- 1 in 6 boys in North America will be physically abused before the age of 18
- 70% of all physical assaults occur to children under the age of 18
- 20% of all child physical abuse victims were abused before the age of 8

…and the Toll it Takes in Later Life

- Children who are abused are more likely to experience depression, develop eating disorders, and experience health problems as adults
- Over 70% of child physical abuse victim later abuse drugs or alcohol
- Almost 50% of women in state prison were physically abused as children
- 75% of teenage prostitutes were previously physically abused

The Montreal Children's Home: Justice and Healing for Physically Abused Children

Founded in 1991, the Montreal Children's Home works to bring justice and healing to the city's most vulnerable children. At our child-friendly facility we offer:

Children's Forensic Interviewing

Our expert Forensic Interviewers are trained to make children feel comfortable, and to allow them to tell their story. Prior to each interview, our staff meets with representatives of the police department and the Department of Human Services. Each of these officials watches the interview through a one-way mirror or on closed-circuit television, thus eliminating the need for the child to tell his or her story over and over again. Each interviewer is trained to work with children in a way that is non-leading, developmentally appropriate, and non-traumatizing. The interviews take place in our child-friendly facility, complete with colorful drawings on the walls, games, books, teddy-bears, and a smiling and supportive staff. The Home also has a bilingual interviewer on staff to work with our Spanish-speaking children. Each year we see children of all ages, from two to eighteen years old, and from all nationalities and neighborhoods in the city.

Victim Advocacy Services

Our team of trained Victim Advocates cares for the child victims and their families throughout the process. While the child is being interviewed, our staff meets with the family or caretaker to provide crisis counseling, determine what additional services are needed, and offer referrals for medical treatment, counseling, and support groups. The Victim Advocate also tracks the court case, guides the child through the process, and attends court proceedings with the child victim. Our staff also offers a number of support groups right in our own facility.

Since our founding, the Montreal Children's Home has grown steadily, and today provides services to an average of 50 child physical abuse victims per month.

> "Without the Montreal Children's Home, the Montreal Police Department couldn't provide the level of service that we need to provide to our child abuse victims."
> - *John Sylvester, Special Victims Unit*

"This city needs the Montreal Children's Home – it is a safe place
for physically abused children."
- Jan Holstein, Assistant State's Attorney

Leading the Way

The Montreal Children's Home had been a leading catalyst for
change in how abused children are served and cared for in the city.
As the catalyst for a team-based approach, the Home has fought to
reduce trauma for children, increase efficiency in the system, and
provide justice and healing to child victims in a safe and timely
manner.

The Home is part of a network of programs across the country that
works to end child physical abuse by implementing child-friendly
forensic interviews and a team-based approach to better care for our
children. As a leader in the field, the Home trains front-line workers
in the city, as well as offers guidance and training to similar
programs throughout North America.

With Your Help, No Abused Child Needs to Feel Alone

Today, the Montreal Children's Home sees just over one-third of the
1,900 child Physical abuse victims in the city each year. While the
number of children we see has grown every year, it is still not
enough. Our goal is simple, but ambitious: by 2012, every single
child victim of physical abuse in Montreal will be served at the
Children's Home.

To accomplish that goal, we will need to expand both our facilities
and staff. Through the generous contributions of our donors, we've
already begun: this winter, we will be moving to a spacious 8,000
square foot facility, complete with additional interview rooms,
private family waiting areas, and more space for investigators from
the police department, staff from the DA's office, and for DHS
social workers. Over the past year, we have hired additional trained
interviewers and advocates, including a bilingual interviewer to
serve our Spanish-speaking children.

What it Costs to Save a Child from a Lifetime of Abuse and Shame

Providing the Home's services to a child who has been victimized by physical abuse costs about $1,000 beyond our government funding stream. This includes the cost to operate our child-friendly facility, provide forensic interviews for victims, and provide ongoing victim advocacy and support services to the child and his or her family.

In 2008, the Home had an operating budget of almost $900,000. Of that amount, over 55% of our budget came from individual donors and corporate and foundation grants. To enable us to serve every child victim in Montreal, we will need to increase our budget dramatically over the coming years to support our increased facility space and staff. For the next three fiscal years, our budget needs to be:

2009 –2010	$1,181,646
2010 –2011	$1,297,879
2011 –2012	$1,460,616

While these goals are ambitious, they are necessary… and we know that we can meet them through the continued generosity of our donors and the community. Every dollar that we raise is going directly to increasing our capacity to serve abused children.

The Montreal Children's Home spends only 9% of its revenue on administration and 7% on fundraising. That means a full 84% of your gift goes directly to supporting programs and services for physically abused children.

How You Can Help Stop the Abuse
… and let a Child Know She is Not Alone

The Home needs your help to reach our goal of serving each and every victim of child physical abuse in Montreal. While your gift to the Home will depend on your own financial situation, we would be pleased to help you make a gift that meets both your needs and those of our children.

One-time gifts are gratefully accepted and used to support our general services, or may be restricted to one particular service or program at the direction of the donor. Pledge payments over time may be arranged according to your individual preferences.

Friends of the Children's Home

In addition to one-time gifts, our "Friends of the Children's Home" program recognizes donors who pledge to support the Home with a gift for each of the next three years. These supporters form the core of financial support for our growth plan and enable us to expand, confident that the fiscal needs for the services we offer will be met. These key donors support us at the following levels:

Guardian: Enables the Home to Serve Five Additional Children per Year.

$5,000+ per year for 3 years will allow the Home to provide complete child-friendly forensic interviewing and victim advocacy / support services to five children per year. ($417 per month)

Advocate: Enables the Home to Serve One Additional Child per Year.

$1,000 per year for 3 years will allow the Home to provide complete child-friendly forensic interviewing and victim advocacy / support services to one child per year. ($84 per month)

Supporter: Enables the Home to Provide Forensic Interviewing for One Additional Child per Year

$500 per year for 3 years will allow the Home to provide a child-friendly forensic interview, including digital videotaping and analysis, plus expert court testimony in cases of substantiated abuse, for one child per year. ($42 per month)

Three-year pledges to the Friends of the Children's Home program may be paid on a monthly, quarterly, or yearly basis. Monthly auto-debiting is available.

Planned Giving

The Home also gratefully accepts gifts through wills, bequests, and estates. Please contact our development office for more information.

Our Team of Supporters Makes it All Possible...
Join Them in Stopping Child Physical Abuse Today

Every year, over 1,000 individuals, businesses, and foundations join together to support the Montreal Children's Home. Their support, and yours, is needed now more than ever. It's time to make sure that every Physically abused child... no matter how hurt, no matter how afraid, no matter how poor... has access to the resources of the Children's Home.

To join our team and support our children, please call our Development Office at 982.287.9520, or e-mail us at jill@savemontrealschildren.ca

Appendix B: Sample Fundraising Plan

Kilkenny Children's Home
Development Plan
2009 – 2010

Background Summary

The Kilkenny Children's Home has begun an exciting new phase of growth which calls for the creation of a larger, more structured, and more entrepreneurial development organization. This development plan builds on the work that has already been completed by the board to lay out the strategy, tactics, and timelines necessary to meet the KCH's ambitious goals. In doing so, this development plan is guided by two key documents:

The Strategic Plan – The KCH's board-approved Strategic Plan defines the agency's ultimate goal: being able to provide the Home's core services to 100% of the population of reported abused children each year. In order to meet this goal, the Strategic Plan lays out a three year program of growth in all areas, including office space, staff, victim support services, collateral materials and marketing needs. The goals of the Home also include an expanded research agenda, and the possibility of expanded services after meeting our 100% goal. This development plan begins with the second year of the growth plan, and presents a strategy for meeting the Strategic Plan's budget needs in years 2 and 3, and into a 4th year.

The Development Audit – The KCH recently completed a comprehensive Development Audit utilizing the consulting services of GHRadnor LLC. This audit provided a clear and definitive overview of the Home's current fundraising capabilities and noted the potential for growth in a number of areas. The Development Audit provides a blueprint for our fundraising growth and this development plan is thoroughly informed by the audit's findings.

Types of Funding

It is important, at this point in the plan, to differentiate between the various funding streams that provide revenue for the KCH:

Philanthropic Fundraising – This includes all money raised from non-governmental sources for the KCH. The three primary types of philanthropic funding the KCH currently engages in includes:

> Individual Giving – Money raised from individuals shall be the primary focus of the KCH's development efforts

> Foundation Giving – Money raised from foundations and grant-writing comprises a significant portion of our fundraising efforts, but is not our primary focus.

> Events – Money raised from fundraising events will continue to be a key part of our plan.

Government Contracts and Funding – While it is important to include the large amount of government revenue that we receive as part of any development plan for the KCH, it is equally important to note that government funding is not the primary focus of our fundraising efforts. The primary focus of our efforts shall be raising philanthropic dollars to support the KCH's work.

Goals and Objectives

The primary goal of this development plan is to provide the funding necessary to carry out the KCH's growth agenda, which will allow the Home to meet the needs of 100% of Kilkenny's homeless children. The board's growth planning budget has set the following revenue goals for the next three years:

7/1/2009 – 6/30/2010	$1,181,646
7/1/2010 – 6/30/2011	$1,297,879
7/1/2011 – 6/30/2012	$1,460,616

Thus, the goal of this plan is to provide a detailed strategy to raise the above budgeted revenues. In order to meet this goal, the Kilkenny Children's Home must meet the following objectives:

- Build a development infrastructure that is capable of handling a fast-growing, dynamic fundraising operation of the size and scope laid out by this plan

- Establish scalable fundraising systems capable of providing maximum efficiency for a relatively small development staff

- Provide easy and concrete methods for cultivating and maintaining relationships with donors and prospects

- Reach outside the Home's current core donors to build an ever-expanding universe of prospects

- Operate in a professional and entrepreneurial manner, utilizing development best practices, ambitious goals, and measurable metrics

Assumptions

In formulating this plan, the Kilkenny Children's Home is operating under the following assumptions:

- The KCH has developed a strong base of friends, prospects, and donors during its history, but has lacked the staff resources to effectively maximize those contacts

- Our board of directors is committed to the Home's growth plan.

- The area of greatest need for the Home is in developing an individual giving program. To date, the KCH has enjoyed strong foundation, government, and event programs, but has lacked the resources to efficiently tap into the individual giving market, which accounts for over 80% of all philanthropic gifts made in the United States

- The current fundraising environment will be a challenging one due to the state of the economy, which has led to dwindling savings, profits, and investment portfolios among our individual and corporate donors and falling endowments among those foundations which support us financially

- A well planned and entrepreneurial fundraising operation will allow the KCH to meet its ambitious revenue goals

Development Infrastructure

In order to effectively carry out this plan and build a professional development network, the Home will need to enlarge and strengthen its current development infrastructure:

Case for Support

The Home should develop strong case of support with several case statements aimed at our various funding prospects which provide both factual and emotional reasons for those individuals, corporations, government agencies and foundations to get involved with the KCH. These case statements must provide client anonymity while at the same time sufficiently draw donors into supporting our efforts. Similarly, the case for support and statements must provide a factual basis for our funding needs while being generic enough to be used in a wide variety of fundraising opportunities. Effective case statements will include compelling stories of the work that we do, coupled with evidence of the societal benefit of our work and the efficient stewardship of donor resources. Case statements should be able to be used by board members, staff members, friends and others who are interested in generating support for our work.

Action Steps (Deadline)
- Research case for support best practices (April 10, 2009)
- Work with KCH program staff to locate / generate necessary information (May 1, 2009)
- Finalize case for support and 2-4 case statements (May 15, 2009)
- Present case and case statements for board approval (July board meeting)

Donor Database

The Home currently uses File Maker Pro to track donors and prospects. The reporting capabilities, relationship-building functions, and prospecting tools provided by the current software package are inadequate to meet the needs of a development organization of our current and future size. Consequently, the KCH should move to a fundraising-specific database package as soon as possible.

Bobbi Schmitt and Rob Davies have already performed significant research into the available software packages, which will substantially inform the database process. Further, the staff has determined that the optimal time for switching to a new database is at the end of the current fiscal year / beginning of the new fiscal year, July 1, 2009. The package must be in place, the data must be migrated, and the staff trained far enough in advance of that date to ensure a successful transition.

Action Steps (Deadline)
- Research database packages, pricing schemes, support, migration, and training issues (May 1, 2009)
- Finalize decision on database package (May 15, 2009)
- New database installed, data migrated, package fully functional (June 15, 2009)
- Staff training complete (June 25, 2009)
- Begin using new database (July 1, 2009)

Uniform Prospect and Donor Tracking Procedures

Once the database is fully operational, the KCH must have standard practices in place for handling new prospects and donors, including appropriate paperwork that may be used by the board, committees, affinity groups, and event hosts. These procedures should allow us to ensure that all prospects and donors are entered into our database and cultivation systems with the appropriate level of information and that allows for correct and efficient follow-up to be made. Therefore, the Home should develop a small set of one-page memos and forms to be used in handling new prospects and donors, or when a donor or prospect is contacted by one of the friends of the Home.

These procedures cannot be effectively established until after our new donor database is in place.

Action Steps (Deadline)
- Develop necessary memos and forms for prospect and donor tracking (August 1, 2009)

Website

Most Home stakeholders agree that the time is right to redesign and update the KCH's website. The website redesign is a portion of the Home's overall marketing agenda, and thus the objectives and timelines for the website redesign will be handled in the agency's forthcoming marketing and public relations plan, and not in this document.

Until such time as that redesign is completed, however, the portions of the KCH's website that deal with fundraising and prospect development are in need of some updated features, copy, and creative design. Similarly, because this development plan will call for an e-mail marketing campaign as part of our donor cultivation plan, presented below, the development office needs to be sure that our current e-mail marketing capabilities will be able to effectively convey our fundraising message.

Therefore, the KCH should conduct a brief audit of our web and e-mail fundraising capabilities and creative, and make such changes as are necessary to effectively carry out our development mission until the overall web redesign is completed.

Action Steps (Deadline)
- Perform web, e-giving and e-mail fundraising capabilities audit and generate list of required changes prior to complete web redesign (June 15, 2009)
- Work with appropriate vendors and stakeholders to complete necessary changes (August 15, 2009)

Staffing

Depending on the success and growth velocity of both this plan and the forthcoming public relations/ marketing plan, the development office should consider the possibility that it may need to bring on an additional staff person at some point in the third year of this plan, or thereafter, to handle the growing donor account services work that will be necessary as we build donor relationships and affinity groups, as well to handle general office support for the development and public relations operations of the KCH. Because of the Home's limited resources, this decision should only be made when it is clear that a lack of additional staff support is hindering our work product.

Board Development Training

As will be seen from the rest of this plan, the active and informed participation of the Board of Directors in our fundraising efforts will be integral to our ultimate success. In addition to their current fundraising activities on behalf of the Home, members of the board will be asked to make donor cultivation calls, help populate both non-ask and ask fundraising events, hold events and expand our donor and prospect universe.

In conversations with board members regarding this plan, many members of the board expressed a desire to learn more about fundraising best practices and to hone their fundraising skills through additional development training.

The development staff, in conjunction with the Development Committee, should plan an ongoing board development training program to assist the board with meeting their fundraising goals on our behalf.

Action Steps (Deadline)
- Discuss board training schedule and goals at next Development Committee meeting and add result to overall development timeline (April 9, 2009)

Board Meeting Development Goals

Traditionally, the development office has been allotted time at the KCH board meetings for development reporting. This time is normally spent updating the board on development receipts and future goals. While the board should continue to receive regular development updates at these meetings, in the future, development time at board meetings should be more heavily weighted towards "activities." These activities should include reviewing prospect lists and assigning contacts, discussing and assigning donor/prospect cultivation calls, brainstorming contacts, events, and targets, and other items that will lead to an increased donor and prospect universe and additional dollars raised.

Donor Communications and Cultivation

Maintaining a uniform, scalable system of donor and prospect communications will be a key factor in leveraging the time and resources of the KCH's small development organization as we grow our donor universe. In pursuing an aggressive cultivation agenda, several prime methods will need to be established for communicating our message and needs:

Collateral Materials

In order to provide non-monetary methods for prospects to get involved with the KCH prior to making a financial commitment to our organization, the Home should prepare a list of volunteer opportunities that are available with our agency, as well as a "wish list" of tangible items that would aid us in carrying out our mission. Similarly, we should develop a comprehensive list of in-kind donations that would be beneficial to our agency to inform our efforts to get new donors excited and involved in our work.

Action Steps (Deadline)
- Research / organize lists of volunteer opportunities, in-kind donations, and "wish list" items at KCH (June 1, 2009)
- Prepare useable, well formatted documents based on these lists (June 10, 2009)

Command Appearance Script and Materials

As the KCH grows its individual, corporate, and foundation giving programs, numerous opportunities will arise for the development staff and/or executive director to hold one-on-one and small group meetings ("command appearances") with prospects to inform them about the Home's mission and current state of affairs. These meetings will often be "non-ask" meetings, similar to the "non-ask events" mentioned below, where the actual ask will take place after the meeting, in subsequent follow-up phone calls and/or meetings.

The KCH should prepare a strong, well-designed script for these meetings, as well as gather the collateral materials that would best support our message, to allow us to conduct effective meetings with relatively short notice.

Action Steps (Deadline)
- Prepare scripts and collateral materials list for command appearance meetings (June 20, 2009)

Non-Ask Events

For several years, the Home offered non-ask tour events to prospective donors on an every other month schedule. These tours were generally successful, but due to a lack of staff resources, the agency was not able to effectively follow-up with prospects that attended, or mine our network for additional attendees. The KCH should re-start a non-ask event program that can be used as a first point of contact with potential funders. These events should take two distinct shapes:

KCH Tour Events - The Home should re-start a system of in-house office tours for prospects to be conducted at our North County location or at any new location.

Outside Events ("KCH in a box") – The Home should actively seek out the opportunity to hold non-ask events in other locations, such as local law firms, supporters' offices, etc.

In order to make the best possible use of our limited resources, the KCH should prepare compelling scripts and materials for these non-ask events, and in our first year should limit the number that is held to allow for maximum leverage of staff time.

Action Steps (Deadline)
- Research the KCH's previous tour program and non-ask event best practices (July 5, 2009)
- Establish schedule of Fall 2009 and Spring 2010 non-ask events, with goal of holding 4-5 events, with 1-2 events being held at outside locations (July 10, 2009)
- Develop and begin implementing prospect strategy for moving prospects to each event. Prospects should include current and former donors and prospects, former committee and board members, auction item givers, and a select group of brand new prospects (July 20, 2009)
- Develop scripts and materials for in-house and outside non-ask events (August 20, 2009)
- Hold first non-ask event (No later than November 1, 2009)

Prospect Cultivation Strategy and Timeline

Our goal for new individual and corporate prospects is to engage them in a non-threatening way, to tell them our story and our needs, and to make them feel like part of our team. Then, after the prospect is fully engaged and we have identified their area of interest, we can ask for funding in an effective manner.

Our first step with any new individual or corporate prospect should be to arrange for them to attend one of our non-ask events, or, if the prospect is at the appropriate potential giving level, arrange to meet with the prospect for a command performance. After the initial contact, we will need to communicate with the prospect on a regular basis to answer questions, continue to tell our story, and eventually seek support.

Our timeline for prospect cultivation will be as follows:

1. Receive information on new prospect from friend of the KCH, event, or other source

2. Perform basic research on prospect giving ability, source of funds, etc.
3. Determine who will make invitation call
4. Invite prospect to non-ask event or suggest command performance
5. Attend event / meeting
6. Within one week of event / meeting, perform follow-up call with prospect to determine level of interest and strengthen relationship.
7. If prospect indicates they are not interested in KCH, drop from list and STOP CULTIVATION. If prospect indicates some level of interest, add to prospect mailing list to receive appropriate communication from KCH
8. For interested prospects at higher levels, develop individual timeline for getting prospect more involved. For lower level prospects, add to ALL KCH communications (including mail asks) and schedule one follow-up call for after prospect has received written / e-mail communications from Home.

Development Communications Strategy and Timeline

In addition to our prospect cultivation plan, it is imperative that the KCH strengthen its program of regular communications with donors and prospects. This program will be comprised primarily of non-solicitation communications for the purposes of building and stewarding our donor/prospect relationships, along with a few well-timed asks. Research shows that donors who are contacted and communicated with using a variety of online and offline formats give bigger gifts and give more often. Thus, our communications strategy will utilize the following varied tactics:

Snail Mail: We will continue to utilize standard postal mail for a number of communications, including our annual report, our newsletter (currently mailed once per year), event invites, and direct mail solicitations (e.g. the annual campaign)

E-Mail: The KCH will begin a program of regular e-mail communications, including one e-mail solicitation per year

<u>Recognition Events</u>: In addition to the non-ask events which will begin in the 2009-2010 portion of this plan, the KCH should begin a series of recognition events for appropriate level donors (e.g. lunch with the executive director for our top donors, a breakfast with a guest speaker for our mid-level donors, etc.) For additional information, see Donor Recognition Plan, below

<u>Phone Calls</u>: Donors at appropriate levels should be thanked, via phone, for their gifts after they are received, and also should be thanked, via phone, for their support at an appropriate time during the year, during a "Know-Your-Donor Campaign" targeted specifically at lower level donors that we don't often talk with.

The KCH's development communications timeline for the 2009-2010 year should be as follows:

Donor/Prospect Level	July 2009	August 2009	Sept. 2009	Oct. 2009
$500 and up	Summer Snail Mail Newsletter	E-Update	Annual Report	Annual Campaign $
$499 and under	Summer Snail Mail Newsletter	E-Update	Annual Report w/Re-engagement questionnaire	Annual Campaign $

Donor/Prospect Level	Nov. 2009	Dec. 2009	January 2010	February 2010
$500 and up	Gala Sponsor Calls; E-update	Donor Recognition Event		E-update
$499 and under	E-update	Donor Recognition Event		Know Your Donor Call Program; E-update

Donor/Prospect Level	March 2010	April 2010	May 2010	June 2010
$500 and up	Gala Mailings $		E-Solicitation $	**Annual Giving Program Launch**
$499 and under	Gala Mailings $		E-Solicitation $	

*In 2010-2011, the Home should determine whether staff resources will permit a Winter Snail Mail Newsletter, which may be mailed in December starting with December 2010.

Donor Recognition Program

The KCH should institute a donor recognition program to thank and encourage our donors and draw them into deeper relationship with the Home. This recognition program will have the following components:

Thank You Procedure: The KCH will continue its practice of ensuring that each large gift-giver receives a personal thank you call and that all gift-givers at all levels receive thank you notes following their gifts. The KCH should develop a script for these thank you calls that is designed to garner information and funnel it into a plan to grow and develop the relationship with that individual giver. In addition, for the 2009-1010 fiscal year, all new donors, regardless of size of gift, should receive a personal phone call, and be invited to a non-ask event. The KCH should seek out board member volunteers to make these calls.

Donor Recognition Event: Beginning this year, the KCH should host a small, informal, inexpensive, non-ask thank you event for donors at all levels, where we reinforce our mission with a quick update, perhaps offer a compelling speaker and an open bar, and let our supporters meet each other and build their relationship to the Home. The KCH should also consider inviting volunteers to this event.

<u>Annual Giving Clubs</u>: In addition to the thank you procedure and the donor recognition event, the annual giving clubs mentioned below will offer a complete range of donor recognition for members at each level.

<u>Action Steps (Deadline)</u>
- Prepare thank you call script, forms, and procedure sheet * Development Director will need to know checks that come in on a weekly basis with event code, and contact source (April 30, 2009)
- Solicit board member volunteers for calls and provide training materials (May board meeting)
- Write event plan for 1st annual donor recognition event to take place in December, 2009 (September 15, 2009)

Annual Giving Program

The key innovation for the KCH during the 2009-2010 fiscal year will be the introduction of a multi-year annual giving program aimed at individual donors. The purpose of using this program as our first major development project are twofold: first, as an efficient way of targeting individual donors and moving our current prospects to make a gift and our current donors to increase their gifts, and second, to provide a stable support system for the Home and begin to pull us out of our current "start from scratch every year" methodology.

Our strategy for starting this program will begin with re-engaging our current high-level donors and prospects through one-on-one meetings and phone calls, and re-engaging our lower level donors by including a questionnaire and note with our annual report mailing to these donors, and making follow-up calls regarding returned questionnaires where appropriate. <u>These calls and meetings will also serve as an opportunity to ask for new gifts this year, prior to the launch of our annual giving program, wherever appropriate.</u>

The KCH will develop 3-4 giving levels, along with an appropriate number of recognition methods for each level. Similarly, the KCH will develop collateral materials explaining the program, including pledge cards asking for a three year commitment to one of these levels, and will brand the program with an appropriate name and logo.

Over the course of this year, as we re-engage our current prospects and donors, we will be preparing for the launch of our annual giving program, in June, 2010. Depending on the response to these meetings and the number of annual giving program prospects in our universe, we will roll out the program in June, 2010 with either a launch/pledge event or with one-on-one and small group meetings. Under either scenario, the KCH should make a big deal out of this launch. All pledges made during the June, 2010 roll out would begin funding in the 2010-2011 fiscal year, and would provide a solid foundation for our fundraising efforts that year. In this or future years, there is also the possibility of adding a challenge / matching gift component to the annual giving program event.

To make this plan effective, we will also need to make changes to The Board Giving Campaign. For 2009-2010, the board giving campaign will continue as normal. However, for 2010-2011, the KCH should ask the board to include the "board giving campaign" as a leadership portion of the annual giving campaign. Thus, for 2010-2011, the board would be asked to make a financial pledge during the annual giving program roll-out in June, 2010, with the funding not occurring until the 2010-2011 fiscal year. Thenceforth, the Board Giving Campaign would serve as a leadership component of each year's annual giving program.

Action Steps (Deadline)
- Develop list of prospects and donors for re-engagement and determine method of re-engagement (August 10, 2009)
- Develop re-engagement questionnaire and materials for low-level donor mail-out (August 20, 2009)
- Begin high-level donor and prospect re-engagement calls and meetings (begin no later than September 10, 2009)
- Complete low-level donor questionnaire follow-up (complete no later than January 10, 2010

- Create annual giving program levels, brand, logo, etc. (February 1, 2010)
- Create collateral materials for annual giving program (February 15, 2010)
- Develop master list of annual giving prospects for launch (March 15, 2010)
- Decide on launch structure and event/meeting planning requirements (March 15, 2010)
- Work with board on leadership gifts / board giving campaign for annual giving program (April 10, 2010)
- Mail invitations to launch events and/or schedule launch solicitation meetings (April 15, 2010)
- Hold Annual Giving Program Launch (June, 2010)

Year 2 (2010-2011)
- Continue program growth; replace donor re-engagement with high level donor and prospect meetings as part of the donor cultivation plan

Year 3 (2011-2012)
- Continue program growth; consider adding annual giving program leadership structure and/or committee

Direct Mail Program

The KCH will continue to mail out its annual campaign appeal letter in the fall of each year, and in year 2 of this plan, will research the benefits of a more comprehensive direct mail prospecting and housefile mailing program.

Affinity Group Program

The Kilkenny Children's Home currently has a strong board structure, as well as a highly effective committee working on The Gala, the Home's marquee annual event. To date, the KCH has not offered many opportunities for its friends and donors to interact and network with each other outside of these committees and the Gala event.

Starting an affinity group program based on members' common interests would not only allow the KCH to offer additional recognition and benefits to its supporters, but would also provide an easy way for our supporters to invite their friends to join them in their support in a non-threatening manner. These affinity groups should be asked to provide knowledge/suggestions, volunteers, and eventually funding to support the work of the KCH.

While there are many affinity groups that may be started to support the Home, the group with the best potential for a quick start-up would be a group of attorneys who supported the KCH. There are a number of attorneys who already contribute time and money to the Home, and these lawyers should provide a solid foundation for our affinity group efforts. Additional affinity groups may be started in subsequent years.

In order to efficiently organize each group, the Home should seek out a core group of potential members to form a steering committee, which will name the group, solicit members, and help drive the affinity group effort. Each group may also have its own collateral materials, as needed, to aid the members in their work on our behalf. Groups should be presented with a multitude of ways to help, including but not limited to monetary contributions.

Action Steps (Deadline)
- Begin prospect list for lawyers affinity group steering committee (February 1, 2010)
- Begin soliciting prospects for steering committee (February 20, 2010)
- Create agenda and collateral materials for steering committee meeting (March 31, 2010)
- Hold lawyers affinity group steering committee meeting (April, 2010)

Year 2 (2010-2011)
- Expand lawyers affinity group
- Create second affinity group for KCH (possible groups: Young Friends of the Home, Business Leaders Supporting Kids)

Year 3 (2011-2012)
- Expand current affinity groups
- Create   third   affinity   group   for   KCH

Major Event: The Gala

The KCH has had great success with the Gala, which should remain the Home's one "marquee event" each year. Each of our funding sources, from individuals to corporations to affinity groups can and should be re-solicited each year for this one event, even if they have already made a substantial gift to the Home during the year.

While this event initially began as a Young Friends of the KCH event, it has begun to morph into an all-Home fundraising event and showcase for our work (through the awards, etc.) The KCH should, with the approval and support of those who have driven the event each year from the board and elsewhere, make this our official fundraising event each year, and drop the "Young Friends" moniker. (The Young Friends group should, however, be restarted with its own event as an affinity group, see above).

Our goal for the Gala should be to substantially grow this event, through the introduction of well-known headliners, business and celebrity partners, event chairs and co-chairs, and by seeking "adoption" of the event by large giving networks (the Eagles, labor unions, etc.)

Action Steps (Deadline)
- Create detailed event plan and timeline for Gala 2010, including review of ticket prices and giving levels (September 15, 2009)
- Create detailed sponsor and ticket sale plan and timeline for Gala 2010, including a plan for substantially growing the event, as mentioned above (September 30, 2009)

Year 2 (2010-2011)
- Continue event growth, consider seeking additional well-known headliners for event

<u>Year 3 (2011-2012)</u>
- Continue event growth, consider adding affinity group pre- or post-event components

Hosted Event Program

Recently, the KCH has begun having great success with "hosted events," small house parties and other gatherings held by board members and supporters to raise money for the Home. These small events serve three purposes: (1) raising money for the Home, (2) raising awareness of the Home, and (3) generating new prospects for future fundraising efforts.

The KCH should develop a scalable program for encouraging and supporting our friends to host events on our behalf by creating an "event in a box:" a handbook detailing how to hold an event on our behalf, along with the supporting materials a prospective event host will need in preparing for their event.

Additionally, a core group of supporters has held extremely successful charity golf tournaments on our behalf for a number of years. These hosted events are an integral part of our funding stream, and should be continued. This group has indicated a desire to have the KCH staff take a larger role in planning this even, which occurs every fall. The Home development staff should speak with the group leadership to determine what level of involvement we need to have this year and over the coming years, and to develop an event plan for this year's event.

In addition, during the 2009-2010 fiscal year, several North County Rotary Clubs are hosting a Black Tie Dinner Event and Fashion Show on our behalf.

<u>Action Steps (Deadline)</u>
- Speak with Golf Committee regarding 2009-2010 Golf Event (June 1, 2009)
- Develop event plan and timeline for KCH's involvement in Golf Event (June 20, 2009)
- Develop "Event in a Box" handbook and materials for use by our supporters (August 31, 2009)

- Develop and begin implementing plan for seeking sponsors for Rotary Event (September 15, 2009)
- Develop strategy for seeking out supporters to host events on our behalf (September 20, 2009)
- Seek one additional hosted event for Fiscal Year 2009-2010 (October   31,   2009)

Year 2 (2010-2011)
- Goal: 2-3 events hosted on our behalf + golf tournament

Year 3 (2011-2012)
- Goal: 3-4 events hosted on our behalf + golf tournament

Foundation Giving

Traditionally, the KCH has had a very strong program soliciting grants from philanthropic and corporate foundations. The Home can and should continue aggressively pursuing grants as a source of funding our program activity and expansion. Bobbi Schmitt will continue to be primarily responsible for grant-writing and prospecting.

To promote larger and more sustained gifts, Rob Davies and Jim Martin will begin a program of meeting with grant-makers and grant prospects to showcase our programs and build deeper relationships with key decision makers. We will also invite current and prospective grant-makers to attend our non-ask events.

Because we will not be adding additional grant-writing staff, our plan for growing our foundation giving will rely primarily on utilizing the above mentioned meetings and the relationships we build to seek larger grants, as well as adding some larger grant prospects to our current solicitation mix.

Action Steps (Deadline)
- Create 2009-2010 foundation giving plan, including detailed prospect lists and timelines (May 31, 2009)
- Develop list of current and prospective grant makers to invite to non-ask events (July 15, 2009)

- Develop list of current and prospective grant makers to invite to one-on-one and small group meetings (September 1, 2009)
- Rob Davies and Jim Martin begin ongoing series of meetings with foundation executives (October 1, 2009)

Year 2 (2010-2011)
- Continue growing program and seeking out larger grants

Year 3 (2011-2012)
- Continue growing program and seeking out larger grants

Government Funding

The state, local, and federal governments all currently provide or direct funding to the Home. This funding comprises a significant portion of our annual revenues. The KCH should continue to seek forums for educating government officials about the good work that we do to both prevent a decrease in government funding as well as seek increases whenever appropriate. In order to do so, the KCH should perform a review of its current government funding and any opportunities for growth, as well as create a list of government officials to target for one-on-one meetings, tours, etc.

Additionally, the KCH has developed a plan for seeking additional, stable government funding by adding a court charge to civil court filings in Kilkenny County (note that this represents a change in the Home's original goal of adding a charge at the state level, which was fraught with difficulty). A generous donor has offered to fund the hiring of a lobbyist for the purpose of both increasing the Home's funding as well as maintaining our profile among governmental stakeholders. The Home should utilize this funding and begin speaking with lobbying firms to determine the feasibility of our plan and the recommended course of action.

Action Steps (Deadline)
- Develop list of government officials to target for relationship-building and plan for doing so (August 15, 2009)
- Perform review of current government funding and potential (September 1, 2009)

- Confirm lobbying gift level and duration with donor (September 1, 2009)
- Hold meetings with prospective lobbying firms to determine feasibility and course of action and solicit proposals (November 15, 2009)
- Review proposals and generate short lobbying plan based on these materials (December 15, 2009)
- Engage lobbying firm to solicit funding stream on our behalf (January 15, 2010)

Planned Giving

During the upcoming fiscal year, the KCH should remain focused on increasing its individual prospect base, starting a comprehensive donor communications program, and launching an annual giving program, as well as maintaining its foundation and event giving. As our programs increase and strengthen, the Home should be prepared to solicit planning gifts and bequests from our friends and supporters.

While this planned giving program will not be a major focus of our fundraising efforts during the coming year, we can and should be prepared to aid those who want to include the KCH in their wills, even if we are not yet marketing this avenue for supporting our work. The best way to be prepared is to create a short document, with the help of our supporters in the legal and non-profit development fields, detailing the options for making a bequest to the KCH.

Action Steps (Deadline)
- Work with supportive professionals to create a simple document detailing the options for making a bequest to the KCH and ensuring that we have the necessary capabilities to accept such bequests (February 15, 2010)

Year 2 (2010-2011)
- Begin including simple language on making a bequest on the KCH website and in other Home documents

Year 3 (2011-2012)
- Evaluate benefits of a larger "planned giving" roll out and, if appropriate, create plan for a larger campaign.

United Way Giving

In addition to becoming a United Way Partner Agency, the KCH has had moderate success recently with generating financial support through the United Way's workplace campaigns. While the Home would prefer to receive contributions directly to avoid administrative costs, we recognize that not only is the United Way Campaign a more convenient way to give for many prospects, but also that many people who might be inclined to give to us through the United Way may otherwise not give at all.

Therefore, the KCH should be sure to include information on the United Way Workplace Campaigns, including our donor choice numbers, in appropriate donor and prospect communications this year, and in Year 2 of this plan, should investigate additional ways of marketing our agency and the option of giving through the United Way to targeted companies throughout the area.

Action Steps (Deadline)
- Include United Way giving information in appropriate donor communications (ongoing)

Year 2 (2010-2011)
- Research best practices for increasing United Way giving
- Develop and implement plan for increasing United Way giving

Year 3 (2011-2012)
- Continue program growth

Major Giving / Capital Giving Options

In addition to the development tactics listed above, should the KCH relocate during the 2009-2010 fiscal year, the Home should consider using this relocation project as a method for soliciting contributions from major donors in a method similar to a capital campaign. Options for large one-time gifts include naming rights, multiple-year endowments of additional staff positions or program costs, and a greatly expanded donor recognition program utilizing our new office space (plaques / giving level wall / etc.)

Additionally, during our donor meetings and throughout the growth of our annual giving program, KCH staff and board members should diligently seek out opportunities for major gifts to build cash reserves, endow programs, and meet individual giving needs.

Miscellaneous Opportunities

In addition to the fundraising tactics laid out above, the KCH should remain mindful of seizing fundraising opportunities as they arise. We should be prepared to listen to the suggestions of our stakeholders and friends, and be prepared to implement the many good ideas that cross our path each year.

Two opportunities that we should be diligent in seeking are the opportunity to be named "official" or "partner" non-profit agency for a local business, civic group, or other network, and the opportunity to hold a participatory fundraising event ("-athon", "drive", school fundraising partnerships, etc.)

Action Steps (Deadline)
- Review progress of donor re-engagement and prospect calls / meetings to determine opportunities for "partner" agency status and participatory fundraising events (December 20, 2009)

Fundraising Needs and Goals

For the 2009-2010 fiscal year, the KCH budget has estimated total expenses at $1,161,901. Of that amount, **the following revenue shall be carried over from the prior fiscal year**, and spent in its entirety in 2009-2010:

George Foundation Grant	$22,700
Anonymous Grant	$91,817
City Initiatives Grant	$125,704
Biscayne Grant	$30,000
Total Balance Carried Forward:	$270,221

In addition, **we expect the following revenue from government sources**:

County Contract (no change from prior year)	$233,912
Municipal Contracts	$10,000
Violent Crime Bill Authorizations	$69,152
Attorney General's Office	$91,345
Additional expected revenue:	$404,409

Total "in hand" funding: **$674,630**

Total additional revenue needed: $487,271

Our revenue projection for fundraising activities in 2009-2010 is as follows:

Foundation Giving / Grants	$150,000
Major Events (The Gala)	$120,000
Hosted Events	
..........Golf Tournament	$50,000
..........Rotary Event	$20,000
..........Additional Hosted Event	$2,500
Direct Mail	
..........Annual Campaign	$24,000
United Way	$17,500
Online Giving and E-mail Solicitation	$5,000
Interest	$2,150
Board Campaign	$20,000
Corporate Giving	$20,000
Individual Giving	$57,500
Total projected revenue:	**$488,650**

Consolidated Action Step Timeline

March, 2009

March 15: Complete solicitation of additional Gala auction item donors

March 16: Gala Planning Committee meeting. Focus: Tickets and Sponsors

March 20: Complete Gala 2009 sponsor non-renewal calls, where necessary

March 20: Roberta Roberts Event: Do Plan, Do items for meetings, do press release she requested, plan for her walk a thon, including collateral materials

March 20: Complete 2009-2010 Development Expense Projection and Budget

March 31: Complete development plan stakeholder conversations; complete plan edits

March 31: Generate call list and script for staff calls to last year's auction item donors who did not renew this year + prospect lists for calls

April, 2009

April 1: Send out Jackie Press release & build basic media list

April 1: Generate list of complimentary invitees for Gala, complete invitation process (whatever method is appropriate) – one should be Amanda Roman and guest

April 1: Annual campaign follow up calls

April 5: Develop event plan for our involvement in Roberta Roberts event

April 9: Discuss board training program with development committee, add result to overall development timeline.

April 10: Research case for support best practices

April 10: Check in with board members re: Gala 2009 ticket and sponsorship sales, and auction items

April 12: Begin stakeholder conversations on PR Plan

April 12: Learn constant contact online and figure out our plan for using it as part of our development communications plan.

April 17: Check in with committed Gala 2009 sponsors who have not submitted check

April 17: Email all board members re: Auction items will not be listed in program unless they are in by 4/20, still accepted after though.

April 30: Prepare thank you call script and training materials for gift thanking procedure

April 30: Complete stakeholder conversations on PR Plan, begin writing PR Plan

April 30: Talk with Rob about expanding Development Committee to include non-board members, start talking about who and when

May, 2009

May Board Meeting: Solicit board member volunteers to participate in non-ask event program

May 1: Work with KCH program staff to locate/ generate necessary information for case for support

May 1: Research database packages, pricing schemes, support, migration, and training issues

May 10:Send out e-mail blast highlighting Roberts event and Walkathon.

May 15: Complete PR Plan

May 15: Create Roberts event booklet with Dickinson poems, sponsor names, KCH info, etc.

May 15: Develop communication plan for July Snail Mail Newsletter

May 15: Write draft case for support

May 15: Finalize decision on database package

May 20: Create Roberts Art sign in sheet for exhibition, and one for event.

May 20: Send out Roberts Art Event press release

May 23: Check in with Roberta Roberts re: art and walkathon events, sponsors, ticket sales, etc.

May 24: Press release for Roberta Roberts Event and exhibit

May 31: Plan for board giving for those who have not given yet this FY

May 31: Develop list of key Gala volunteers and stakeholder for next year's committee. Plan thank you social event.

June, 2009

JUNE EVENT: Roberta Roberts hosted event
June 1: Speak with Golf Committee regarding 2009 Golf Event (no later than this date)
June 1: Provide Roberta Roberts with, KCH flyers, annual reports, envelopes, etc.
June 10: Develop communication plan for September Annual Report
June 20: Prepare scripts and collateral materials list for command appearance meetings
June 20: Develop event plan and timeline for KCH's involvement in Golf Event

July, 2009

JULY COMMUNICATION: Snail mail newsletter
July 5: Research KCH's previous tour program and non-ask event best practices
July 30: Finalize Gala 2010 Line-by-Line
July 30: Research / organize lists of volunteer opportunities, in-kind donations, and "wish list" items at KCH. Prepare useable, well-formatted documents based on volunteer opportunities, in-kinds, and wish list items

August, 2009

AUGUST COMMUNICATION: E-update
August 1: Develop necessary memos and forms for prospect and donor tracking
August 10: Develop communication plan for October Annual Campaign mailing
August 10: Develop list of prospects and donors for re-engagement and determine method of re-engagement for Annual Giving Program and donor-engagement calls / meetings. Include board members calling low and midlevel people for re-engagement, including training, materials, and scripts.
August 10: Establish schedule of 2009-2010 non-ask events, with goal of holding 4-5 total events, 1-2 of which are held at outside locations

August 10: New database installed, data migrated, package fully functional

August 15: Work with appropriate vendors and stakeholders to complete changes identified in web fundraising capabilities audit

August 15: Develop list of government officials to target for relationship building and plan for doing so

August 15: Perform web, e-giving, and e-mail fundraising capabilities audit and generate list of required changes prior to complete web redesign

August 20: Develop scripts and materials for in-house and outside non-ask events

August 20: Develop re-engagement questionnaire and materials for low-level donor mail-out of Annual Report

August 31: Develop "Event in a Box" handbook and materials for use by our supports in hosting events on our behalf

August 31: Finalize 2009-2010 foundation giving plan, including detailed prospect lists and timelines [This is a new due date, pushed back from June]

August 31: Develop and implement strategy for moving prospects to our non-ask events

including list of current and prospective grant donors to invite to non-ask events

September, 2009

SEPTEMBER COMMUNICATION: Annual Report

September 1: Develop list of current and prospective grant makers to invite to one-on-one meetings

September 1: Perform review of current government funding and potential

September 1: Confirm lobbying gift level and duration with donor

September 10: Begin high-level donor and prospect re-engagement calls and meetings (no later than this date)

September 15: Write event plan for 1st annual donor recognition event to take place in December, 2009

September 15: Create detailed event plan and timeline for Gala 2010, including review of ticket prices and giving levels, plus plan for auction, including massive data entry and mailing effort to start

September 15: Develop and start implementing plan to sell sponsorships for Rotary Event

September 20: Develop strategy for seeking out supporters to host events on our behalf

September 30: Create detailed sponsor and ticket sale plan and timeline for Gala 2010, including a plan for substantially growing the event

October, 2009

OCTOBER COMMUNICATION: Annual Campaign direct mail piece

OCTOBER EVENT: Golf Event

October 1: Rob Davies and Jim Martin begin ongoing series of meetings with foundation executives, subject to their availability (no later than this date)

October 10: Develop prospecting plan for November's Gala 2010 sponsor calls

October 31: Seek out one additional hosted event for this fiscal year (no later than this date)

November, 2009

NOVEMBER COMMUNICATIONS: Gala 2010 sponsor calls; E-update

November 1: Hold first non-ask event no later than this date

November 15: Hold meetings with prospective lobbying firms to determine feasibility and course of action and solicit proposals (complete no later than this date)

December, 2009

DECEMBER EVENT: Donor Recognition Event

December 15: Review proposals and generate short lobbying plan based on these materials; choose firm to engage

December 20: Review progress of donor re-engagement and prospect calls / meetings to determine opportunities for "partner" agency status and participatory fundraising events

January, 2010

January 10: Complete low-level donor re-engagement questionnaire follow-up

January 15: Develop communication and call plan for February's Know Your Donor Call Program

January 15: Engage lobbying firm

February, 2010

FEBRUARY COMMUNICATION: E-update; Know Your Donor Call Program

FEBRUARY EVENT: Rotary Gala Event and Fashion Show

February 1: Create annual giving program levels, brand, logo, etc.

February 1: Begin prospect list for lawyers affinity group steering committee

February 15: Create collateral materials for annual giving program

February 15: Work with supportive professionals to create a simple planned giving document; perform review of our capabilities for accepting such gifts

February 20: Begin soliciting prospects for lawyers affinity group steering committee

March, 2010

MARCH COMMUNICATION: Gala invitation mailings

March 15: Develop master list of annual giving program prospects for launch

March 15: Decide on annual giving campaign launch structure and event/meeting planning requirements

March 31: Create agenda and collateral materials for lawyers affinity group steering committee meeting

April, 2010

APRIL EVENTS: Lawyers affinity group steering committee meeting, Gala 2010

April 10: Work with board on leadership gifts / board giving campaign for 2010-2011 as part of annual giving campaign launch

April 15: Mail invitations to annual giving campaign launch events and/or start scheduling launch solicitation meetings

About the Author

Joe Garecht is the founder of The Fundraising Authority, which provides fundraising consulting and coaching programs for non-profits worldwide. Joe is a sought after speaker and trainer and is the creator of the Rapid Growth Fundraising System ™.

Prior to starting The Fundraising Authority, Joe served as a non-profit Executive Director and Development Director for several organizations as well as a Fundraising Director for numerous large political campaigns.

Joe's other books include *The Silent Auction Handbook, The Non-Profit Fundraising Formula,* and *Raising Money Without Going Crazy.* You can find Joe online at TheFundraisingAuthority.com

Joe, his wife and four children live in the Philadelphia area.

Made in the USA
Middletown, DE
15 April 2016